The Churchill-Eisenhower
Correspondence, 1953–1955

EDITED BY PETER G. BOYLE

The Churchill-Eisenhower
Correspondence, 1953–1955

The University of North Carolina Press

Chapel Hill and London

Library of Congress Cataloging-in-Publication Data

Churchill, Winston, Sir, 1874–1965.
    The Churchill-Eisenhower correspondence, 1953–1955 / edited by
Peter G. Boyle.
        p.   cm.
    Includes bibliographical references.
    ISBN 0-8078-1910-7 (alk. paper)
        1. Churchill, Winston, Sir, 1874–1965—Correspondence.
    2. Eisenhower, Dwight D. (Dwight David), 1890–1969—Correspondence.
    3. Prime ministers—Great Britain—Correspondence.   4. Presidents—
    United States—Correspondence.   5. Great Britain—Foreign relations—
    United States.   6. Great Britain—Foreign relations—1945-   .
    7. United States—Foreign relations—Great Britain.   8. United
    States—Foreign relations—1953–1961.   I. Eisenhower, Dwight D.
    (Dwight David), 1890–1969.   II. Boyle, Peter G.   III. Title.
    DA566.9.C5A4   1990
    327.41073—dc20   89-77572
                                                                     CIP

Crown copyright records in the Public Record Office are reproduced by
permission of the Controller of Her Majesty's Stationery Office.

The Eisenhower letters in the Dwight D. Eisenhower Library are reproduced
by permission of John S. D. Eisenhower.

The paper in this book meets the guidelines for permanence and durability of
the Committee on Production Guidelines for Book Longevity of the Council
on Library Resources.

Manufactured in the United States of America

94 93 92 91 90   5 4 3 2 1

CONTENTS

ILLUSTRATIONS

ACKNOWLEDGMENTS

I am very appreciative of the assistance which I have received in the preparation of this edition from archivists, librarians, colleagues, and friends.

I wish to record my gratitude to President Eisenhower's son, John Eisenhower, and to Her Majesty's Stationery Office for permission to publish the letters of President Dwight D. Eisenhower and Prime Minister Winston S. Churchill which are contained in this edition. Acknowledgment is made to the Master, Fellows, and Scholars of Churchill College in the University of Cambridge for permission to use photographs selected from the Churchill Press Photographic Collection in the Churchill Archives Centre, to the Dwight D. Eisenhower Library for the use of one photograph from their collection, and to Associated Press, United Press, and Her Majesty's Stationery Office for permission to publish photographs of which they hold copyright.

For financial assistance I acknowledge support from the University of Nottingham Research Fund during a sabbatical term in 1986 when the initial research was undertaken.

I am grateful to the staffs of the Dwight D. Eisenhower Library, Abilene, Kansas, and the Public Record Office, Kew, Surrey, for all of their assistance to me during my periods of research and for their responses to my inquiries by mail.

I am grateful to my University of Nottingham colleague, Robert Frazier, who read the manuscript and made many helpful suggestions.

For assistance on a number of points of detail I record my appreciation to Stephen Ambrose, Angela Chandler, Jill Edwards, Robert Ferrell, Elizabeth Gilliatt, Martin Gilbert, General Andrew Goodpaster, Milton Gustafson, Lesley James, Anthony Montague Browne, Peter Morris, Sir David Pitblado, John and Katherine Robinson, Lord Sherfield, Ann Whitman, and Lady Williams of Elvel.

I am grateful to Lisa Brockway for word-processing the manuscript, to Freda Duckitt for secretarial assistance, to Alan Odell for transferring computer disks, and to Mary Reid for copyediting.

My greatest debt is to Lewis Bateman, my editor at the University of North Carolina Press. It was his suggestion to me, after I had delivered a paper based on the Churchill-Eisenhower correspondence at the convention of the Society for Historians of American Foreign Relations in 1986, that I edit the Churchill-Eisenhower correspondence. It was, I feel, an excellent suggestion. I am grateful to him also for his editorial assistance throughout the preparation of the book.

The assistance which I have received from so many quarters has saved me from many errors of fact and of judgment. For any errors which remain I of course accept responsibility.

ABBREVIATIONS

Abbreviations in Letters

Alex	Lord Alexander of Tunis
Anthony	Anthony Eden
Bedell	Walter Bedell Smith
Bernie	Bernard Baruch
Clemmie	Clementine Churchill
Foster	John Foster Dulles
Mamie	Mamie Eisenhower
Pug	Lord Ismay
The Admiral	Lewis Strauss
The Prof	Lord Cherwell

Abbreviations in Text and Notes

CAB	Cabinet
EDC	European Defense Community
FO	Foreign Office
FRUS	*Foreign Relations of the United States*
NATO	North Atlantic Treaty Organization
PREM	Prime Minister
PRO	Public Record Office, Kew, Surrey
R	Republican
SACEUR	Supreme Allied Commander, Europe
SEATO	Southeast Asia Treaty Organization
WFIS	Whitman File, International Series, Eisenhower Library, Abilene, Kansas

In her *Guide to Documentary Editing*, Mary Jo Kline suggests that editors ought to state their editorial principles in their introduction.[1] The Churchill-Eisenhower correspondence does not raise the problems involved with collections of documentary material from a wide scattering of different locations, but there are several matters of editorial principle and of factual information regarding the letters which should be provided.

Copies of the Churchill-Eisenhower letters are located in the Eisenhower Library in Abilene, Kansas, and in the Prime Minister's Papers in the Public Record Office in Kew, Surrey.[2] Copies of most, but not all, of the letters are contained in both collections. A list of the letters which are not found in both collections, with details of their location, is provided in Appendix 2.

Additional photocopies of a number of letters can be found in various Foreign Office and State Department files. The State Department file, "President and Secretary of State Correspondence with Heads of Government, 1953–64," is still closed, however. Letters from this file which have been published in *Foreign Relations of the United States* are identical to the originals in the Whitman File in the Eisenhower Papers at the Eisenhower Library in Abilene or in the Prime Minister's Papers in the Public Record Office in Kew.[3] A further number of letters that have been published, in part or in whole, in *Foreign Relations of the United States* have been taken from the collection in the Eisenhower Library or from copies in various State Department files. Some letters have also been published in the final volume of Martin Gilbert's official biography of Churchill.[4] These previously published letters constitute only a very small percentage of the letters in the present edition, which is a full collection with the exception of the few letters that remain classified.

A first matter of concern to an editor of letters is to ascertain that the letters were actually sent and that copies in the editor's possession are not drafts which were never sent or which were altered in transit. Warren Kimball provides many examples of Churchill-Roosevelt letters which were never sent.[5] Moreover, examples can be found of communications from Churchill to figures other than Eisenhower which were altered without his knowledge before delivery. Harold Macmillan, for instance, writes of the manner in which Roger Makins, who was a Foreign Office official, General Henry Maitland ("Jumbo") Wilson, and Macmillan altered messages dealing with the situation in Yugoslavia in 1944. "I found a Yugoslav crisis which Roger had dealt with very well," Macmillan noted in his diary. "The P.M. wants to send messages to Tito; but as his messages were full of inaccuracies of fact, Roger and Jumbo have held them up. I think that we shall probably have to send them and the best thing to do is to amend them without letting on at home."[6] Macmillan's revelation is all the more pertinent in light of the fact that the Foreign Office official, Roger Makins, was British ambassador to the United States in 1953–55, and it was through him that Churchill's letters to Eisenhower were delivered.

A first principle in editing letters, therefore, is to rely upon a copy in the archives of the recipient rather than of the sender. Wherever possible, the copy in the recipient's archives should be checked against the copy in the sender's archives. In the Churchill-Eisenhower letters, this has generally been possible as copies of most letters are in both archives. In instances where copies were not in the recipient's archives but were in the sender's, additional evidence was required that the letter was actually sent. This evidence consisted of acknowledgment of receipt of the letter or reference to it in the succeeding letter of the other party. The only exceptions, where such evidence was not found, were a few minor notes of congratulation on such matters as a birthday. Where copies of letters were found in both archives, the texts were found to be identical. Roger Makins was perhaps willing, on Harold Macmillan's authority, to alter a Churchill message to Tito, but he did not on his own authority alter personal letters from Churchill to Eisenhower in the 1953–55 period.

A second matter of concern relates to the composition of the letters. It is necessary to determine whether the letters were written personally by Churchill and by Eisenhower, or whether they were drafted in government departments and perfunctorily signed by the prime minister and the president. There are, except in a very few instances, no extant early drafts and redrafts of either Churchill or Eisenhower letters, so that it is only possible to ascertain the degree of personal composition from internal evidence and from the testimony of aides.

In Eisenhower's case a number of the letters were based on State Department drafts which Eisenhower read carefully and discussed with Dulles before transmission. In other cases, however, as Eisenhower's chief of staff, General Andrew Goodpaster, and his personal secretary, Ann Whitman, have both testified, the letters were composed entirely by Eisenhower and seen by no one before transmission. In such instances, according to Ann Whitman, Eisenhower would write a letter to Churchill in his own hand; his secretary typed it; the president read it and made a few alterations; the letter was retyped; and the president signed and transmitted the letter without showing it to anyone else.[7]

In Churchill's case there is evidence of the circulation of drafts of some letters within the Foreign Office for comment before final drafting and transmission.[8] In July 1954 Churchill said in Cabinet that "It had been his practice as prime minister, both during the war and since the present government took office, to exchange personal messages with heads of government and more particularly with the president of the United States. Most of the messages had been dispatched by the Foreign Secretary who would always suggest that reference should be made to the Cabinet if he thought this necessary."[9]

For the most part, however, the letters were not based on government department drafts but were composed and dictated by Churchill personally. Sir David Pitblado, Churchill's principal private secretary, expresses the view that the letters to Eisenhower "were entirely WSC personal composition." Anthony Montague Browne, another of Churchill's four private secretaries, agrees, writing that "My recollection of WSC's correspondence with Eisenhower is that . . . he dictated them himself. The Foreign Office more than once suggested drafts, and bits were incorporated, but with a volley of dismissive snorts of contempt both at content and literary style."[10] Lady Williams, one of the secretaries to whom Churchill dictated, recalls that "Churchill very rarely used prepared drafts for this correspondence. . . . He enjoyed dictating to a secretary: he liked the sound of his own words and I say this meaning that there was no hint of vanity in this pleasure. . . . Briefs were sometimes given to him by Departments, especially by the Foreign Office and the Treasury. He would read from them carefully but, to the best of my recollection, he would put them aside and use his own words."[11] Lady Williams's recollection is confirmed by Elizabeth Gilliatt, another of Churchill's secretaries.[12]

The letters were sent by diplomatic bag, which would generally mean delivery the next day. Churchill's letters to Eisenhower were delivered through the British embassy in Washington, D.C., while Eisenhower's letters to Churchill were delivered through the American embassy in London. Dates of the same letter in the recipient's and sender's archives often differ by one day, indicating the date of transmission and the date of delivery by the embassy, which was usually a day later. In this edition the date of transmission has been printed.

Letters were headed The White House or 10 Downing Street. The signature and salutation were in handwriting; the rest of the letter was typed. In transcribing the letters from the copies in the archives to this printed edition, the address has been omitted, as it would be needless repetition, and the signatures and salutations are printed as the rest of the letter, though it should be noted that in the original letters they were personally handwritten. Shorter messages were sent by cable without salutation or signature.

The letters have been transcribed exactly as in the original. Where misspellings or typographical errors occur in the original they have been transcribed in this printed edition, but there are in fact very few such errors and none of great significance.

A small number of the letters remain classified. Two letters have one paragraph withheld, while four are wholly classified. Requests to the Record Office, 10 Downing Street, and through the Freedom of Information Act in the United States did not result in the opening of these letters. The list of dates of these classified letters is provided in Appendix 1.

Annotation has been kept to a minimum. The editorial principle followed has been to provide the reader with background information necessary to allow a sufficient knowledge of the matter which the recipient of the letter would have had. This has been provided by means of footnotes, headnotes, and the index. Footnotes at the end of each letter provide brief identification of individuals and events. Occasional headnotes provide a slightly lengthier background account of a number of issues, such as Egypt, Stalin's successors, and sharing of atomic information. Relatively frequent headnotes are provided in the early part of the text, explaining issues at the first reference to them, but headnotes become much less frequent as the same issues are discussed and developed. The index provides a guide to the first reference to events and personalities at which identification is made, whereas identification and background information is not repeated at later references.

The effort has been made to resist the temptation open to editors to give overly detailed background information. "Excessive informational annotation is the 'occupational disease of editors,' " as Mary Jo Kline puts it—quoting a fellow writer on documentary editing.[13] Headnotes, Kline warns, can become small monographs which range widely beyond the immediate subject.[14] Moreover, out of zeal to point out the significance of some points in the documents, an editor can steal the thunder by making the point in an introduction or headnote, so that the reader is very familiar with the point before reaching it in the document. In this edition the attempt has been made to provide sufficient information required by the reader to understand the letter as it would have been understood by the recipient, but with the minimum of editorial intrusion.

Notes

1. Mary Jo Kline, *A Guide to Documentary Editing* (Baltimore: Johns Hopkins University Press, 1987), p. 11.

2. Whitman File, International Series, Boxes 16–17, Dwight D. Eisenhower Library, Abilene, Kansas; PREM 11 1074, Public Record Office, Kew, Surrey.

3. "President and Secretary of State Correspondence with Heads of Government, 1953–64," Department of State lot file 66 D 204; *Foreign Relations of the United States, 1952–54* (Washington, D.C.: U.S. Government Printing Office, 1986), vol. 6, *Western Europe and Canada*, pp. 966, 975–76, 977–78, 1015–17.

4. For example, *FRUS, 1952–54*, 6:970–74, 1012–14, 1037–48; *FRUS, 1952–54*, vol. 5, *Western European Security*, pp. 1711–13; *FRUS, 1952–54*, vol. 9, *The Near and Middle East*, pp. 1989–91; Martin Gilbert, *Never Despair, 1945–65*, vol. 8 of *Winston S. Churchill* (London: Heinemann, 1988), pp. 810–11, 830–31, 959–60.

5. For example, Warren Kimball, ed., *Churchill and Roosevelt: The Complete Correspondence*, 3 vols. (Princeton: Princeton University Press, 1984), 1:115, 138; 2:206, 260; 3:125, 361 (hereafter cited as *Churchill and Roosevelt*).

6. Harold Macmillan, *War Diaries: Politics and War in the Mediterranean, January, 1943–May, 1945* (London: Macmillan, 1984), p. 524.

7. Andrew J. Goodpaster to Peter G. Boyle, November 14, 1987; Ann Whitman to Peter G. Boyle, October 21, 1987, personal correspondence in editor's possession.

8. For example, FO 800 838 US//53//27, February 20, 1953; PREM 11 421, May 6, 1953; PREM 11 1074, March 2, 1954, PRO.

9. Cabinet Conclusions, CAB 128//27, July 8, 1954, PRO.

10. Sir David Pitblado to Peter G. Boyle, September 30, 1988; Anthony Montague Browne to Sir David Pitblado, August 3, 1988, personal correspondence in editor's possession.

11. Lady Williams of Elvel (née Jane Portal) to Peter G. Boyle, July 9, 1988, personal correspondence in editor's possession.

12. Elizabeth Gilliatt to Peter G. Boyle, July 29, 1988, personal correspondence in editor's possession.

13. Kline, *Guide to Documentary Editing*, p. 187; James Thorpe, *Principles of Textual Criticism* (San Marino, Calif.: Huntington Library, 1972), p. 201.

14. Kline, *Guide to Documentary Editing*, p. 187.

The Churchill-Eisenhower
Correspondence, 1953–1955

"It is my understanding that you and I hope to maintain if only intermittently a personal correspondence, which will provide opportunity to help clarify intentions and explain reasons for decisions, when this seems appropriate."[1] In this manner President Dwight D. Eisenhower wrote to Prime Minister Winston Churchill on February 2, 1953, two weeks after Eisenhower's inauguration as president of the United States. "I was so glad to get your letter of February 2," Churchill replied, "and to feel that a private correspondence will continue apart from regular official communications."[2] The correspondence continued regularly throughout the time when Churchill and Eisenhower were both in office, until Churchill's retirement in April 1955. It provides fascinating insights into the relationship between the two statesmen and their countries as well as their views of world affairs of their time.

Churchill and Eisenhower were well acquainted by 1953. They first met in December 1941, when Churchill came to the United States for meetings with President Franklin Roosevelt following America's entry into the Second World War. "One day when I was at the White House in 1941," Churchill later recalled, "FDR arranged to have me meet some American officers and Ike came in."[3] They came to know one another very well during the war, and despite not infrequent disagreements over particular issues their mutual respect and affection steadily deepened. When Eisenhower was given command in 1942 of TORCH, the Allied operation in North Africa, Churchill flew on several occasions to Eisenhower's headquarters, and he was very favorably impressed. "The concord and confidence of Eisenhower's headquarters," Churchill wrote to Roosevelt, "and the order and conviction of the commanders actually charged with the operations was most bracing."[4] Toward the end of 1943 Churchill wrote that "We have full confidence in General Eisenhower. He is the soul of loyal cooperation between the Allies."[5]

In times of controversy in the latter stages of the war, Churchill defended Eisenhower resolutely. With the Allied setback in the Battle of the Bulge in December 1944, for example, Churchill asked Roosevelt to understand that "in case any troubles should arise in the press, Her Majesty's Government have complete confidence in General Eisenhower and feel acutely any attacks made on him."[6] Toward the end of the war, in spite of serious disagreements over strategy in the Balkans and the speed of advance to Berlin and Prague, Churchill wrote that he wished "to place on record the complete confidence felt by Her Majesty's Government in General Eisenhower, our pleasure that our armies are serving under his command and our admiration of the great and shining qualities of character and personality which he has proved himself to possess in all the difficulties of handling an allied command."[7]

Yet, although Churchill was full of praise of Eisenhower's ability as a military leader, he felt that Eisenhower was naive on political issues. On the delicate matter of dealing with the Vichy French leader Jean Darlan in North Africa in 1942, for example, Churchill, Warren Kimball suggests, "continued to treat Eisenhower as a political innocent."[8] Churchill therefore sent Harold Macmillan to North Africa to guide Eisenhower on matters which required political skill and expediency. On an even more serious issue, Churchill regarded Eisenhower as blind to political considerations with regard to the Soviet Union in 1944–45 in the military strategy which was pursued in the closing stages of the war. The American insistence on ANVIL, the invasion of southern France, and rejection of Churchill's scheme for an Allied advance into the Balkans from Italy constituted "the most acute difference I ever had with General Eisenhower," Churchill later wrote.[9] For his part, Eisenhower resented that toward the end of the war "troop maneuvers had acquired a political significance that demanded the intervention of political leaders in the development of broad operational plans."[10] Moreover, even in the early stages of the war, although Eisenhower acknowledged Churchill's wide experience and knowledge in military matters, the general was often irritated by the prime minister's interference in details of military operations.[11]

From the end of the war until 1950 Churchill's contact with Eisenhower was relatively slight. Churchill was more concerned with his relationship with the new president, Harry Truman. When he met Truman at the Potsdam Conference in July 1945, he was impressed by Truman's "gay, precise sparkling manner and obvious power of decision."[12] Even after Churchill's surprising defeat in the British general election in 1945, he and Truman continued to have a close relationship, especially after Truman accompanied him to Fulton, Missouri, where he delivered his Iron Curtain speech in March 1946. In 1948 Churchill congratulated Truman on his reelection. Noting that he had an American mother, Churchill wrote to Truman, "Of course it is my business as a foreigner or half a foreigner to keep out of American politics, but I am sure I can now say what a relief it has been to me and most of us here to feel that the long continued comradeship between us and also with the Democratic party in peace and war will not be interrupted."[13] Churchill had earlier written a significant letter to Eisenhower when the latter had decided against a possible candidacy for president in 1948. "My feeling is," Churchill wrote, "that you were right not to intervene on this occasion. Because if you had stood as a Democrat, it would have looked like going to the rescue of a party which has so long held office and is now in difficulties. On the other hand if you had stood as a Republican it would have been hard on the party whose president you served. However, luckily there is plenty of time."[14]

Churchill and Eisenhower met only once between 1945 and 1950. Following his Iron Curtain speech on March 5, 1946, Churchill came to Washington and on March 8–9 he and Eisenhower led a small party to Williamsburg, Virginia, where Churchill addressed the Virginia legislature, advocating that Britain and America should "walk together in majesty and peace."[15] But although Churchill and Eisenhower exchanged letters from time to time, for the most part they went their own ways in the late 1940s. Churchill was out of office and leader of the Opposition, and he devoted a great deal of his time to writing his six-volume history of the Second World War. Eisenhower became U.S. Army chief of staff until he retired from the army in February 1948 to accept the presidency of Columbia University.

In December 1950, however, Eisenhower was recalled to military duty as the first SACEUR, supreme allied commander in Europe of NATO forces. Churchill welcomed Eisenhower's appointment, saying in the House of Commons that "There is no man in the world who can do that job so well."[16] In October 1951 Churchill returned to office as prime minister following the Conservative victory in the British general election. He met Eisenhower as SACEUR on several occasions in 1951–52 and they renewed their wartime comradeship, until Eisenhower resigned as SACEUR in May 1952 to become a candidate for the Republican nomination for president.

Churchill did not welcome the Republican victory in 1952. His private secretary, Sir John Colville, records that when Churchill received news of the election result, "Winston said to me: 'For your private ear, I am greatly disturbed. I think this makes war much more probable.' "[17] Churchill felt that the belligerence of the Republican proposals in their election platform combined with their inexperience in office was a very dangerous combination. He expressed his alarm, for example, in a report to Foreign Secretary Anthony Eden of a conversation with Thomas Dewey, Republican candidate for president in 1944 and 1948, at a dinner in New York on January 7, 1953. "On the spur of the moment," Churchill recorded, "he said that an alternative plan might be for the United Kingdom and the United States to make a joint declaration (comparable to our guarantee to Poland in 1939) that if Communist China attempted to occupy Indo-China, Burma or any other country in the Pacific area, we and the Americans would declare war. I tell you all of this to show you the rough weather that may well be ahead in dealing with the Republican party. . . . Much patience will be needed."[18]

Churchill felt that Eisenhower himself was steadier in his views and that he represented the moderate wing of the Republican party. But Churchill feared that Eisenhower might be too weak or insufficiently politically astute to restrain the more extreme elements within the Republican party. Churchill felt, therefore, that an important part of the Anglo-American relationship should be British efforts to act as a restraining influence on America against the pursuit of volatile and dangerous extremes of policy which the new Republican administration might be inclined to pursue. He met Eisenhower in New York on January 5 and January 7, 1953, between Eisenhower's election and inauguration, and he felt a little more reassured. Sir John Colville recorded that "The Prime Minister told me, after Ike had left, that he had felt on top of him this time: Ike seemed to defer to his greater age and experience to a remarkable degree."[19]

For his part, Eisenhower was very well disposed toward Britain and toward Churchill. In 1945 he wrote that Churchill was "an extraordinary character and to me at least is practically the personification of British life."[20] In a letter to his lifelong friend Swede Hazlitt, Eisenhower wrote of the qualities of a great man and concluded that Churchill "comes nearest to fulfilling the requirements of greatness in any individual I have met in my lifetime."[21] Eisenhower's long-serving secretary, Ann Whitman, in expressing Eisenhower's feelings for Churchill, writes simply, "He adored Churchill."[22] Eisenhower's affection for Britain was equally unquestioned. In his diary he noted that Britain was America's "greatest natural friend."[23] His success as a wartime commander had been due above all to his ability to maintain close Anglo-American military cooperation, and in December 1944 he had said that after the war he hoped to spend "the afternoon and evening" of his life working for Anglo-American amity.[24] Yet while Eisenhower was a very good friend of Britain, he took a broader view of international affairs than a reliance on Anglo-American partnership as the panacea for all the world's ills, which tended, he thought, to be Churchill's position. Eisenhower felt that Churchill, who was seventy-eight in 1953, was too old and was living in the past, trying to revive the exclusive Anglo-American relationship of wartime years, whereas the world had moved on by the 1950s. "Winston is trying to relive the days of World War II," Eisenhower noted in his diary on January 6, 1953. "In those days he had the enjoyable feeling that he and our president were sitting on some rather Olympian platform with respect to the rest of the world and directing world affairs from that point of vantage."[25]

The personal relations between Churchill and Eisenhower were a reflection of their more basic concern with the national interests of their countries. At the end of the war in 1945, amidst the glow of triumph Britain faced a perilous future. She was exhausted economically, faced a dire threat from Soviet expansion in Europe, and feared American withdrawal into isolationism and the reemergence of Anglo-American rivalry as in pre–World War II years. The Anglo-American "special relationship" was largely a creation of the Second World War. Despite later mythology on the subject, the British and Americans had not always walked shoulder to shoulder as transatlantic cousins with common interests and common ideals. On the contrary, as one recent historian has put it, "The first thing that must strike anyone who thinks objectively about the Anglo-American relationship is the contrast between its coolness for most of its duration and its warmth in modern times."[26] From the American War of Independence and the War of 1812 through the nineteenth century, Britain and the United States for the most part viewed one another with mutual suspicion and hostility. A rapprochement at the turn of the century improved relations somewhat, but there were serious matters of dispute in the period of American neutrality in World War I, from 1914 to 1917. The two nations then fought at one another's side in 1917–18, but the peace settlement ended in American disillusionment and suspicion that the wily British had duped the idealistic Americans.

Americans, it was felt in the United States, had fought a war to make the world safe for democracy, whereas the terms of the Treaty of Versailles showed that Britain was more concerned with narrow national and imperial interests. In the interwar years issues such as war debts poisoned Anglo-American relations, while the personal relationship was distant between British and American leaders of these decades, such as U.S. presidents Warren Harding, Calvin Coolidge, Herbert Hoover, and Franklin Roosevelt and British prime ministers such as Stanley Baldwin and Ramsay MacDonald. Indeed, the last British prime minister of the prewar era, Neville Chamberlain, although he had an American mother, had strong anti-American prejudices. As he noted bitterly on one occasion, "It is always best and safest to count on nothing from the Americans but words."[27]

As the historian David Reynolds has emphasized, it was the unexpected fall of France in June 1940, together with the Nazi-Soviet pact of August 1939, which created a desperate threat to Britain's security that could be met only by cooperation with the United States.[28] At the same time, growing American fears for the longterm security of the United States in the face of increasing Axis might made the United States look toward Britain as the only power which stood between America and the Axis. These mutual security requirements formed the basis of the Anglo-American World War II alliance. In the course of the war the relationship undoubtedly developed into much more than a bare security arrangement. The degree of warmth and closeness of cooperation and camaraderie in the war years justified the term "special relationship." World War II, as one historian has written, "saw a co-ordination between the political authorities of two sovereign states possibly unsurpassed in history."[29] Nevertheless, throughout the war years there were underlying tensions, so that there was a very real prospect that the wartime relationship would evaporate with the defeat of the common enemy and the prewar relationship of rivalry and suspicion would be resumed. This prospect was made into a very strong possibility by serious postwar differences, especially over economic issues, atomic matters, American criticisms of British colonialism, and American pressure for a united Europe. These differences were reconciled and the two nations were brought together again, however, by the new common threat which faced them in the late 1940s from the Soviet Union.[30]

The gravity of Anglo-American differences in the mid-1940s should not be underestimated. On economic issues, for example, disagreements with the United States exacerbated the dire financial straits in which Britain emerged from the war. During the Second World War Britain expended a quarter of her national wealth. As one historian has phrased it, "It was as if all the resources and treasures which in the days of her pre-eminence had been built up by Victorian thrift and enterprise had now been flung, with a kind of calculated prodigality, upon the pyre of total war."[31] The British harbored a lingering resentment that the United States had remained neutral and grown rich in 1939–41 (as in 1914–17) while Britain had borne the burden at tremendous cost. Britain was very grateful for wartime economic aid from the United States by means of Lend-Lease, but was resentful over conditions attached to it, such as the requirement that recipients commit themselves to the goal of the elimination of all forms of discriminatory treatment in international commerce. This stipulation reflected the belief which had been developed in the U.S. State and Treasury departments in the 1930s that economic nationalism was one of the major causes of the tensions and disorders which culminated in World War II and that the United States should lead the world to a new economic order which would prohibit cartels, quantitative agreements, imperial preferences, and other such trading restrictions and create an open economic world of liberalized trade and convertible currencies. Britain accepted these ideas to some extent but wished to proceed gradually and to protect such interests as Commonwealth connections and the sterling area. Britain was resentful that the United States took the opportunity during the war to impose conditions regarding trade and economic issues which the British considered to be against their longterm interests and which would lead to a postwar economic world order favorable to the United States.[32]

Even more so, after the war Britain regarded the terms of the American loan of 1946 as a further instance of American exploitation of British weakness for the longterm economic advantage of the United States. Although many Americans regarded the terms of the $3.75 billion loan as very generous, with its low rate of interest of 2 percent over fifty years, the British had sought a grant rather than a loan and they were aggrieved by such conditions as the requirement to make the pound convertible with the dollar within a year, which led to a convertibility crisis in 1947.[33] Even in the case of the Marshall Plan, which on the surface appeared to be the epitome of altruistic American generosity, the British were on the one hand grateful for American aid through the plan, from which Britain received a larger amount than any other country, but on the other hand the British were offended by the heavy-handed bureaucratic methods by which the Americans administered the aid. The Marshall Plan was established as a four-year program of economic aid, 1948–52, but appropriations were set by Congress annually, with recipient countries required to give an account of the manner in which the previous year's aid had been used in order to receive aid the following year. British officials squirmed over the criticisms made of British policy, especially by Anglophobes in Congress, yet due deference needed to be shown in order to receive aid. Fundamentally, Britain felt humiliated that she was in a position of dependency on the United States. As the Cabinet Mutual Aid Subcommittee noted, "U.K. dependence on U.S. economic aid is not in the longer term compatible with our position as a great power with worldwide responsibilities. Nor is it conducive to cordial relations with the United States."[34]

While disagreements over economic issues were often aired in public, the most important single source of Anglo-American dispute in these years was kept secret, namely, atomic issues. British scientists had worked in America on the atomic bomb during the war, and Churchill and Roosevelt made two agreements, the Quebec agreement of 1943 and the Hyde Park aide-mémoire of 1944, which seemed to promise Britain a continuation of cooperation and a supply of information after the war both for civil and military purposes. In 1946, however, Congress passed the McMahon Act, which barred the dissemination of atomic information by the United States to any other country, including Britain. The Labour government of Clement Attlee felt that the United States had reneged on an agreement on an issue of the highest importance. But the United States refused to go beyond some relatively minor concessions in the so-called Modus Vivendi of 1948. Consequently, the British government embarked on its own atomic program, at a considerably higher cost without American cooperation, and with a deep sense of grievance against their wartime ally over this issue.[35]

Britain was also irritated by sanctimonious American criticisms of British colonial policy and by American pressure on Britain to join a united Europe. America had always taken a public stand of anticolonialism, and, in her position of preeminent power at the end of World War II, the United States denounced the colonialism of the European powers, especially Britain, and pressed for self-government for colonial peoples. The Labour government, which was facing great problems in implementing self-government in India and in withdrawing from Palestine, did not find helpful what were regarded as ill-informed and self-righteous American criticisms.[36] Moreover, Americans laid great emphasis on European unity as a panacea for Europe's economic and security problems, while the British favored a gradual move toward unity of the continental European powers, with Britain playing an associative rather than a fully integrated role. By means of the Marshall Plan, and by threats to withhold further aid unless there was more evidence of closer European unity, the Americans tried to force Britain to loosen her ties to the Commonwealth and the sterling area and to become part of a united Europe. The British resented this pressure and felt that the Americans failed to appreciate the importance of Britain's worldwide as well as European role. The United States, in Britain's view, had only a superficial understanding of the problems involved in bringing about European unity and put forward hastily conceived, impractical schemes. As one British official, Paul Gore-Booth, put it, progress toward constructive measures for European integration was constantly hampered by "some of the wilder American ideas."[37]

Hence, in the two or three years after 1945 Britain and the United States became embroiled in serious disagreements over substantial issues which were difficult to resolve. By 1947–48, however, as one writer expresses it, "The prospective challenge from Moscow had a powerfully concentrating effect on policy-makers' minds. And it largely diffused antipathies at the popular level. The Yanks had come to fight the Nazis. They would return to deter the Bolsheviks."[38]

In the last years of World War II the British were more apprehensive over Soviet policy than the United States. Not only Churchill himself but the British Foreign Office became convinced that Stalin had no intention of keeping the wartime agreements but was bent on the expansion of communism as far as possible. The British Foreign Office in 1945–46 felt that the United States was unrealistically optimistic that agreements could be reached with the Soviet Union and postwar cooperation attained. Ernest Bevin, the new foreign secretary in the British Labour government, briefly hoped that a Labour government could achieve better relations with the Soviet Union and that Left could meet Left. But Bevin, who was fundamentally a staunch anti-Communist from his earlier career in the trade union movement, soon concluded that any such hopes were forlorn, and he accepted the analysis of his Foreign Office that the Soviet threat of expansion through Europe posed a grave threat to Britain. Since Britain, however, was too weak to deal with this threat alone, the fundamental requirement of British foreign policy in the late 1940s came to be to draw the United States into cooperation with Britain and the West European powers in order to contain the Soviet Union.[39]

The British were critical of the volatility of American foreign policy and the rapid and unpredictable changes of mood on the part of American public opinion. The British were pleased, however, by the gradual overall change in American opinion between 1945 and 1947 to the viewpoint that it was utopian to hope that the wartime cooperation with the Soviet Union could continue after the war. Britain had feared above all an American retreat into isolation, as after the First World War. Instead, however, the Truman Doctrine in 1947 reflected America's commitment to international involvement in the containment of communism. Britain welcomed this trend in American policy, which the British had used their influence to help to bring about. The Marshall Plan had features which irritated the British, but these were far outweighed not only by the benefits of economic aid but by the process which was involved in the Marshall Plan of drawing the United States into Europe. The Americans meantime came to regard Britain as their bridge with other allies in Europe and their essential junior partner in the containment of the Soviet threat. The culmination of these trends in British and American policy came with the signing of the North Atlantic Treaty in April 1949 and the formation of NATO.

By the end of 1950, however, British fears had arisen again over the volatility of American policy and its tendency to swing from one extreme to the other. Whereas in 1945 Britain feared American withdrawal into isolationism, leaving Britain alone against the Russian bear, by 1950 the British feared that provocative and extreme anti-Communist American policies could lead to war with the Soviet Union or with China. When North Korea invaded South Korea in June 1950, Britain supported the resolute action of President Truman in defense of South Korea. Nor did Britain dissent from the decision that United Nations forces should cross the 38th parallel and invade North Korea in October 1950. However, the subsequent Chinese intervention in Korea in 1950 led Britain to seek a compromise peace acceptable to China, but the United States angrily rejected compromise proposals and instead pressed her allies to vote for a United Nations resolution condemning China as an aggressor, which the British regarded as provocative and unhelpful in the attempt to reach a settlement. At the same time, General Douglas MacArthur's inflammatory statements alarmed the British and aroused fears of an expanded war with China.[40] Moreover, these developments took place against a background within the United States of the Red Scare and McCarthyism. In February 1950 Senator Joseph McCarthy, the junior senator from Wisconsin, made his first speech concerning Communists in the State Department, and this brought to a crescendo the hysterical anticommunism of the Red Scare which had been building up since 1945 and which continued until McCarthy's condemnation by the U.S. Senate in December 1954. The British were aghast by the excesses of McCarthyism and feared that it would add to the political pressures on the U.S. administration to pursue extreme policies in foreign affairs.[41]

Furthermore, while Britain had welcomed the change in American defense policy in 1950 from the very low defense expenditures of the late 1940s, American policy in this matter seemed to swing from one extreme to the other. By late 1950 and early 1951, not only had American defense expenditure increased by enormous amounts, but the U.S. government applied pressure, by means of the military assistance program, to persuade allied countries to increase their defense expenditure significantly. The British government was willing to respond, although left-wing figures such as Aneurin Bevan objected. By 1951, however, even the Conservatives felt that defense expenditure had risen too sharply and that American military assistance had not materialized in the amount anticipated, so that some cutbacks would be necessary.[42]

When Churchill and the Conservatives returned to power following the British general election in December 1951, the acute crises of 1950–51 over Korea, McCarthy, China, and other such matters had abated somewhat, especially after the dismissal of General MacArthur in

April 1951, which the British welcomed. Relations between the Truman and Churchill administrations were good, and the British favored Adlai Stevenson and the Democrats rather than Eisenhower and the Republicans in 1952. Following Eisenhower's election a particular fear of Churchill and Foreign Secretary Anthony Eden concerned Eisenhower's choice of secretary of state. Churchill deeply disliked and feared John Foster Dulles, whom he regarded as the worst embodiment of narrow-minded, dogmatic, extreme American anticommunism. In November 1952 Eden was in the United States and tried to persuade Eisenhower not to appoint Dulles as secretary of state. But Eden had to report the failure of his mission, writing to Churchill that the "man we don't like is still making all the running" and that "we must do the best we can with him." Churchill found this difficult. As Sir John Colville describes Churchill's attitude to Dulles, the latter's " 'great slab of a face' was one he disliked and distrusted."[43] To Eisenhower, Dulles was eminently well qualified to be secretary of state. Dulles had almost been preparing for the office for half of his life. The grandson of a secretary of state, John W. Foster, John Foster Dulles had been an adviser to Thomas Dewey, an adviser to President Truman, and the negotiator of the Japanese peace treaty in 1951. But Eisenhower's reason for choosing Dulles was not only on grounds of his qualifications but also for political reasons. Eisenhower, a moderate Republican, had defeated the conservative senator from Ohio, Robert Taft, to win the Republican nomination for president in 1952. Eisenhower therefore needed to appease the right wing of the Republican party in order to achieve party unity. Dulles's appointment helped this process of reconciliation between the factions within the Republican party.[44]

Against this background of the issues as they had developed since the Second World War, then, the Churchill-Eisenhower correspondence commenced in January 1953. During the period of its duration, until Churchill's retirement in April 1955, the correspondence provides fascinating insights into the relationship between the two statesmen and their response to the issues of international affairs of their time, such as relations with the Soviet Union following Stalin's death, German rearmament, the European Defense Community, Egypt, the Korean armistice, Indochina, Formosa, and atomic energy.

The Introduction, then, has been designed to set the scene by giving the background of the Churchill-Eisenhower relationship up to 1953. It concludes by posing a number of questions that the reader might bear in mind and which are assessed in the Conclusion. Did the Anglo-American "special relationship" become closer and more intimate in the Churchill-Eisenhower era or did the special nature of the relationship gradually wane? How realistic was Churchill's aim to hold a summit meeting and seek a détente with the Soviet Union and how valid were Eisenhower's reservations? How far did Churchill succeed in restraining what he viewed as the extremes of a volatile American foreign policy? Does the correspondence reveal Churchill as an old man clinging to power for too long or does it reveal a world figure continuing to make a valuable contribution in his Indian summer? What evidence does the correspondence reveal with regard to the evaluation of Eisenhower as a statesman?

The purpose of this edition of the Churchill-Eisenhower correspondence is to present the letters and to allow the readers to form their own judgments. Nevertheless, an editor may be permitted in a brief introductory or concluding essay to make an assessment which might be a contribution of some value to scholarship. Robert Griffith, for example, in his edition of *Ike's Letters to a Friend*, has above all served scholarship by publishing the fascinating collection of Eisenhower's letters to his friend, Swede Hazlitt, but Griffith's interesting brief introductory essay is a useful contribution to Eisenhower scholarship.[45] It is hoped, therefore, that the introductory and concluding essays in this edition may be contributions of some value to scholarship on Churchill and Eisenhower. Any such contribution is, however, minor and transitory. The letters of Churchill and Eisenhower themselves, on the other hand, constitute historical documents of great significance and absorbing interest.

Notes

1. Dwight D. Eisenhower to Winston S. Churchill, February 2, 1953.

2. Churchill to Eisenhower, February 7, 1953.

3. C. D. Jackson to J. Davenport, March 19, 1946, C. D. Jackson Papers, Box 32, Dwight D. Eisenhower Library, Abilene, Kansas.

4. Churchill to Roosevelt, June 6, 1943, *Churchill and Roosevelt*, 2:232.

5. Churchill to Roosevelt, October 14, 1943, *Churchill and Roosevelt*, 2:529.

6. Churchill to Roosevelt, January 7, 1945, *Churchill and Roosevelt*, 3:498.

7. Churchill to Roosevelt, April 1, 1945, *Churchill and Roosevelt*, 3:603–4.

8. *Churchill and Roosevelt*, 2:17.

9. Winston S. Churchill, *Closing the Ring*, vol. 5 of *The Second World War* (London: Cassell, 1952), p. 218.

10. Dwight D. Eisenhower, *Crusade in Europe* (New York: Doubleday, 1948), p. 399.

11. David Eisenhower, *Eisenhower at War, 1943–45* (New York: Random House, 1986), p. 55.

12. Winston S. Churchill, *Triumph and Tragedy*, vol. 6 of *The Second World War* (London: Cassell, 1953), p. 545.

13. Churchill to Truman, November 8, 1948, President's Secretary's Files, General File, Winston Churchill 1947–50, Harry S. Truman Library, Independence, Missouri.

14. Churchill to Eisenhower, July 27, 1948, in *Columbia University*, vol. 10 of *The Papers of Dwight D. Eisenhower*, ed. Louis Galambos (Baltimore: Johns Hopkins University Press, 1984), p. 139.

15. Louis Galambos, ed., *Eisenhower, The Chief of Staff*, vol. 7 of *The Papers of Dwight D. Eisenhower* (Baltimore: Johns Hopkins University Press, 1978), p. 686.

16. *Parliamentary Debates* (Hansard), 5th ser., vol. 486, House of Commons, col. 2022, April 19, 1951.

17. John Colville, *The Fringes of Power: Downing Street Diaries, 1939–1955* (London: Hodder and Stoughton, 1985), p. 654.

18. Prime Minister to Foreign Office, January 8, 1953, FO 800 US//53//1, PRO.

19. Colville, *Fringes of Power*, p. 661.

20. Galambos, *Eisenhower, The Chief of Staff*, p. 686.

21. Robert Griffith, ed., *Ike's Letters to a Friend, 1941–58* (Lawrence: University Press of Kansas, 1984), p. 140.

22. Ann C. Whitman to Peter G. Boyle, October 21, 1987, personal correspondence in editor's possession.

23. May 15, 1947, in *The Eisenhower Diaries*, ed. Robert C. Ferrell (New York: W. W. Norton, 1981), p. 142.

24. David Eisenhower, *Eisenhower at War*, p. 552.

25. Ferrell, *Eisenhower Diaries*, p. 223.

26. David Watt, "Introduction: The Anglo-American Relationship," in *The "Special Relationship": Anglo-American Relations since 1945*, ed. William Roger Louis and Hedley Bull (Oxford: Clarendon Press, 1986), p. 1.

27. Keith Feiling, *Neville Chamberlain* (London: Macmillan, 1946), p. 325.

28. David Reynolds, *The Creation of the Anglo-American Alliance, 1937–41* (London: Europa, 1981), pp. 96–120.

29. H. C. Allen, *Great Britain and the United States* (London: Odhams Press, 1954), p. 781.

30. Robin Edmonds, *Setting the Mould: The United States and Britain, 1945–50* (Oxford: Clarendon Press, 1986).

31. H. G. Nicholas, *The United States and Britain* (Chicago: University of Chicago Press, 1975), p. 106.

32. Alan Dobson, *U.S. Wartime Aid to Britain, 1940–46* (London: Croom Helm, 1986).

33. Robert M. Hathaway, *Ambiguous Partnership: Britain and America, 1944–47* (New York: Columbia University Press, 1981), pp. 230–48.

34. Mutual Aid Subcommittee, "U.S. Aid in 1953–54: Draft Memo for Ministers," August 12, 1952, CAB 134//762, PRO; Peter G. Boyle, "The British Foreign Office and American Foreign Policy, 1947–48," *Journal of American*

Studies 16, no. 3 (December 1982): 373–89; Michael J. Hogan, *The Marshall Plan: America, Britain and the Reconstruction of Western Europe, 1947–52* (Cambridge: Cambridge University Press, 1987).

35. Margaret Gowing, *Independence and Deterrence: Britain and Atomic Energy, 1945–52*, 2 vols. (London: Macmillan, 1974).

36. Lord Beloff, "The End of the British Empire and the Assumption of Worldwide Commitments by the United States," in Louis and Bull, *Special Relationship*, pp. 249–60; William Roger Louis, *The British Empire in the Middle East, 1945–51: Arab Nationalism, the United States and Post-War Imperialism* (New York: Oxford University Press, 1986).

37. Paul Gore-Booth, "Record of Conversation with Mr. H. Labouisse," October 22, 1948, FO 371 71828 UR 7321//399//98, PRO; Edmonds, *Setting the Mould*, pp. 182–194.

38. Richard H. Ullman, "America, Britain and the Soviet Threat," in Louis and Bull, *Special Relationship*, p. 104.

39. Peter G. Boyle, "The British Foreign Office View of Soviet-American Relations, 1945–46," *Diplomatic History* 3, no. 3 (Summer 1979): 307–20; Alan Bullock, *Ernest Bevin: Foreign Secretary, 1945–51* (London: Heinemann, 1983); Victor Rothwell, *Britain and the Cold War, 1941–47* (London: Cape, 1982).

40. Burton I. Kaufman, *The Korean War: Challenges in Crisis, Credibility and Command* (Philadelphia: Temple University Press, 1986); Rosemary Foot, *The Wrong War: American Policy and the Dimensions of the Korean Conflict, 1950–53* (Ithaca: Cornell University Press, 1985).

41. Earl Latham, *The Communist Controversy in Washington: From the New Deal to McCarthyism* (Cambridge: Harvard University Press, 1966); Thomas C. Reeves, *The Life and Times of Joe McCarthy* (London: Secker and Warburg, 1978).

42. Peter G. Boyle, "Britain, America and the Transition from Economic to Military Assistance, 1948–51," *Journal of Contemporary History* 22, no. 3 (July 1987): 521–38; Kenneth O. Morgan, *Labour in Power, 1945–51* (Oxford: Clarendon Press, 1984), pp. 339–46.

43. New York to Foreign Office, November 12, 1952, PREM 11 352 T212//52, PRO; New York to Foreign Office, November 21, 1952, PREM 11 352 T221//52, PRO; Peter G. Boyle, "The 'Special Relationship' with Washington," in *The Foreign Policy of Churchill's Peacetime Administration, 1951–55*, ed. John W. Young (Leicester: Leicester University Press, 1988), pp. 32–33.

44. Townsend Hoopes, *The Devil and John Foster Dulles* (Boston: Little Brown, 1973), pp. 135–41; James T. Patterson, *Mr. Republican: A Biography of Robert A. Taft* (Boston: Houghton Mifflin, 1972), p. 583.

45. Griffith, *Ike's Letters to a Friend*, pp. 1–11.

ONE

Response to Stalin's Death
January 29–May 8, 1953

During the first few months of the time when Churchill and Eisenhower both held office as prime minister and president respectively, they established the habit of regular correspondence. The most important topics in early 1953 were Egypt and, following the death of Joseph Stalin in March 1953, relations with the Soviet Union.

European Defense Community

Eisenhower's first letter to Churchill was of an official nature, written on the occasion of the visit to Europe of U.S. Secretary of State John Foster Dulles and Mutual Security Agency director Harold Stassen. Dulles and Stassen toured European capitals for a week, January 31–February 8, 1953, to discuss current problems, in particular the European Defense Community (EDC). They met Churchill, Eden, and other British officials in London on February 4, 1953.

EDC was a controversial proposal designed to allow West German rearmament in a manner which would be politically acceptable to other European countries. At the September 1950 meeting of the North Atlantic Council in New York, the United States insisted that West German rearmament was an essential element in strengthening European security and that if the European powers would not accept this, the United States might not become part of an integrated NATO command. France, deeply disliking the idea of German rearmament, proposed the Pleven Plan for a European Defense Community, presented by René Pleven, French minister of defense. This called for a European army, into which national contingents would be integrated at the level of the smallest possible unit. There would not, therefore, be a German army but German battalions distributed among European brigades. The force would be under a European minister of defense, with a European Defense Council of Ministers and a com-

mon European defense budget. The EDC treaty was signed in May
1952, but it required ratification by signatory states to come into force.

Britain had deep reservations with regard to EDC. Churchill frequently referred to it as "a sludgy amalgam," and Britain gave reluctant support out of deference to American wishes. In November 1951
Eden declared that Britain would work in partnership with EDC rather
than become a full member. The other European nations and the
United States criticized Britain for lack of enthusiasm in supporting
EDC and in hindering European unity in general. Churchill had made
a celebrated speech in Zurich in 1946 regarding a United States of
Europe. Americans, including Eisenhower, did not fully appreciate
that this was a proposal for unity of the continental European countries, with a loose association on the part of Britain, rather than unity
of all European countries, including Britain, which the United States
favored. Eisenhower and Dulles put pressure on the continental European powers to ratify the EDC treaty and on Britain to give more
enthusiastic support. In August 1954, however, the French National
Assembly rejected EDC by 319-264, and the scheme collapsed. Instead, Eden took the initiative in complex maneuvers which led to
West German entry into NATO in 1955.

EISENHOWER TO CHURCHILL

January 29, 1953

My dear Mr. Prime Minister:

I have asked Secretary Dulles and Mr. Stassen to convey to you and
your colleagues my warm personal greetings. I am very glad that they
will have the opportunity of visiting London during their trip to Europe and to talk to you and your associates. I shall always remember
with pleasure my own visits to the United Kingdom and the cordial
and warm reception I invariably received there. I am sure that the
visit of Secretary Dulles and Mr. Stassen will be equally pleasant and
profitable.

The purpose of the trip undertaken by Secretary Dulles and Mr.
Stassen is to obtain first-hand information about the problems which
we and our NATO partners face in pursuing our common goals of
peace, security, and economic health. The passage of time has reinforced my conviction that this joint enterprise is one of the most
important developments in modern history, because it is clear that our
combined strength is far greater than the sum total of its individual
parts. It is for this reason that I have watched with great satisfaction

the far-reaching steps which have been taken toward the integration of the European community, and I retain the most fervent hope that the continental European nations will continue to move forward toward a more complete unity.

In particular, I have been impressed by the support which your government has given to the creation of a European defense community. I believe that your continued support and encouragement are of the utmost importance in the successful completion of this great undertaking which will lay a more solid foundation for peace and progress throughout the free world.

I wish to express my personal admiration for your vital contribution to European unity and Atlantic cooperation, and to assure you that my government will continue to cooperate in every practicable way to advance the mutual interests of our respective peoples.

I enjoyed our recent talks in New York, and hope that you have had a pleasant and restful stay in Jamaica.[1]

Sincerely,
Dwight D. Eisenhower

1. After his talks with Eisenhower in New York on January 5 and 7, Churchill went to Jamaica, where he frequently vacationed.

Formosa

Eisenhower's first letter of a more personal nature deals mainly with Formosa, an issue on which British and American views diverged widely. On the day this letter was written, February 2, 1953, Eisenhower delivered his State of the Union message in which he announced a change in American policy toward Formosa. New instructions were given to the U.S. Seventh Fleet in the Formosa Straits that it should continue to protect the Chinese Nationalists on Formosa from attacks by the Chinese Communists but that it should no longer, as instructed by a directive of June 27, 1950, prevent the Chinese Nationalists from making attacks upon the Chinese Communists on the mainland.

When Mao Tse-tung and the Communists came to power in 1949 and Chiang Kai-shek and the Nationalists withdrew to Formosa, the United States was initially inclined, in late 1949 and early 1950, to take no action in the event of an anticipated Chinese Communist invasion of Formosa. Policy changed with the growing political pressure on the Truman administration as a result of charges of being "soft on Communism" and with the outbreak of the Korean War on June 25, 1950. On June 27, 1950, Truman ordered the Seventh Fleet to maintain order in the area of Formosa and to keep war limited to Korea by preventing attacks by the Communists against Formosa or by the Nationalists against the mainland. Britain supported American policy in Korea but disassociated herself from American policy with regard to Formosa.

With Communist Chinese intervention into the Korean War in October 1950, it seemed odd for the American navy to be engaged in the protection of the Chinese mainland from attack while American forces were engaged in hostilities with Chinese Communist troops in Korea. In practice, the Nationalists made many raids on the mainland, which the Seventh Fleet was unwilling or unable to prevent. Nevertheless, Eisenhower felt that a change in directive to the Seventh Fleet was necessary and would serve American military and diplomatic interests in China and Korea, while it would also provide a useful sop to right-wing Republicans who had long called for the "unleashing of Chiang." The British accepted that the current American policy with regard to Formosa was anomalous and politically difficult to sustain. The British feared, however, that a public pronouncement of an end of the prohibition on attacks by the Nationalists would appear provocative to the Chinese Communists and suggest a willingness on the part of the United States to widen the war in the Far East. Despite British misgivings, Eisenhower was determined on a change of policy regarding Formosa. On January 27 the Foreign Office was officially informed of Eisenhower's intended statement on Formosa in his State of the Union message. On January 31 the Foreign Office sent a telegram expressing British regret over the American decision, which the British government felt would have unfortunate repercussions internationally without compensating military or diplomatic advantages in helping to bring an end to the war in Korea.

EISENHOWER TO CHURCHILL

February 2, 1953

Dear Prime Minister,

Over the weekend, I had your cable referring to our intention of relieving the Seventh Fleet of responsibility for defending China.[1]

Of course, I have no means of knowing what will be the effect of this order if the Communists are determined to hunt for any excuse in order to justify some indefensible action on their part. Your message made a point of the fact that no great military advantage would result from our decision. This is likely true. But there is a very definite psychological point involved—even self respect. The United States is in the peculiar position of battling Chinese Communists in Korea; while, at the same time, under the old order, of accepting the humiliating position of defending Communist China against a possible attack.

You may be right in your guess that the United Nations will, initially at least, disapprove of our decision. Nevertheless, I am making it quite clear in my statement that we intend nothing aggressive—that we are just tired of being dupes.

No one could be more desirous than I of developing a common political attitude among the Western nations with respect to our Asiatic problem. Never will you or your associates find anything but the greatest of sympathy from us in our effort to reach logical, common attitudes and policies in that region. But, to save me, I cannot see why any of our friends have a right to expect of the United States that it maintain such an anomalous attitude as was required of it under the original order.

I assure you again that there is nothing belligerent in my feeling—in fact, there is possibly in this whole world not a less belligerent person than I am!

This message is nothing but a personal communication. It is not, of course, a part of the diplomatic exchanges between the British Government and the United States Government. But it is my understanding that you and I hope to maintain, even if only intermittently, a personal correspondence, which will provide opportunity to help clarify intentions, and explain reasons for decisions, when this seems appropriate.

With warm personal regard,

As ever,
Eisenhower[2]

1. Foreign Office to Washington, January 31, 1953, FO 371 105196 FC 1018/9, PRO.
2. After this letter, Eisenhower did not again use his surname in his signature but signed himself as "Ike," "D.E.," or "Ike E."

Atomic Energy

Churchill's reply was above all an expression of pleasure that Eisenhower had begun the personal correspondence which Churchill so wished. It is significant, however, that in this first letter Churchill raised a matter on which he hoped to extract substantial concessions from Eisenhower, namely, atomic energy.

At the beginning of the Second World War British scientists were further advanced than their American counterparts in the field of atomic energy. Nevertheless, in 1941, even before America's entry into the war, Churchill willingly agreed to a request from Roosevelt that British scientists share atomic information with the Americans, and in 1942 Churchill agreed to the establishment of the Manhattan Project, with the transfer to the United States of work on the atomic bomb. But Churchill became concerned that Britain was being denied its proper share of atomic information, and he attempted to solve the matter in agreements with Roosevelt, especially the Quebec agreement of August 1943 and the Hyde Park aide-mémoire of June 1944. By the Quebec agreement each side agreed not to use the atomic bomb without the consent of the other, while, with regard to the peaceful uses of atomic energy, the U.S. president was left with discretion to share information as he saw fit, a discretion which Churchill assumed that the U.S. president would exercise generously toward Britain. With the informal style of Churchill-Roosevelt diplomacy, the agreement was not properly lodged in U.S. bureaucratic files, and a copy was found later in the American records only in a misplaced file in the Navy Department.

After the war the United States wished international control of atomic energy and the McMahon Act of 1946 prohibited disclosure of atomic information by the United States to other countries. The British government felt bitterly that the Americans had not honored the wartime agreements. The Labour government headed by Clement Attlee initiated an ambitious program of atomic energy development by Britain for both military and civil purposes, but this program received virtually no scientific or technical information from the United States. The matter was one of the sorest points in Anglo-American relations in the late 1940s, though the dispute was not made public since the Attlee government developed its program with great secrecy. When Churchill returned to office in 1951 he was pleased to discover the progress made by Attlee on the British development of atomic energy. He was very critical, however, of the Labour government's inability to gain information from the United States. Churchill was hopeful that he could make Anglo-American relations closer in general and that this would result in particular in American agreement to increase atomic information to Britain.

Churchill discussed the matter with Eisenhower in New York on

January 5, 1953, and he showed Eisenhower a copy of the Quebec agreement of 1943. Eisenhower was sympathetic to Britain on the matter. Moreover, the successful British test of an atomic bomb in 1952 weakened the case for continuing to withhold information. Eisenhower sought amendments to the McMahon Act to allow more disclosure to Britain. Congressional opposition, however, made progress difficult and although amendments to the McMahon Act were passed in 1954 it was not until the late 1950s that a fuller flow of atomic information to Britain took place.

CHURCHILL TO EISENHOWER

February 7, 1953

My dear Ike—if I may so venture—[1]

I was so glad to get your letter of February 2, and to feel that our private correspondence will continue apart from the regular official communications. I hope you believe that I understand all the reasons that led to your declaration.[2] If it had been necessary, I would have explained to the House of Commons the distress of millions of Americans whose relations are under fire in Korea because of the prolonged stalemate, and the apparent association of the United States Seventh Fleet with the security of the Communist country that is firing on them. I feel it in my bones, and it grieves and stirs me every day. If you could find time to read Anthony's speech, which I enclose, you will see how earnestly he put this aspect before the House;[3] and there was no doubt that it is fully accepted by all except perhaps an eighth of the Members, and most of them would come into line on a grave issue.[4] What I do hope is that where joint action or action affecting our common destiny is desired, you will let us know beforehand so that we can give our opinion and advice in time to have them considered. Now that you are in the saddle and can deal with long term policies, this ought to be possible. Anthony and I are resolved to make our cooperation with the United States effective over the world scene. I am sure that you will not hesitate to tell him frankly all your thoughts on these matters when you see him. He will know mine.

Let me know if I should send you the facsimile of my agreement with Roosevelt about the atomic bomb. When we talked you said you would like it, but maybe you have found one in your own archives. I am hopeful that now that we are making the bomb ourselves, we could interchange information to mutual advantage.

I am very glad it is all arranged for Anthony and Rab Butler to come over next month.[5] I shall stay here myself and mind the shop.
[. . .][6]

I am sure you will realise that in these matters I do not wish to ask favours of the United States but only action or inaction for our mutual advantage.

Yours ever,
Winston S. Churchill

1. In only four other letters did Churchill "so venture" as to address Eisenhower as Ike. Churchill's normal salutation was "My dear Friend," while Eisenhower consistently used the form, "Dear Winston."

2. Eisenhower pronouncement on Formosa, February 2, 1953.

3. Speech by Anthony Eden, British foreign secretary, 1951–55, *Parliamentary Debates* (Hansard), 5th ser., vol. 510, House of Commons, cols. 2057–67, February 15, 1953.

4. Left-wing Labour members of Parliament, such as Aneurin Bevan, Sidney Silverman, and Emrys Hughes.

5. Anthony Eden and R. A. Butler, chancellor of the exchequer, came to Washington for talks on March 4–7, 1953.

6. Paragraph classified.

CHURCHILL TO EISENHOWER

February 9, 1955

My dear Mr. President,

Thank you very much for your letter of January 29 and for your kind greetings.[1]

We have been very glad to have your Secretary of State and Mr. Stassen with us for a short visit, and I am sure that the discussions which they had with the Foreign Secretary and myself and some of our colleagues were most valuable to both sides.

We entirely agree with you about the paramount importance of the North Atlantic Treaty Organisation, on the strength of which our whole future depends. A good deal of attention was given during our talks with Mr. Dulles to the problems of the European Defence Community. There was complete agreement that it was desirable to make rapid progress in setting up the Community. We were able to tell Mr. Dulles of our most recent communication to the six Powers about our military association with them. We hope that this will lead to really close practical co-operation and also help to solve the immediate problem of securing French ratification. We agreed to urge our Dutch friends to ratify the treaty at the earliest opportunity without necessarily waiting for the French and the Germans to ratify.

We shall be discussing these questions with the French Ministers this week. We have certain ideas for equally close co-operation with the E.D.C. in the political field. You can rely upon us to continue to give every support and encouragement to this great undertaking. I have noted with great pleasure the successful talks Mr. Dulles has just had in Bonn with the federal Chancellor and I am sure they will be a great help to Dr. Adenauer in completing German ratification.[2]

I need hardly assure you of our determination to work as closely as possible with your Government in all matters affecting our common interests. Our collaboration within the wider society of the Atlantic community is indeed essential to the attainment of our goals of peace, security and prosperity.

Yours sincerely,
Winston S. Churchill

1. Churchill replied to Eisenhower's more personal letter of February 2 before his reply to the more formal communication of January 29.

2. Dulles met Dr. Konrad Adenauer, chancellor of West Germany, in Bonn on February 5, 1953.

EISENHOWER TO CHURCHILL

February 12, 1953

Dear Winston,

I shall write you at length another time, but meantime I wanted to send you this note to thank you very much for your letter of the seventh.

I read Anthony's speech with great interest and thought it was fine. We are looking forward to his visit.

With warm personal regard,

As ever,
D.E.

Egypt

One of the most difficult issues in Anglo-American relations in the early 1950s was Egypt. Britain had gradually increased influence in Egypt throughout the nineteenth century as Ottoman power declined.

In 1875 Britain purchased the khedive's shares in the Suez Canal, and Egypt became important to Britain as a means to ensure an orderly and secure route to India. In 1882 British troops were sent to Egypt, originally as a temporary measure to suppress an antiforeign revolt, but British forces remained in Egypt until 1954. Egypt was nominally independent but was effectively an informal part of the British Empire, especially with regard to defense and foreign affairs. The Anglo-Egyptian treaty of 1936 gave greater theoretical independence to Egypt while it formalized Britain's rights regarding her military base in Suez. The 1936 treaty enabled Britain to retain Egyptian acquiescence during World War II, when the Suez base was of vital importance in the war in North Africa. After 1945 successive Egyptian governments demanded a cancellation or drastic revision of the 1936 treaty and British withdrawal from Egypt. Egyptian pressure increased following the overthrow of King Farouk in a military coup in July 1952. The new government was headed by General Mohammed Naguib but power lay with the Revolutionary Command Council, which fell increasingly under the control of Lieutenant Colonel Gamal Abdel Nasser, who finally ousted Naguib in April 1954.

By the early 1950s Britain's need for the Suez base had greatly diminished, since nuclear weapons had altered strategic considerations, Turkey had joined NATO, the eighty thousand British troops in Suez were needed as a strategic reserve at home, and above all because the base was useful only with local acceptance and had become useless with local hostility and terrorist attacks on British troops. The 1936 treaty was due to expire after twenty years, and the British were prepared to negotiate earlier revision and withdrawal. Britain wished, however, to retain the ability to reactivate the base in wartime. Britain had a number of negotiating positions, ranging from the best to the worst terms for withdrawal, referred to as cases A, B, and C. Britain hoped also to draw Egypt into Middle East defense against Soviet penetration, especially by Egyptian membership in the Baghdad Pact, along with Turkey, Iraq, and Pakistan.

The American attitude toward Egypt was ambivalent. On the one hand, the United States condemned British imperialism in Egypt. On the other hand, the Americans supported British efforts to strengthen Middle Eastern defense in the containment of possible Soviet penetration into the area. The British became very irritated by moralizing American criticisms of British colonialism and even more so when open American sympathy toward Egypt undermined Britain's negotiating position. Anglo-American differences became even more acute when the United States, in its efforts to increase influence in Egypt and to win Egyptian adherence to an anti-Soviet defense organization, was less cautious than Britain in supplying arms to Egypt—arms which might be used against British soldiers.

In October 1954 a new treaty was signed by which the British withdrew from the Suez base, with the right to return in the event of an attack by a foreign power on Egypt, on another Arab country, or on Turkey. In 1956, a year and a half after Churchill's retirement, an attack on Egypt came not from an outside power, thereby requiring a British return to defend Egypt, but from Britain herself, in collusion with France and Israel. The British action was vigorously condemned by the United States, which pressured Britain into withdrawal. The Suez crisis of 1956 marked the nadir in postwar Anglo-American relations.

CHURCHILL TO EISENHOWER

February 18, 1953

My dear friend,

Thank you very much for your kind letter of February 12. I now write to you about the Suez Canal and M.E.D.O.[1]

We reached an agreement with the late United States Administration about the minimum arrangements necessary before we began to withdraw our forces. I do not know the level on your side which our discussions with your people had reached; Acheson and Bradley certainly knew.[2] The talks took place here between December 31 and January 7 and the conclusions were set out in agreed papers copies of which I enclose. I have given my assent to these plans, epitomized on page 11, paragraph 1, in the five sub-heads a, b, c, d, and e, and in A in the Appendix on page 7, because of the enormous advantages which might flow from our joint action.[3]

There is no question of our seeking or needing military, physical, or financial aid from you. Alex[4] assures me that our forces in the Canal are in ample strength to resist any attack, and even if necessary, in order to prevent a massacre of white people and to rescue them, to enter Cairo and Alexandria, for which all preparations have been made for some time at 96 hours' notice. Moreover, nearly half the effective Egyptian Army, about 15,000 men, stands on the Eastern side of the Canal watching Israel. They could be easily forced to surrender perhaps indeed merely by cutting off supplies. As for Egypt herself, the cutting off of the oil would, as you know, exercise a decisive effect. There is therefore no question of our needing your help or to reinforce the 80,000 men we have kept at great expense on tiptoe during the last year. The advantages of our working together on the lines agreed with your predecessors are so great that a successful result might be achieved without violence or bloodshed and without exposing you to any military obligation.

We feel however that our Ambassador, Stevenson, requires to be guided by one of our strongest military personalities.[5] The Socialist Government sent Field-Marshal Slim out there in 1949 and 1950, and he did extremely well in his visits.[6] He has profound knowledge of the military situation and was indeed until recently responsible as C.I.G.S. for advising us upon it. I am sure you know him well. He would head our delegation if the Australian Government will agree to postpone for a few weeks his assumption of their Governor-General-ship. If not, it might be Slessor or Portal or Tedder, as the Air has a lot to say.[7] I wonder whether you would consider favourably placing a first class American military figure with Ambassador Caffery?[8] You have many versed alike in policy and defence.

Thus we should present to the dictator Naguib an agreed plan which represents far-reaching concessions on our part, sustained by Britain and the United States and by outstanding representatives thoroughly soaked in the Middle East problem. This would, I am sure, give the best chance of making a tolerable arrangement for M.E.D.O. without a renewal of Anglo-Egyptian strife. Let me repeat that if all fails the United States would in no circumstances be involved in military operations.

I shall be most grateful if you will let me know what you think of these ideas.

Kindest regards,
Winston

1. Middle East Defense Organization.
2. Dean Acheson, U.S. secretary of state, 1949–53; General Omar Bradley, chairman, Joint Chiefs of Staff, 1950–53.
3. *FRUS, 1952–54*, 9:1967, n. 5.
4. Field Marshal Lord Alexander of Tunis, British minister of defense.
5. Sir Ralph Stevenson, British ambassador to Egypt.
6. Field Marshal Sir William Slim, chief of the Imperial General Staff, appointed governor-general of Australia in 1953.
7. Sir John Slessor, chief of the Air Staff. Lord Portal of Hungerford and Lord Tedder of Glenguin were previous chiefs of the Air Staff.
8. Jefferson Caffery, U.S. ambassador to Egypt.

CHURCHILL TO EISENHOWER

February 20, 1953

I sent you yesterday by air an important letter about Egypt. I was so glad to hear today that your Government endorse the agreement we reached with your predecessors in January. I shall be very grateful for an early answer.

Kindest regards. Winston

CHURCHILL TO EISENHOWER

February 22, 1953

I am sending you the text of a statement about Field-Marshal Slim which we propose to issue tomorrow or on Tuesday a few hours after the Australian Government have announced that his assumption of office as Governor-General is temporarily postponed.[1] It has been necessary for the Australians and ourselves to take this course as Slim was due to sail for Australia on Tuesday.

We have not, of course, referred in any way to your participation, for which we so greatly hope.

Winston

1. The proposed statement announced a request by the British to the Australian government for Slim to be permitted to postpone his assumption of office in order to participate in the negotiations with the Egyptian government.

CHURCHILL TO EISENHOWER

February 23, 1953

At Menzies' request[1] I have agreed to defer British announcement sent with my message of 22nd February until we have your reply. Meanwhile publicity is being confined to a general statement that Slim is postponing his departure for Australia in order to be available to us for consultations about the Middle East.

Amended text follows.[2] Timing has been very difficult owing to Slim having to disembark his baggage today which must give rise to speculation. Also I did not know about George Washington's Birthday, for which I send my sincere apologies.[3]

Winston

1. Robert Menzies, prime minister of Australia.
2. Proposed statement, February 22, and amended statement, February 23, WFIS, Box 16.
3. George Washington's birthday, February 22, was a public holiday in the United States.

EISENHOWER TO CHURCHILL

February 24, 1953

I read your personal letters regarding Egypt with great interest and confess with some concern. However, as you know, we are in general accord with the agreed position arrived at during the January conference in London. I would rather not make final decision on the other matters you mention, such as military representation during Suez discussions until Dulles and I have had an opportunity to discuss the entire problem with Eden, who I understand arrives next Wednesday.

As you know, I have highest regard for Slim and personally feel his participation in discussions will have good and stabilizing effect.

With warm regard,

As ever,
Your Old Friend,
Ike

CHURCHILL TO EISENHOWER

February 25, 1953

My dear friend,

I had a talk with Aldrich[1] when he delivered your message this morning. The time factor is important to me and Menzies as Slim is needed in Australia by the end of April, but of course if you so prefer, the decision can await Eden's talks with you and Dulles.

I am sure you will consider my suggestion in relation to Ridgway's front now so advantageously extended to Turkey.[2] All the Egyptian theatre lies behind Ridgway's right wing and if cast away might be a source of weakness to the whole position in Western Europe. The

Canal of course is a lateral communication in the whole potential front which I believe you would wish to see sustained southward from the North Cape to Korea. Our British interest in the Canal is much reduced by the post-war changes in India, Burma, etc., and we got on all right round the Cape for a long time in the War. I cannot regard it as a major British interest justifying the indefinite maintenance of eighty thousand British troops at immense expense. There are lots of places where they could be used better or the money saved.

On the other hand we are not going to be knocked about with impunity and if we are attacked we shall use our concentrated strength to the full.

It seems to me that you might by standing with us in the approach to Naguib on the lines on which we have agreed bring about a peaceful solution in the truest harmony with the military and moral interests of the anti-Communist front. This is no question of British Imperialism or indeed of any national advantage to us, but only of the common cause. If an Anglo-American team, military and diplomatic, puts our agreed plan firmly to Naguib all may come out well without bloodshed, and other blessings would flow from the success of this decisive accord. Please think of a potential regrouping of forces as a part of your bitter problem in Korea.

We were very pleased to see the line Ambassador Caffery has taken since your hand was on the tiller.

Please talk everything over with Anthony including the atomic point I made to you. I hope that he can be shown the same kind of picture I was given at the Pentagon last year.[3]

> Every good wish,
> Your much older friend,
> Winston

1. Winthrop Aldrich, U.S. ambassador to Britain, 1953–55.
2. General Matthew Ridgway, SACEUR.
3. Churchill was given a full personal briefing on U.S. atomic matters by the Defense Department on his visit to Washington in January 1952.

EISENHOWER TO CHURCHILL

March 5, 1953

Dear Winston,

I have studied your recent telegram and will discuss the whole subject with Anthony whom I hope to see this evening.[1] I am sure the conversations here with Foster Dulles and other members of this government will be mutually profitable.

With all good wishes,
Sincerely,
Ike

1. Anthony Eden visited Washington with R. A. Butler, March 4–7, 1953.

Stalin's Successors

Following Stalin's death on March 5, 1953, a collective leadership, in theory, ruled in the Soviet Union. Its principal figures were Georgi Malenkov, chairman of the Council of Ministers; Nikita Khrushchev, first secretary of the Communist party; Vyacheslav Molotov, foreign minister; Marshal Nikolai Bulganin, minister of defense; and Lavrenti Beria, minister of state security. Initially Malenkov appeared to be the effective new leader. He succeeded to both posts previously held by Stalin, chairman of the Council of Ministers (referred to in the West as prime minister) and first secretary of the Communist party (later changed in title to general secretary). Within two weeks of his succession, however, Malenkov gave up the post of first secretary of the Communist party to Khrushchev, and it became clear that a struggle for power within the collective leadership was taking place. In June 1953 Beria was charged with treason, and in December 1953 he was found guilty and shot. In February 1955 Malenkov was demoted from the post of chairman of the Council of Ministers. Bulganin succeeded Malenkov as chairman of the Council of Ministers and ruled jointly with Khrushchev. But Khrushchev's power steadily grew until by 1957, following the failure of the plot by the so-called antiparty group, Khrushchev's sole leadership was unquestioned.

In the months after Stalin's death, a series of friendly gestures was made by the new Soviet leadership, such as a conciliatory speech on East-West relations by Malenkov on March 15, 1953, the easing of travel restrictions for foreign diplomats, and the granting of permission for Russian wives of some non-Russians to leave the country. These moves were interpreted by some in the West as evidence of the possibility of détente but by others as a deceptive peace initiative designed to lull Western public opinion into a false sense of security. Churchill inclined toward the former view, while Eisenhower inclined toward the latter.

CHURCHILL TO EISENHOWER

March 11, 1953

My dear friend,

I am sure that everyone will want to know whether you still contemplate a meeting with the Soviets. I remember our talk at Bernie's[1] when you told me I was welcome to meet Stalin if I thought fit and that you understood this as meaning that you did not want us to go together, but now there is no more Stalin I wonder whether this makes any difference to your view about separate approaches to the new regime or whether there is a possibility of collective action. When I know how you feel now that the personalities are altered I can make up my own mind on what to advise the Cabinet.

I have the feeling that we might both of us together or separately be called to account if no attempt were made to turn over a leaf so that a new page would be started with something more coherent on it than a series of casual and dangerous incidents at the many points of contact between the two divisions of the world. I cannot doubt you are thinking deeply on this which holds first place in my thoughts. I do not think I met Malenkov but Anthony and I have done a lot of business with Molotov.

I am so glad we have reached an agreement about joint negotiations in Egypt.[2]

Kindest regards. Winston

1. Talks on January 5 and 7, 1953, at the New York apartment of Bernard Baruch. Baruch and Churchill became acquainted in World War I when they were respectively the chairman of the War Industries Board and minister of munitions. Baruch was Churchill's host on several visits by Churchill to the United States.

2. Joint approach by U.S. and U.K. military and diplomatic representatives to the Egyptian government.

EISENHOWER TO CHURCHILL

March 11, 1953

Dear Winston,

The subject raised in your message of today has been engaging our attention here for some days. We are convinced that a move giving to the world some promise of hope, which will have the virtues of simplicity and concreteness, should be made quickly. A number of ideas have been advanced, but none of them has been completely acceptable.

At our meeting in New York I by no means meant to reject the possibility that the leaders of the West might sometime have to make some collective move if we are to achieve progress in lessening the world's tensions. Rather I meant that there could easily arise circumstances that would indicate action on a unilateral basis, and that it was therefore necessary that at bottom our two countries should always have confidence that neither would do anything to damage the other in such an eventuality.

Even now I tend to doubt the wisdom of a formal multilateral meeting since this would give our opponent the same kind of opportunity he has so often had to use such a meeting simultaneously to balk every reasonable effort of ourselves and to make of the whole occurence [sic] another propaganda mill for the Soviet. It is entirely possible, however, that your government and ourselves should agree upon some general purpose and program under which each would have a specific part to play.

Warm regard,
Ike

CHURCHILL TO EISENHOWER

March 19, 1953

My dear Friend,

I am very sorry that you do not feel that you can do much to help us about the Canal Zone. Naturally I am glad that we are broadly speaking agreed upon the merits and upon what we must get. I know that we can count on your goodwill. A month has passed since I wrote my first letter to you and I fear it will be impossible for us to keep Field Marshal Slim any longer from his task in Australia. I hope however that though you may not be able to help us positively it will not look as if the United States is taking sides against us. I am like the American who prayed "Oh Lord, if you cannot help me don't help the bear." It would be a very great pity if differences about the method of approach were represented as differences of policy between our two countries and still worse if they became public.

We are discharging an international duty and are resolved not to be bullied any further by Naguib either in the Canal Zone or in the

Sudan.[1] I have reached my limit. We are neither unable nor afraid to deal with Naguib by ourselves. But even if we have to continue keeping 80,000 troops in the Canal Zone I assure you that in no circumstances will Her Majesty's Government abandon the United Nations crusade in Korea. At present we seem to be heading for a costly and indefinite stalemate both in the Middle East and the Far East instead of helping each other to reach conclusions agreeable to world peace at both ends.

Tito seems full of commonsense.[2] He is definitely of the opinion that the death of Stalin has not made the world safer, but he believes that the new regime will probably feel their way cautiously for some time and even thinks there may be divisions among them. Malenkov and Beria, he says, are united but Molotov is not so closely tied. Anthony and I are doing all we can to urge him to improve his relations with the Italians and also with the Romans. He is very anxious about what would happen if he were attacked all alone. We have said we do not think a local war in Europe is likely or even possible. He was not therefore in particular danger. I pointed out to him the risks we had shown ourselves ready to run by having an American Bomber base in this Island. The point did not seem to have occurred to him.

Kindest regards,
Winston

1. Egypt made claims to the Sudan, which Britain resisted.
2. Marshal Tito of Yugoslavia visited Britain in March 1953. Britain tried to persuade Yugoslavia to settle the dispute over Trieste, which was finally resolved in October 1954.

EISENHOWER TO CHURCHILL

March 19, 1953

Dear Winston,

I am a bit puzzled as to the real meaning of your recent note to me. By no means have I, or my associates, indicated or implied that we are not in agreement with your Government in what you are trying to do in the Canal Zone. On the contrary, Anthony and I reached a clear understanding of what we should strive to get under the various alternatives laid down by the staff, and both of us were very clear that the offer we would be making would be so fair to the Egyptians that we hoped it could not possibly be rejected.

While he was here, I raised one question involving procedure. The question was: "How does the United States get into this consultation?"

It was obvious that no one had thought very much on this point and it was recognized a very awkward situation could result for our representative, and, indeed, for the negotiations themselves, if an American should show up without some prior invitation and agreement between the principals, namely, your Government and the Egyptian Government.

My point is this: If the United States walks into a conference with you, against the wishes of the Egyptian Government, then the only obvious interpretation would be that our two governments, together, are there to announce an ultimatum. An uninvited guest cannot possibly come into your house, be asked to leave, and then expect cordial and courteous treatment if he insists upon staying.

So far as I know, this is the only point that has blocked the initiation of the conference. But until it is ironed out, I do not see how we can possibly get into it.

I am sure that Anthony will confirm to you that I expressed exactly these sentiments to him when he was in my office.

Please be assured that I have no idea that either of us should be bullied by Naguib. We have objectives in common and they are vital objectives, so vital indeed that I do not think we should be inflexible on procedure.

I am much interested in what you say about Tito. I am glad that you and Anthony have been urging him to improve his relations with some of his neighbors.

With warm personal regard,

Sincerely,
D.E.

CHURCHILL TO EISENHOWER

April 5, 1953

My dear Friend,

Thank you so much for your letter. You know the importance I attach to our informal interchange of thoughts.

Of course my Number One is Britain with her eighty million white English-Speaking people working with your one-hundred-and-forty million.[1] My hope for the future is founded on the increasing unity of the English-Speaking world. If that holds all holds. If that fails no one can be sure of what will happen. This does not mean that we should seek to dominate international discussions or always try to say the same thing. There are some cases however where without offending the circle of nations the fact that Britain and the United States took a joint initiative might by itself settle a dispute peaceably to the general advantage of the free world.

It was for this reason that I hoped that Anglo-American unity in Egypt and also in the Levant including Israel, would enable us without bloodshed to secure our common military and political interests. I did not think it would have been wrong for Slim and Hull[2] with our two Ambassadors to have presented the package to Naguib and then seen what he had to say about it. This was on the basis that you would not be asked by us to contribute money or men to any fighting if things went wrong as they may well do now.

However, you have decided that unless invited by Naguib, who like all dictators is the servant of the forces behind him, we cannot present a joint proposal. We therefore have to go it alone. I think however that the fact that Britain and the United States are agreed upon what should be done to preserve an effective base there seems as far as it has gone, already to have had a modifying and helpful influence. Mere bluster by Naguib has not so far been accompanied by any acts of violence.

There is a view strongly held on the Opposition side of Parliament that we ought to abandon Egypt altogether. It is argued that the interests in the Middle East which we bear the burden of defending are international and NATO interests far more than British. The post-war position of India, Pakistan and Burma makes the Suez Canal in many ways more important to them than to us. Even in the War, as you will remember, for three years we did without the Suez Canal. We can keep our contacts with Malaya and Australasia round the Cape as we did then. We could maintain our influence in the Levant and Eastern Mediterranean from Cyprus and our interests in the Persian Gulf from Aden. The great improvement of the right flank of the Western Front achieved by the Yugo-Tito-Greeko-Turko combination has made the danger of a physical Russian attack upon Palestine and Egypt definitely more remote in distance and therefore in what is vital namely in TIME. It is pointed out that if we brought our troops home and under their rearguards our worthwhile stores valued at about £270 million and also cancelled the £200 million so-called sterling debts (incurred in defending Egypt in the War) we should experience great relief.

If your advisors really think that it would be a good thing if we washed our hands of the whole business I should very much like to be told. It is quite certain that we could not justify indefinitely keeping eighty thousand men over there at more than £50 million a year to discharge an international task in this area. If with your influence this burden could be largely reduced the great international Canal could continue to serve all nations, at any rate in time of peace, without throwing an intolerable burden upon us. It is for these reasons which have nothing to do with Imperialism that I persevere.

As all this seems to have something to do with history in which we have both occasionally meddled, I am sure you will not mind my putting the matter before you as I see it.

With kind regards,
Yours very sincerely,
Winston

1. Britain and the British Empire.

2. General John F. Hull, U.S. Army vice-chief of staff, selected as U.S. military representative for talks with the Egyptian government.

CHURCHILL TO EISENHOWER

April 5, 1953

My dear friend,

Anthony and I have been thinking a good deal, as we know you have also, about the apparent change for the better in the Soviet mood. I am sure we shall be in agreement with you that we must remain vigilantly on our guard and maintain all that process of defensive rearmament from which any real improvement must have resulted. We think, as I am sure you do also, that we ought to lose no chance of finding out how far the Malenkov regime are prepared to go in easing things up all round. There seems certainly to be great possibilities in Korea and we are glad of the steps you have taken to resume truce negotiations.[1]

For our part we are sending our Ambassador back to Moscow with instructions to try to settle with Molotov a number of minor points which concern Britain and Russia alone and have caused us trouble in the last few years.[2] None of these are of major importance: they include such matters as the recent Soviet notice of intention to terminate the temporary Anglo-Soviet Fisheries Agreement of 1930, the cases of certain individual British subjects in Russia, exchange rates and restrictions on movements. Talks on them may give us some further indication of the depth of the Soviet purpose. We shall of course gladly keep your people informed of how we progress.

It may be that presently the Soviets will make overtures for some form of direct discussion of world problems, whether on a Four Power basis or in some other manner. I assume of course that we shall deal in the closest collaboration with any such overtures if they are made.

I am sending you today a reply to your letter of the 19th about Egypt.[3]

Winston

1. An American proposal of February 22, 1953, regarding the exchange of sick and wounded prisoners met with Communist acceptance on March 28 and a Communist suggestion of resumption of armistice talks, which had been suspended since October 1952.

2. The British ambassador to the Soviet Union, Sir William Hayter, was recalled to London for consultations following Stalin's death.

3. Above, Churchill to Eisenhower, April 5, 1953.

EISENHOWER TO CHURCHILL

April 6, 1953

Dear Winston,

Thank you very much for your cabled message which reached me this morning. I feel sure that you will find our thinking on the subject largely paralleling your own. We feel that it is entirely possible that you will realize your hope of exploring further into the sincerity of the Soviet intentions through your impending negotiations with them on fisheries and so on.

I am considering the delivery of a formal speech, with the purpose of setting concretely before the world the peaceful intentions of this country.[1] I would hope to do this in such a way as to delineate, at least in outline, the specific steps or measures that we believe necessary to bring about satisfactory relationships with resultant elimination or lowering of tensions throughout the world. These steps are none other than what our governments have sought in the past. I have been working on such a talk for some days and will soon be in a position to show it to your Ambassador, who will of course communicate with you concerning it. While I do not presume to speak for any government other than our own, it would be useless for me to say anything publicly unless I could feel that our principal allies are in general accord with what I will have to say. I am particularly anxious that this be true of Britain, and I think it also necessary to check with France and, as regards Germany, with Adenauer who arrives here tomorrow.

This whole field is strewn with very difficult obstacles, as we all know; but I do think it extremely important that the great masses of the world understand that, on our side, we are deadly serious in our search for peace and are ready to prove this with acts and deeds and not merely assert it in glittering phraseology. This presupposes prior assurance of honest intent on the other side.

With warm regard,
Ike

1. Delivered to the American Society of Newspaper Editors in Washington, D.C., April 16, 1953.

EISENHOWER TO CHURCHILL

April 7, 1953

Just before your letter of April fifth reached my desk, I learned that Anthony is to undergo a major operation.[1] Please convey to him my warm greetings and my most prayerful wishes for his early recovery. I have a great respect for his wisdom and integrity; the free nations cannot spare his sound counsel in these parlous times.

It would be difficult for me to find a single line in your letter with which I disagree, even if I were minded to look for such an opportunity. The convictions expressed in my former letter to you merely paralleled the old proverb about leading a horse to water. I assume that Naguib wants, above all else, to remain in power in Egypt. To do that, he has to have a large proportion of the population with him. To satisfy the population's intense emotionalism with respect to national prestige, he must appear always to be treated in the world's councils as a complete equal. Consequently, a meeting on his own territory should be arranged, if possible, by his invitation.

If this is to be brought about, then we need really skillful negotiators to get him to realize how big he would look to his own people if he should issue an invitation and both of our governments should accept.

As to the abilities of our own Ambassadors—either yours or ours—in Egypt, I know nothing. They may be quite skillful and imaginative; likewise, they may be the reverse. In any event, our two Ambassadors went to see Naguib and were rebuffed.[2] This is the unpleasant fact that must be taken into consideration as we lay plans to go further.

Possibly one way, now, to go about the affair is for your own representative to start negotiations with Naguib and, when there arise in those negotiations the question of additional arms for Egypt—which might in part be provided by us—the question of America's interests and the conditions on which these arms would be furnished, would seem to create a natural opening for an invitation of our representatives to the conference. As quickly as we should receive any kind of intimation of welcome, General Hull would be on his way.

Our general agreement with you as to the things that ought to be done in that area and our readiness to do our best in bringing these things about, stand just as they did when we so expressed ourselves to Anthony during his visit.

But we are convinced that if your government and ours should press Naguib with some sort of ultimatum to the effect that he had to come into a conference with the two of us or we would simply walk out and desert the region, then he would have no recourse but defiance. He would realize, of course, that as a result he might eventually go under. But he would calculate that, by acceptance, he would go under without delay.

There is another subject of vital interest to us both and concerning which I have spoken to you a number of times. It is the need, in Europe, for uniform progress on the Common Defense Plan and for greater political and economic unity. In recent weeks I have been consulting with official and unofficial representatives from some of the countries in Western Europe. Almost without exception, they have said that a more emphatic public endorsement by Great Britain of these projects would be helpful, particularly in securing the support of most of the Socialist Party in France, which is more or less the key to that country's probable action.

Permit me to say again that I should very much like to see you seize some appropriate opportunity to make a major address on the general subject of greater European military and economic unity, stating in your own inimitable and eloquent way the things that you have already announced that Britain is ready to do in support of these purposes. Such might just happen to be the decisive influence.

With warm regard,
Ike

1. Eden entered hospital for an operation to remove gallstones.
2. On March 14, 1953, the British and American ambassadors to Egypt, Sir

Ralph Stevenson and Jefferson Caffery, met Naguib, who declined to issue an invitation to the U.S. government to take part in negotiations on the Canal Zone.

CHURCHILL TO EISENHOWER

April 9, 1953

My dear Ike,

The sixth and last volume of my History of the Second World War was finished before I took office again and will be ready for publication, here and in the United States, towards the end of this year.[1] It deals with the period from the launching of "Overlord" down to the Potsdam Conference—a period of almost unbroken military success for the Allied arms but darkened by forebodings about the political future of Europe which have since been shown to have been only too well founded.

It contains, of course, a good many references to yourself, and I am writing to ask whether you would like to see these before the book comes out. I know that nothing which I have written will damage our friendship. But, now that you have assumed supreme political office in your country, I am most anxious that nothing should be published which might seem to others to threaten our current relations in our public duties or to impair the sympathy and understanding which exist between our countries. I have therefore gone over the book again in the last few months and have taken great pains to ensure that it contains nothing which might imply that there was in those days any controversy or lack of confidence between us. There was in fact little controversy in those years; but I have been careful to ensure that the few differences of opinion which arose are so described that even ill-disposed people will be unable now to turn them to mischievous account.

I think therefore that you can be confident that the publication of this final volume will do nothing to disturb our present relationship. And I can imagine that, in these first few months of your new responsibilities, you will not find much time to turn back to those "far-off things and battles long ago." If, however, you would prefer to have seen, before publication, those passages which refer directly to yourself, I will gladly have the extracts made and sent to you.

Yours sincerely,
Winston S.C.

1. Winston S. Churchill, *Triumph and Tragedy*, vol. 6 of *The Second World War* (London: Cassell, 1953).

CHURCHILL TO EISENHOWER

April 11, 1953

My dear friend,

Thank you so much for sending me an advance copy of your proposed speech. This is indeed a grave and formidable declaration. You will not, I am sure, expect me to commit Her Majesty's Government to the many vital points with which it deals except to say that we are, as ever, wholly with you in the common struggle against communist aggression.

I believe myself that at this moment time is on our side. The apparent change of Soviet mood is so new and so indefinite and its causes so obscure that there could not be much risk in letting things develop. We do not know what these men mean. We do not want to deter them from saying what they mean. Hitherto they have been the aggressors and have done us wrong at a hundred points. We cannot trade their leaving off doing wrong against our necessary defensive measures and policies which action demands and has procured.

Nevertheless, great hope has arisen in the world that there is a change of heart in the vast, mighty masses of Russia and this can carry them far and fast and perhaps into revolution. It has been well said that the most dangerous moment for evil governments is when they begin to reform. Nothing impressed me so much as the doctor story.[1] This must cut very deeply into communist discipline and structure. I would not like it to be thought that a sudden American declaration has prevented this natural growth of events.

All this comes to a particular point upon Korea. I was hoping that at least we should secure at this juncture a bona fide, lasting and effective truce in Korea which might mean the end of that show as a world problem. Indeed, if nothing more than this happened everyone would rejoice. I hope that you will consider what a tremendous score it would be for us all if we could bring off this truce. It seems to me very unlikely that the terms you require for a later political settlement of Korea as set out in your statement would be accepted as they stand by the other side. I fear that the formal promulgation of your five points at this moment might quench the hope of an armistice.[2]

Anthony and I have in mind important comments we could make on your text, but we are not putting them forward now as we hope that our arguments will persuade you to bide your time. We cannot see what you would lose by waiting till the full character and purpose of the Soviet change is more clearly defined and also is apparent to the whole free world. I always like the story of Napoleon going to sleep in his chair as the battle began, saying "Wake me when their infantry column gets beyond the closest wood."

In Anthony's unfortunate but temporary illness I have had to take over the Foreign Office. But this telegram is addressed to you as part of our personal correspondence. I am however showing it to Makins and Aldrich.

Pray let me know what you decide.

Kindest regards,
Winston

1. In January 1953 nine Soviet doctors, including Stalin's personal physician, confessed to charges of plotting against the Soviet regime. In April 1953 Beria revealed that the plot was a fabrication designed to prepare for a purge and that the confessions had been extracted by torture. Two of the doctors had died in prison, but the other seven were released.

2. Eisenhower's five points were cessation of hostilities and exchange of prisoners; free elections in the reunited part of Korea; American economic aid to all parts of Korea; a neutral zone in North Korea along the Yalu River; and ultimate withdrawal of all foreign troops from Korea.

EISENHOWER TO CHURCHILL

April 11, 1953

Dear Winston,

I deeply appreciate your offer to allow me to go over certain excerpts from your forthcoming book, and I am grateful for your expressed anxiety to avoid saying anything that could possibly hurt our relations either directly or indirectly. Although I am so pressed at the moment that I could not go over them personally, Bedell Smith, who, as you know, was my constant companion in the days of which you are now writing, would be glad to perform this service for me. His current position as our Under Secretary of State also makes him peculiarly sensitive to any possible expressions of thought that could have a jarring effect upon our mutual relations. Consequently, if you will send the excerpts to Bedell he will go over them and return them to you at the earliest possible moment.[1]

With regard to your concern about the speech that I must give on April 16th, I have a considerable sympathy with your point that we must be careful to avoid anything that would make the Russians retreat into their shell, if they are, in fact, sincere in extending certain feelers for peace. Nevertheless the time has come in this country when something must be said by me on the whole subject, and of course it cannot be a meaningless jumble of platitudes. I shall consequently soften the parts concerning Korea, and change certain other expressions so that there can be no misinterpretation of our position to be fully and completely receptive in any peace proposals, while at the same time never letting down our guard. I think we must all realize it is primarily our own growing and combined strength that is bringing about a change in the Russian attitude, and that if this is a sincere change we must not be belligerent or truculent. This is the attitude for which I shall strive in this talk.

As for the matter of timing, of course no one can accurately gauge the probable influence of an early statement as opposed to a later one. However, since I am obligated beyond any possibility of withdrawal to making a speech on this general subject, I suggest that you cable at once any comments that you and Anthony may wish to make after reading what I have to say in this message. While I cannot agree in advance to be guided by all of them, I shall certainly consider them prayerfully.

1. General Walter Bedell Smith, Eisenhower's chief of staff during World War II and under secretary of state, 1953–54.

CHURCHILL TO EISENHOWER

April 12, 1953

Thank you so much for your kind message. I do not seek any share of responsibility in the speeches you make to the United States although they play so vital a part in the fortunes of the world. You may be sure that we shall stand by you on fundamentals. The question of timing did however press upon me. It would be a pity if a sudden frost nipped spring in the bud, or if this could be alleged, even if there was no real spring. I do not attempt to predict what the Soviet change of attitude and policy, and it seems to me of mood, means. It might mean an awful lot. Would it not be well to combine the re-assertions of your and our inflexible resolves with some balancing expression of hope that we have entered upon a new era? A new hope has, I feel, been created in the unhappy, bewildered world. It ought to be possible to proclaim our unflinching determination to resist Communist tyranny and aggression and at the same time, though separately, to declare how glad we should be if we found there was a real change of heart and not let it be said that we had closed the door upon it.

Since you kindly invite me to make a few detailed comments I venture to append a few suggestions. (See my immediately following telegram).

I have to make a speech on the 17th and hope to use the theme "we are firm as a rock against aggression but the door is always open to friendship."

About the book. I am delighted that Bedell should vet it for you and I will communicate with him.

Anthony's operation this morning is reported to have been completely successful and was absolutely necessary.

CHURCHILL TO EISENHOWER

April 12, 1953

These are my comments:—

1. No reference is made to the North Atlantic Treaty Organization while great stress is laid upon the E.D.C. Would it not be well to place E.D.C. within the wider scope of our developing North Atlantic Community?

2. There is also no reference to the problem of China and the Far East generally. Could not this be covered by adding to your paragraph about Korea some words about the need to find a basis for future peace in the whole Far Eastern area?

3. Thirdly we are not sure what is meant about the "reunited part of Korea." Does it mean South Korea and North Korea less the neutral zone? In considering such a "neutral zone" much would depend upon the width.

4. In your section about armaments the thought behind paragraph 2 is new to me.[1] As you alone produce at least three times the Soviet steel production this would not be likely to suit their fancy.

5. Sub-paragraphs 3 and 4 about the control of atomic energy are, I presume, a continuance of the position which Bernie Baruch's committee took up in 1946 and on which we have rested ever since and must continue to rest.[2]

6. Finally I am entirely with you on not letting Adenauer down. He seems to me the best German we have found for a long time.

1. Eisenhower's draft suggested a limitation by all nations to a small fixed percentage of total production of certain strategic materials, particularly steel, which could be devoted to military purposes.

2. Churchill correctly presumed that Eisenhower referred to the Baruch plan on international control of atomic energy, proposed in the United Nations in June 1946.

EISENHOWER TO CHURCHILL

April 13, 1953

Dear Winston,

Thank you very much for your prompt reply to my cablegram. I agree with the tenor of your comments and shall certainly strive to make my talk one that will not freeze the tender buds of sprouting decency, if indeed they are really coming out.

Ike

CHURCHILL TO EISENHOWER

April 13, 1953

I thought that now Slim is no longer available the best man to replace him in our negotiations with the Egyptians would be General Sir Brian Robertson, Commander-in-Chief, Middle East Land Forces. I am sure you know him well. The Ambassador will lead our delegation with Robertson as his co-delegate. Therefore, if, as I still hope, you can join us at a later stage, Robertson will be in almost exactly the same position as Hull. Robertson is being relieved of his Command for this purpose a month earlier than would otherwise have been the case.

This announcement will be made on 16th April, and will be preceded on 15th April by an invitation from us to the Egyptians to open negotiations. I intend that there shall be a definite and formal opening. We hope this will be before the end of April.

CHURCHILL TO EISENHOWER

April 15, 1953

Thank you so much for your last message. All good luck. Winston

CHURCHILL TO EISENHOWER

April 21, 1953

My dear friend,

Thank you so much for your letter of April 7 about Egypt on which I am pondering. I conveyed your message to Anthony who was cheered by it. He is having a hard time but is progressing.[1] As you know, we are having our first meeting with the Egyptians on the 27th and nothing will be agreed to by us except as part of a "package" settlement.

Your speech about Russia was well received here by all Parties.[2] I append my statement and that made by Herbert Morrison in reply.[3] No dissent was expressed in any part of the House.

I should like to know what you think should be the next step. Evidently we must wait a few days for their reply or reaction. It is not likely that the Soviets will agree about the release of the Satellites or a unified Korea. There will, however, be a strong movement here for a meeting between Heads of States and Governments. How do you stand about this? In my opinion the best would be that the three victorious Powers, who separated at Potsdam in 1945, should come together again. I like the idea you mentioned to me of Stockholm.[4] I am sure the world will expect something like this to emerge if the Soviets do not turn your proposals down abruptly.

If nothing can be arranged I shall have to consider seriously a personal contact.[5] You told me in New York you would have no objection to this. I should be grateful if you would let me know how these things are shaping in your mind.

Yours ever,
Winston

1. On April 12, 1953, Eden had an operation to remove gallstones, a relatively straightforward matter. Tragically, the surgeon by error cut his biliary duct, thereby creating a much more serious health problem than the original ailment. An operation to remedy the situation was conducted immediately but was only partially successful. In June 1953 Eden went to Boston for another operation, involving a newly devised technique by a Boston specialist of the insertion of a tube in his biliary duct. This operation was successful and after recuperation Eden returned to the Foreign Office in October 1953.

2. Eisenhower's speech to the American Society of Newspaper Editors, Washington, D.C., April 16, 1953.

3. Herbert Morrison, M.P., Labour party spokesman on foreign affairs.

4. In New York, January 5, 1953, Eisenhower suggested Stockholm as a possible venue if a summit meeting took place.

5. Churchill meeting with Soviet leaders without the Americans.

EISENHOWER TO CHURCHILL

April 25, 1953

Dear Winston,

I am glad to learn from your message of April 22 that Anthony is progressing and hope he will soon be completely restored.

Your comments about the reception of my recent speech were most welcome and I warmly appreciate the support contained in your statement in the House of Commons and Mr. Morrison's reply.

As to the next step, I feel that we should not rush things too much and should await the Soviet reply or reaction longer than a few days. There is some feeling here also for a meeting between Heads of States and Governments, but I do not think this should be allowed to press us into precipitate initiatives. Premature action by us in that direction might have the effect of giving the Soviets an easy way out of the position in which I think they are now placed. We have so far seen no concrete Soviet actions which would indicate their willingness to perform in connection with larger issues. In the circumstances we would risk raising hopes of progress toward an accommodation which would be unjustified. This is not to say, of course, that I do not envisage the possible desirability at an appropriate time that the three Western Powers and the Soviets come together. We should by all means be alert.

My thinking concerning a personal contact at this moment runs somewhat along the same line. The situation has changed considerably since we talked in New York and I believe that we should watch developments for a while longer before determining our further course. However, if you should find it necessary for some special and local reason to seek a personal contact, we would hope for as much advance notice as you could possibly give us.

With warm regard,
Ike E.

EISENHOWER TO CHURCHILL

April 25, 1953

This morning I read that you have become a member of the Order of the Garter.[1] My most sincere congratulations both to the Order and to the new member. I am delighted to hear that Anthony is better. To him also my warm regard.

Ike

1. The queen conferred on Churchill the Order of the Garter and he became Sir Winston Churchill.

CHURCHILL TO EISENHOWER

May 4, 1953

I thought of sending something like the following to Molotov:
Begins:
I had hoped you and Eden might soon be having a talk about things as you know each other so well, but his unfortunate illness will prevent this for some time. I wonder whether you would like me to come to Moscow so that we could renew our own war-time relation and so that I could meet Monsieur Malenkov and others of your leading men. Naturally I do not imagine that we could settle any of the grave issues which overhang the immediate future of the world, but I have a feeling that it might be helpful if our intercourse proceeded with the help of friendly acquaintance and goodwill instead of impersonal diplomacy and propaganda. I do not see how this could make things worse. I should of course make it clear I was not expecting any major decisions at this informal meeting but only to restore an easy and friendly basis between us such as I have with so many other countries. Do not on any account suppose that I should be offended if you thought the time and circumstances were unsuitable or that my thought and purpose would be changed. We have both of us lived through a good lot. Let me know how you and your friends feel about my suggestion.

Ends.

The sort of date I have in mind would be three or four days in the last week of May. All good wishes.

Winston

EISENHOWER TO CHURCHILL

May 5, 1953

Dear Winston,

Thank you for yours of May fourth giving me the lines of a message you are thinking of sending to Molotov. Foster and I have considered it deeply and since you sought my views I must say that we would advise against it.

You will pardon me, I know, if I express a bit of astonishment that you think it appropriate to recommend Moscow to Molotov as a suitable meeting place. Uncle Joe used to plead ill health as an excuse for refusing to leave territory under the Russian flag or controlled by the Kremlin.[1] That excuse no longer applies and while I do not for a minute suggest that progress toward peace should be balked by mere matters of protocol, I do have a suspicion that anything the Kremlin could misinterpret as weakness or over-eagerness on our part would militate against success in negotiation.

In my note to you of April twenty-fifth I expressed the view that we should not rush things too much and should not permit feeling in our countries for a meeting between heads of states and government to press us into precipitate initiatives. I feel just as strongly now as I did ten days ago that this is right, and certainly nothing that the Soviet Government has done in the meantime would tend to persuade me differently. I do not feel that the armistice negotiations are going well and this to me has been the first test of the seriousness of Communist intentions.[2] Far from there having been any communist actions which we could accept as indications of such seriousness of purpose the Pravda editorial repeats all the previous Soviet positions[3] and we are now faced with new aggression in Laos.[4]

But in my mind the most important considerations are the results which might be expected to flow from such a personal contact and the effect of such a meeting on our allies, the free world in general and the Russians themselves. It would of course finally become known that you had consulted me, and it would be difficult for me to explain the exact purpose of the visit. Beyond this, failure to consult the French would probably infuriate them, especially when the situation in Indochina is hanging in the balance. If they were consulted in advance, the result would almost certainly be a proposal for a four-party conference, and this, I am convinced, we are not ready for until there is some evidence, in deeds, of a changed Soviet attitude.

Many would expect dramatic and concrete achievements from a personal visit to Moscow by the Prime Minister of Great Britain. Whatever you said publicly about the purposes of your solitary pilgrimage, I suspect that many in the Far East as well as the West would doubt you would go all the way to Moscow merely for good will. I feel this would be true in this country, and the effects on Congress which is this week taking up consideration of our Mutual Defense Program and extension of our Reciprocal Trade Act, would be unpredictable.[5] It seems to me that in this crucial period when the Soviet peace offensive is raising doubts in people's minds, the things we must strive for above all others are to maintain mutual confidence among the members of NATO and other free nations and to avoid any action which could be misinterpreted.

Naturally the final decision is yours, but I feel that the above factors are so important that I should in all candor and friendship lay them before you.

As ever,
Ike E.

1. Stalin attended meetings outside the Soviet Union in 1943 in Tehran in the northern half of Iran, which was Soviet occupied in World War II, and in 1945 at Potsdam in the Soviet-controlled eastern zone of Germany.

2. When Korean War armistice negotiations resumed at Panmunjom on April 26, 1953, difficulties were raised by the Communist side, especially on the exchange of prisoners of war.

3. An editorial in *Pravda*, April 25, 1953, stressed the continuity and correctness of Stalin's course in foreign affairs.

4. In the spring of 1953 three divisions of Vietminh forces led by General Vo Nguyen Giap crossed from North Vietnam to harass French forces on the Plain of Jars in Laos.

5. The Mutual Security Program encompassed previous economic, military, and technical assistance under the Marshall Plan and the Defense Assistance Act. It required annual appropriations. The Reciprocal Trade Agreements Act granted the president authority to reduce the current tariff rate by 5 percent per annum and to lower to 50 percent of the value of the commodity all rates in excess of that figure. It met with much opposition from protectionists and from those who feared that freer trade aided Communist nations.

CHURCHILL TO EISENHOWER

May 7, 1953

My dear friend,

Thank you for your telegram of May 5th. According to my experience of these people in the war we should gain more goodwill on the spot by going as guests of the Soviets than we should lose by appearing to court them. This was particularly the case when Anthony and I spent a fortnight in Moscow in October, 1944. I am not afraid of the "solitary pilgrimage" if I am sure in my heart that it may help forward the cause of peace and even at the worst can only do harm to my reputation. I am fully alive to the impersonal and machine-made foundation of Soviet policy although under a veneer of civilities and hospitalities. I have a strong belief that Soviet self-interest will be their guide. My hope is that it is their self-interest which will bring about an easier state of affairs.

None of the four men who I am told are working together very much as equals, Malenkov, Molotov, Beria and Bulganin, has any contacts outside Russia except Molotov.[1] I am very anxious to know these men and talk to them as I think I can frankly and on the dead level.

It is only by going to Moscow that I can meet them all and as I am only the head of a Government, not of a state, I see no obstacle.[2] Of course, I would much rather go with you to any place you might appoint and that is, I believe, the best chance of a good result. I find it difficult to believe that we shall gain anything by an attitude of pure negation and your message to me certainly does not show much hope.

I will consult with my colleagues upon the position and your weighty adverse advice. At any rate, I will not go until after your budget has been settled by Congress[3] which would mean my delaying till after the Coronation[4] and about the end of June. Perhaps by then you may feel able to propose some combined action. I deeply appreciate the care and thought you have bestowed on my suggestion.

I have also today telegraphed as acting Foreign Secretary to Foster Dulles about the United States offering arms to Egypt at this critical juncture. I presume this telegram will also be laid before you.[5]

With kind regards,
Winston

1. Omits reference to Khrushchev, regarded by Soviet experts in the Foreign Office and State Department as the fifth member of the joint leadership, and in the course of time the most powerful.

2. The monarch, Queen Elizabeth II, was head of state in Britain. Churchill, as prime minister, was head of government. Eisenhower, as president of the United States, was both head of state and head of government.

3. The United States fiscal year ran from July 1–June 30, so that final decisions on budgeting issues were made in June.

4. Coronation of Queen Elizabeth II, June 2, 1953.

5. *FRUS, 1952–54,* 9:2060–61.

Iran

From 1933 a British oil company, the Anglo-Iranian Oil Company (AIOC), controlled the extraction and marketing of Iranian oil. In the late 1940s the United States became critical of British exploitation of Iran by means of a low AIOC royalty payment and of British domination of the Iranian oil business, which American oil companies wished to enter. On the other hand, the United States supported Britain in the determination to prevent Soviet penetration into Iran. Growing Iranian resentment against Britain reached a climax with the exile of the shah and the coming to power of Prime Minister Mohammed Mossadeq, who in May 1952 nationalized the AIOC concession. Britain organized a boycott of Iranian oil and reinforced naval units in the Persian Gulf, while British intelligence planned a covert operation to overthrow Mossadeq. The Truman administration opposed British use of force, fearing that it might lead to Soviet intervention. The Central Intelligence Agency favored cooperation with the British covert operation, but Truman and Acheson sought a negotiated settlement, involving acquisition by American oil companies of part of the AIOC concession in Iran. This was unacceptable to Britain, as were similar proposals made by Eisenhower's secretary of the treasury, George Humphrey, to the British chancellor of the exchequer, R. A. Butler. Eisenhower increasingly viewed Mossadeq as a tool of radical elements dependent for support on the Iranian Communist party, the Tudeh party. Eisenhower therefore gave his blessing to a covert operation planned by Kermit Roosevelt of the CIA to utilize a hired mob to overthrow Mossadeq, which was accomplished on August 19, 1953. The shah was restored to power and an oil agreement was reached with a new international consortium in which AIOC had a 40 percent interest and American oil companies a 40 percent interest.

EISENHOWER TO CHURCHILL

May 8, 1953

Dear Winston,

I like to have your letters.

Your latest one to me was on the subject of your possible visit to Moscow. I gave you my frank comments, and these included the views of my principal advisers, such as Foster Dulles and others. I did try to make it clear that I recognized very clearly your right to make your own decision in such matters. Certainly I share one simple thought with you—this thought is that I would not admit that any consideration of protocol or of personal inconvenience had any slightest weight as compared to a possible chance of advancing the cause of world peace. My own comments to you were addressed solely and exclusively to the possible effects of your projected visit on friends—and others not so friendly.

As of the moment, I am far more concerned in the specific trouble spots of the world. Korea, of course, there still is. Alongside of it we must place in our concern Southeast Asia—with especial emphasis on the new invasion in Laos—and the frustrating situations in Iran and Egypt. This makes no mention of famine conditions in Pakistan and the still unsettled quarrel between that country and India over the Kashmir problem.[1]

I know that some of our people had talks with your Mr. Butler about a possible new approach to the Iranian affair. In my own official family, George Humphrey was very hopeful that he might be of assistance in getting that situation straightened out, but now he tells me that a letter from Mr. Butler rejects the suggestion we had to offer. This was the offer involving the suggestion that a number of our major oil companies might buy out British interests and start afresh in that region. Mr. Humphrey reported to me that your Government felt it very unwise to make any further attempts to settle the Iranian problem, even through the expedient of selling out to a group of commercial companies.

Of course I do not know for certain that we here could have made the necessary arrangements to have permitted these companies to go ahead without the risk of prosecution under our anti-trust laws, but it is disturbing to gain the impression that your Government now considers the situation absolutely hopeless and believes that it would be preferable to face the probability of the whole area falling under Russian domination than to look for a new approach. We appreciate, of course, your concern for proper respect for contracts in the world; we thoroughly understand your conviction that anything that could be interpreted as additional retreat on your part might set loose an endless chain of unfortunate repercussions in other areas of the globe. Nevertheless, I still regard that area as one of potential disaster for the Western world.

Foster showed me your communication about the Egyptian affair.[2] It is possible that I have not thoroughly understood the background in which should be viewed the existing impasse. I was told that some very protracted negotiations between the Egyptians and ourselves, looking toward the supply to them, by us, of a meager quantity of arms, had been held up for a long time pending a satisfactory solution of the Sudan problem.

I had understood that by agreement with your Government, we were to proceed with the transfer of a small amount of equipment (finally reduced to about five million dollars worth) upon the satisfactory completion of that agreement. It is my impression that the Egyptians knew of this general intention on our part.

Later, when there began to appear in press reports some intemperate remarks—even threats—by the Egyptian authorities against our British friends, we began to drag our feet on fulfilling our part of the bargain. The Egyptians, of course, have pressed us again and again on the matter, and we get a bit embarrassed because of their right to charge us with failure to carry out an agreement. We can, of course, adopt the attitude that, because of some of their extraordinary and threatening statements, we are compelled to make certain that they do not intend to use these arms against our friends. In fact, it is my impression that we have long since done this. It is, however, quite difficult to refuse even to talk about the matter or to go so far, for example, as to decline to allow the Egyptian official to see a list of the kind of articles that would be available. I believe that the initial items to be transferred involved only such things as helmets and jeeps.

Now, of course, we can continue to drag our feet for a while. But I do most deeply deplore having gotten into a position where we can be made to feel like we are breaking faith with another government. It is possible that some years ago we may have been too hasty in promising to include Egypt among those countries to whom we would give some help in preparing necessary defense forces, but that is water long over the dam.

With respect to this particular item, we will at least do nothing further until after Foster has had his talk with Naguib.[3] While it is possible that some hopeful break will develop out of that meeting, I must say that I am extremely doubtful.

As of this moment I still think that we have no recourse except to continue the steady buildup of Western morale and of Western economic and military strength. This is the great "must" that confronts us all, but whenever you have an idea—even a piece of one—that might suggest a possibility of us diminishing the burdens that we are compelled to lay upon our collective peoples, please let me know about it. I should certainly like to ponder it.

I hope my comments do not offend—I assure you again I welcome yours.

Won't you please convey to Anthony my very best wishes and the earnest hope that he will soon be returned to full health?

With warm regard to your good self,

As ever,
Ike E.

1. The claim of both India and Pakistan to Kashmir after independence from Britain in 1947 created a chronic unresolved dispute between the two countries.

2. *FRUS, 1952–54,* 9:2060–61.

3. On May 11, 1953, Dulles held a meeting with Naguib in Cairo.

Stroke and Recovery
May 21–December 1, 1953

In May and June 1953 the Churchill-Eisenhower correspondence centered above all on arrangements for a meeting between the two in Bermuda. Eisenhower insisted on the inclusion of the French. After frustrating delays as a result of the fall of the French government on May 22, 1953, and French inability to form a new government for over a month, Churchill's desire for a meeting appeared to be on the point of fulfillment, only for the plans to be thwarted by Churchill's stroke on June 23, 1953, leading to the postponement of the Bermuda Conference. During the period of Churchill's recuperation over the summer of 1953 correspondence with Eisenhower continued but with a much less frequent exchange of letters than in early 1953.

The focus of Eisenhower's attention in the spring and summer of 1953 was primarily on the Korean War, which culminated in an armistice on July 27, 1953. By the autumn Churchill was again seeking a meeting with Eisenhower, which, he hoped, might lead to a summit with the Soviets. Eisenhower continued to insist on the inclusion of the French in the talks rather than the Anglo-American duo preferred by Churchill, and Eisenhower was reserved on the possibility of the three-power talks leading to a summit with the Soviet Union. In December 1953 a meeting at last took place between Churchill, Eisenhower, and the French prime minister, Joseph Laniel.

EISENHOWER TO CHURCHILL

May 21, 1953

This confirms our telephone conversation this afternoon and this evening.[1] I have informed Paris that you are in agreement with me in connection with René Mayer's suggestion.[2] Pursuant to our understanding, you in London and I in Washington will make an announcement simultaneously with Mayer's appearance before Parliament at approximately 3.30 p.m. Paris time tomorrow substantially as follows: "Our three governments have been in consultation with the view of holding an informal high level meeting between the United States, Great Britain and France. We have agreed that such a meeting is desirable at a date convenient to all of us. A primary purpose will be to further develop common viewpoints with these friends on the many problems that must be solved co-operatively so that the cause of world peace may be advanced." It is understood between us, and I have conveyed to Mayer our understanding, that this proposed meeting is not in any way to be tied to Four Power talks with the Soviet Union or to be considered as preliminary thereto. I have informed Mayer that a tentative acceptable place of meeting would be Bermuda and a date sometime after June 15 would be agreeable to both of us. The arrangements, particularly with regard to any time or place of meeting, are to be developed later.

1. Churchill and Eisenhower rarely talked on the telephone, especially since Churchill was hard of hearing.

2. René Mayer, prime minister of France, suggested a three-power meeting to Eisenhower, May 20, 1953.

CHURCHILL TO EISENHOWER

May 21, 1953

I will make the following statement in the House of Commons about 3.30 p.m. (B.S.T.):

"President Eisenhower has expressed a wish for a personal meeting with M. Mayer and myself on June 17th to discuss our common problems. Her Majesty's Government feel that such an exchange of views could only be of advantage at the present time. It has been agreed that Bermuda, where an American base lies, would be a suitable meeting place. The 17th of June is a convenient date to the President and so far as Her Majesty's Government are concerned it will enable the discussions with the Commonwealth Prime Ministers to be completed in accordance with the plans we have already agreed with them. All arrangements are being prepared accordingly and a similar announcement in the French Chamber is, I believe, being made today."

EISENHOWER TO CHURCHILL

May 22, 1953

Dear Winston,

I apologize for getting you on the telephone at an hour that must have been inconvenient for you.[1] However, I felt it necessary to cable an answer promptly to Mr. Mayer, and I certainly wanted to make no kind of suggestion on the matter of a personal meeting without prior consultation with you. Because Anthony was in the hospital, I knew of no one else to talk to except yourself.

Your cable reached me the first thing this morning. I am delighted that you are stressing the importance of a friendly, informal talk among the three of us because of its own value. I agree with you that a lot of good ought to flow from such a meeting.

As we cabled you late last evening, I was mistaken as to the duration of my mid-June trip to the Western part of the country. It will be possible for me to reach Bermuda on the evening of the fifteenth, provided that date will be convenient also for you and Mr. Mayer. Incidentally, one of the reasons that I suggested our State of Maine as a suitable meeting place is because of the lovely weather there this time of year.[2]

I assume that the three governments will be communicating among themselves concerning detailed arrangements for the conference. My personal thought is that each delegation should be quite small. I hope that the three top men can practically limit themselves to friendly discussion and informal conversations. I am personally restive if not irritable under the restriction of formal agenda. I understand, of course, that each of us should have one or two associates along so that detailed matters can be studied and put into proper form for any action we may find it desirable to take.

I particularly like the idea of the three of us bringing along our wives which in my opinion would increase the value of the meeting as a symbol of the friendship existing among us.

With warm regards.

As ever,
Ike E.

1. Eisenhower telephoned at 6 p.m. Washington time, 11 p.m. London time. To Churchill, a notorious night owl, this was not inconvenient.
2. Eisenhower had suggested Maine as a location for a meeting, but Churchill preferred Bermuda.

CHURCHILL TO EISENHOWER

May 23, 1953

Delighted with your letter of 22nd. Am cabling about arrangements later. Kindest regards to you both from Clemmie[1] and me.

Winston

1. Churchill's wife, Lady Clementine Churchill.

Korea

From the spring of 1951 the Korean War became a stalemate, with the two sides dug in on a line close to the 38th parallel and with no progress made in the armistice talks at Panmunjom, which were suspended in October 1952. On December 2–5, 1952, Eisenhower fulfilled a campaign promise to go to Korea between his election and inauguration, which was widely regarded as an implicit promise to end the Korean War. Churchill was also eager to see an end to the war, which he regarded as a distraction from the major area of importance in Europe and as an impediment in relations with the Soviet Union. But Churchill was wary of Eisenhower's willingness to consider stepped-up military action, including a veiled threat to use atomic weapons, in order to break the deadlock in negotiations and bring about a peace settlement.

On February 22, 1953, the United Nations commander in Korea, General Mark Clark, wrote to his opposite number proposing an exchange of sick and wounded prisoners. On March 28 the Communist side accepted the proposal and suggested resumption of the armistice talks. When the talks resumed in April the most difficult stumbling block was the prisoners of war issue. A compromise was finally accepted on June 4 to transfer prisoners to the care of a neutral repatriation commission, under the guard of Indian troops, with an agreement that after 120 days prisoners who still did not wish to be repatriated should not be forced to return to their home country.

The United States was skeptical of the neutrality of the commission, which was comprised of Czechoslovakia, Poland, India, Switzerland, and Sweden, and American negotiators proposed a 4-1 majority for decisions. Despite an attempt by South Korean president Syngman Rhee to sabotage the agreement by allowing twenty-five thousand prisoners to escape on June 18, the POW compromise, together with an American security treaty with South Korea, made possible an armistice, which was signed on July 27, 1953, bringing the Korean War to an end.

EISENHOWER TO CHURCHILL

May 23, 1953

I have carefully considered your message in reply to discussion which Bedell Smith had with representatives of Her Majesty's Embassy on the Korean Armistice Negotiations.[1] I feel that the position Bedell set forth was eminently reasonable especially in view of the fact that we are the parties who are resisting an unprovoked aggression. I had hoped his proposals could have provided the basis upon which we all could have taken a final stand. It is essential that a firm unified stand be taken if the Communists are to be convinced that the United Nations will never forsake the principle of non-forcible repatriation, either in statement or in fact. Upon this there can be no possibility of misunderstanding. The matter has been thoroughly discussed and considered by members of my administration and with Congressional leaders in the light of your message. Although we have grave doubts concerning the conviction of some of the Allies that we can depend upon a simple majority vote we are prepared also to agree to such a voting formula for the Commission provided that the Terms of Reference for the Commission are such as to ensure beyond any reasonable doubt that coercion and force will not be used against the prisoners. This is not a question of detail or procedure but involves the integrity of the basic principle for which we have so long fought and stoutly defended.

The Terms of Reference and basic procedures which will be set forth by the United Nations Command at Panmunjom on May 25 will be clear, simple, and essential for the maintenance of the principle upon which we are all agreed. If an armistice is to be obtained upon any acceptable basis it will be essential that the Communists clearly understand that there can be no deviation from the essential elements of the position to be taken by the United Nations Command. Any sign of weakening in our unity or resolve would again be exploited by them to the disadvantage of all of us. I am sure that you will appreciate that any failure on the part of our principal Allies fully to support the position so clearly reasonable and fair and going so far to meet the views of those Allies would have most adverse effects upon American public and Congressional opinion at this critical time.

With respect to Syngman Rhee's attitude I quite agree that we cannot allow him to dictate policy to our two countries. Yet I beg of you not to forget that Korea is the one place where we have an inspired resistance by the peoples themselves to the Communist enemy. The Koreans are valiantly resisting in numbers that far exceed the combined contributions from all of us. The inspiration for that struggle largely comes from President Rhee.

I believe that a prompt public and unequivocal statement that the United Kingdom was fully consulted and fully supports the position which the United Nations Command is taking in the forthcoming Executive Sessions would assure an armistice promptly, if in fact the Communists want one on the basis acceptable to us.

1. Bedell Smith met British and Dominion representatives in Washington on May 19, 1953. Churchill, as acting foreign secretary, sent a message on May 22, 1953, on British government reaction to the conversations, *FRUS, 1952–54*, 15:1072–73.

CHURCHILL TO EISENHOWER

May 24, 1953

My dear friend,

Thank you for your most kind message of May 22nd. I am very glad your plan has gone off so well in both our countries. I hope to attend the Naval Review on the 15th, but would be able to fly to Bermuda that night arriving the following day. If you could arrive on the evening of the 16th the 17th could be the nominal day for the beginning of our talks if the French can agree. I like all you say about having very few people, no formal agenda and the three top men talking two and three together about our affairs. Clemmie is looking forward greatly to coming.

My present idea is that we should all three stay in the Mid-Ocean Golf Club. I have received high reports of this and Winthrop Aldrich thought you would probably be attracted by it. I do not play golf any more so I shall bring my paint-box. I think that the three of us with our personal staffs—say 8 to 10 each—might stay here while other officials of the delegations will be accommodated separately in suitable hotels. The three of us would have separate accommodation in the Club with our own separate dining arrangements where we would entertain each other as convenient. The main room at this hotel would be suitable for any more formal meetings at which I should certainly invite you to preside as you are the Head of State and we are only politicians.

The Governor, Sir Alexander Hood, will give an official dinner at Government House. About reporters, I think that the press of all three countries should be asked to choose a limited delegation of not more than say 30 in all, including television representatives. The people I shall bring with me besides Clemmie will be two private secretaries; perhaps Sir Norman Brook, the Cabinet Secretary; Makins from our Washington Embassy and one or two Foreign Office experts, particularly on the Far East.

If arrangements on these lines are agreeable to you I will suggest them to the French. I am looking forward so much to seeing you. With kindest regards,

W.S.C.

EISENHOWER TO CHURCHILL

May 26, 1953

Dear Winston,

I appreciate your suggestions for the Bermuda meeting. Needless to say, the proposal for the three of us to stay at the Mid-Ocean Golf Club is personally appealing. However, may I suggest that even though we do not order our lives to meet press reaction, we are meeting on very serious matters, and consequently one of the hotels would seem to be preferable to the golf club as a meeting place. The other arrangements you outline seem eminently satisfactory.

I am glad that we are in agreement that our delegations should not be large and I will let you know as soon as I have talked to Foster and made up my mind on the composition of our group. With regard to press representation I think we would have considerable difficulty in limiting ourselves to the extent you suggest. But isn't this a matter which can be discussed further by our appropriate people?

While I am most grateful for your thought in inviting me to preside at the formal meetings, it seems to me that as our host you should preside at the opening, at least.

It would still be possible for me to arrive on the evening of the 16th provided that proves practicable for the French which I seriously doubt.[1] We asked our people in Paris whether they thought Mayer's commitment to be in Turkey at that moment would create the same obstacle to a mid-June meeting for a new government as it did for the old. Ambassador Dillon[2] reported over the weekend that the visit of the French Prime Minister and the Foreign Minister to Ankara is now scheduled from June 23 to June 27, inclusive, and that June 29 seemed the earliest date at which the new Prime Minister could reach Bermuda unless the Turkish visit is again postponed. I should not like to press the French to postpone this again.

I see no objection to your inquiring directly of the French whether they think they could meet the Mid-June date, although I hardly think that the present Ministers will feel that they can commit the future Prime Minister before he is selected and obtains parliamentary investiture.

Mamie[3] and I are looking forward to seeing you both.

With warmest regards, Ike E.

1. On May 22, 1953, Mayer lost a vote of confidence in the French National Assembly. Efforts to form a new government were unsuccessful until Laniel formed a government on June 26, 1953.
2. Douglas Dillon, U.S. ambassador to France.
3. Eisenhower's wife, Mrs. Mamie Doud Eisenhower.

CHURCHILL TO EISENHOWER

May 28, 1953

Yours of the 27th. The official name is Mid-Ocean Club. I put "golf" in to attract you. Actually the golf links are around this otherwise admirable hotel. Any arrangements agreeable to you can easily be made. Formal meetings could be held at Government House and I would open the proceedings only by asking you to preside. This follows the Yalta precedent if that is still a help.

It now looks as if the French uncertainties may impose a much longer delay upon our meeting. I like the idea of Reynaud coming as he knows the story and has lived through it.[1] He is quite right to demand some security of tenure. Nevertheless I feel the delay is unfortunate.

I will cable you again as soon as the French situation clears. Meanwhile I am making all preliminary arrangements.

I hope that our declaration of support will be of help at Panmunjom.

Let me thank you warmly for your kindness in responding so readily to Makins' suggestion about Anthony's airplane. The doctors have today decided he should leave on the 5th and as the Canadian Government plane already here is going back on that date this will be the easiest course.[2] Please allow me to mention your kind offer when the arrangements are announced.

All good wishes.
Winston

1. Paul Reynaud unsuccessfully attempted to form a government. Reynaud was prime minister when France fell in 1940, and was deported to Germany during the war, but he was familiar with political problems relating to German rearmament and was willing to support this.

2. Eden came to Boston on June 5, 1953, for an operation.

CHURCHILL TO EISENHOWER

May 29, 1953

In the talk between Bedell and Makins on May 23 the idea was mentioned that perhaps the United States might make some approach to Moscow to help agreement at Panmunjom. I don't know how it all passed, but since the matter has been discussed I hope you won't mind my giving you my opinion. I think it would be a pity for the United States to make an approach to Moscow at this juncture and that it would only be taken by them as a sign of weakness. You are the overwhelmingly powerful figure in the ring and we are supporting you in your effort to make the Communists accept.

It would be quite a different thing for me to send a personal and private message to Molotov and indeed I had thought of doing this anyhow. My message would be in effect—

(Begins)

You will no doubt have seen about the Bermuda Conference. I am hoping that it may result in bridges being built not barriers between East and West. It would I am sure be a help if this Punmunjom Prisoners of War business were got out of the way.

(Ends)

The position would then be the United States maintaining a formidable front and Britain, bound to them by unbreakable ties, giving a friendly hint. Let me know how you feel about this.

I am so glad to read just now your remarks about Taft's speech.[1] I look back with dark memories to all that followed inch by inch upon the United States's withdrawal from the League of Nations over 30 years ago. Thank God you are at the helm.

1. At a press conference on May 28, 1953, Eisenhower expressed disagreement with the view put forward by Senator Robert A. Taft (R-Ohio) that the

United States should abandon efforts to work through the United Nations on Korea. Taft was a prominent isolationist in the 1930s.

EISENHOWER TO CHURCHILL

May 30, 1953

Dear Winston,

The Mid-Ocean is perfectly satisfactory to me, especially since it appears that each of us can have a few of his principal people around him. I will deem it an honor to share the Mid-Ocean Club with you and our French confrere. Incidentally, I hope that there will be no objection to my bringing along with Mrs. Eisenhower her mother and her woman companion. Could you let me know on this point? Of course, the overflow part of the American governmental delegation will be stationed on our air base in Bermuda.

I earnestly hope to keep my entire official delegation down to something on the order of a dozen to fifteen, but I cannot greatly influence the size of the press, radio and photographers sections. These people, of course, travel under their own steam and secure their own accommodation without specific governmental approval. A great proportion of the foreign press representatives stationed in Washington will insist upon going and, of course, the American press will want to be heavily represented. I imagine that they soon will be trying to reserve every hotel in Bermuda for their operations, and I am frank to say that I do not know how we can do anything at this end to control this matter. In fact, it is possible that we would not want to control it for the reason that I should think it would be best for all of us that the entire world was saturated with information that we were enjoying a friendly, informal and profitable get-together.

I sincerely hope that the meeting will not be too long delayed, but we must wait patiently until the French can make up their minds.

I appreciate your declaration of support in connection with Panmunjom. Makins has kept you informed of our special problems and I know you understand them. We should have a report from Clark sometime Sunday night.

With respect to the message to our Ambassador in Moscow, it was not at all any formal representation or appeal of any kind. Our Ambassador was merely instructed to make the observation in connection with other business he was conducting with Molotov that we had, of course, made our final offer at Panmunjom.

Ike

CHURCHILL TO EISENHOWER

May 30, 1953

My dear Friend,

Your message of 30th.

I am so glad that Mid-Ocean Club will suit you. I am assured it is the best pick and as it is stated to hold eighty guests there should be plenty of room. It will be splendid if Mrs. Eisenhower's mother and companion will come too.

My official circles will be kept very small like yours. I agree with you that the press cannot be limited. Sir Norman Brook, the Secretary of the Cabinet, and about to become a Privy Councillor, will look after details for me and keep any members of your staff you nominate fully informed on any points that arise. I am sure that you do not want to be bothered with details.

I am glad about the message to your Ambassador in Moscow. I shall send Molotov a telegram on my own responsibility on the lines that I mentioned to you.

About the date. The French delay in forming a Government may be considerable and anyhow they have their Turkish business on the 23rd or 24th. It looks to me that the 29th may well have to be our target. Let us try to keep four or five days for our stay. I was sorry about Reynaud whose attitude was manly and patriotic.[1]

> With kindest regards,
> Yours ever,
> Winston

1. Reynaud refused to make sufficient compromises with other French political parties which were needed to form a government.

CHURCHILL TO EISENHOWER

June 4, 1953

In the course of my talk with the Turkish Prime Minister and his Foreign Secretary on Monday, June 1, the Prime Minister said that they had just received a telegram from Ankara to the following effect:

Molotov had sent them a most friendly message saying that in 1945 Georgia and Armenia had made substantial territorial claims to Turkish territory in settlement after the war and also that the

U.S.S.R. had claimed military control of the Bosphorus and Dardanelles.[1] Molotov now wished to assure the Turkish Government that these demands no longer formed part of Soviet policy and should be considered as withdrawn.

The Turkish Prime Minister asked me what I thought of this. I said that it showed how wise Turkey had been to join the N.A.T.O. front.[2] The Turkish Prime Minister replied that this was exactly the impression he and his colleagues had sustained. I then said that of course it might be either part of a plan to divide the allies or, as we should all hope, part of a new Soviet policy to have a détente and easier relations all round. The course for all of us seemed simple, namely, while welcoming any improved change of heart, to hold firmly together and to our present policy. He appeared to agree cordially with this.

1. The claim made in 1945 for provinces in northern Turkey by Georgia and Armenia, two of the fifteen republics of the Soviet Union, were in effect made by the Soviet government.
2. Turkey became a member of NATO in 1952.

EISENHOWER TO CHURCHILL

June 4, 1953

Dear Winston,

I fully agree with you that June 29 should be our target date for Bermuda and that the meeting should last about four days. Foster will of course come with me and he will be accompanied by a small group of advisers, generally corresponding to the group which Makins has indicated will accompany you. Douglas MacArthur II, who is Counselor of the Department of State, will be the opposite number of Norman Brook and will coordinate details for us. Brook can get in touch with him at any time.

I understand through Makins that your view is that the purpose of the meeting should be announced as one of a general exchange of views and that it will be informal and without official agenda. I agree with this. Regarding your suggestion that there be no daily press briefings, I do believe there will have to be some sort of daily briefing of the press by the three press officers, even if not much of substance is handed out. In fact, I think it would be good for the press to know that we are getting along well together. I am instructing my people to discuss the substance and the timing of the announcement as well as press arrangements with your representatives here, and of course this as well as other matters such as the June 29 date will have to be coordinated with the French.

My plane will be flying to Bermuda about mid-June, returning the following day, and Makins might desire to send Gore-Booth[1] or some other representative on this short trip for a preview of preliminary arrangements.

As Makins is accompanying you, I will probably have to invite Ambassadors Aldrich and Dillon, but these two and any additions that we may have to make would not impose on your hospitality, as they can be accommodated at our air base in Bermuda.

With warmest regards, Ike

1. Paul Gore-Booth, press attaché in the British embassy, Washington, D.C.

CHURCHILL TO EISENHOWER

June 5, 1953

Our Ambassador in Paris tells me that M. Parodi, Secretary General to the Ministry of Foreign Affairs, has telephoned to say that he has been in touch with M. Bidault[1] and with the Secretariat of the President of the Council. These both agree that, subject to a reserve about the constitutional position, June 29th would be acceptable. Parodi said that although there was no French Government he would take it upon himself to say that arrangements could go ahead accordingly for that date.

In these circumstances I am making all arrangements for starting our talks on the 29th. I shall leave on the 27th and arrive in Bermuda the 28th so that I can receive you.

W.S.C.

1. George Bidault, a former French foreign minister, became foreign minister again in the government which was finally formed by Joseph Laniel.

EISENHOWER TO CHURCHILL

June 5, 1953

I have received your message with reference to Bermuda date. We shall proceed correspondingly from this side subject to the consideration pointed out by Foster yesterday that we must in the last analysis be prepared to accommodate ourselves to the French situation and not seem to put them under external pressures as they are solving their governmental problem at home.

I look forward to our meeting.

EISENHOWER TO CHURCHILL

June 10, 1953

From my discussion with Foster about the findings of his recent trip, I am particularly concerned about Egypt. While I will wish to talk to you personally about this matter in Bermuda, there seems to be a real danger that the situation there will not hold that long without further action.

I was happy to hear that you agreed with Foster's statement of our position on May 12, 1953, at Cairo.[1] He reaffirmed that position in his radio report to the American public on June 1. I fully concur in his views.

From Foster's personal observation and from all other reports which reach us, I have come to the conclusion that some step should be made soon to reconcile our minimum defense needs with the very strong nationalist sentiments of the Egyptian Government and people. It appears that it is not possible to conclude a settlement on the basis of Case A in its entirety, despite its desirability from a military point of view. As we had agreed when it was thought we might negotiate side by side, there may have to be some concessions which will permit a quick start on withdrawal of UK troops and produce an adequate if not ideal arrangement for maintenance of the Base. Dept. of State is sending to Amembassy London a formula which illustrates what we have in mind and which your staff can examine if you so desire. To assist further with this problem, if you desired and if it proved helpful with the Egyptians, I would be prepared to assign US technicians to participate in the maintenance of the Base.

In addition to the question of maintenance there is, of course, the problem of assuring availability of the Base in time of need. Pending more formal arrangements, a private undertaking by Egypt that the Base would be made available in case of general war to the Arab States and to the Allies of Arab States might serve the purpose. You could invoke your treaties with Jordan and Iraq and we might also be able to utilize our special relationship with Saudi Arabia.

Also, on the conclusion of agreement on evacuation and the future maintenance of the Base, Naguib might publicly invite the United Kingdom and the United States to help develop the defense of Egypt, including training and equipping of the Egyptian forces. In response to this initiative, we could jointly negotiate the necessary formal defense requirements of the West, as well as assistance to Egypt. The results of these negotiations could be made public. Meanwhile, as I think you know, Foster, at your request, is presently deferring any arms aid to Egypt.

Once agreements of the nature described were reached with the Egyptians, we would be prepared to insist uncompromisingly on their being carried out in good faith. This determination could be made unequivocally clear to the Egyptians.

I am sorry to bother you with this before we can talk together at Bermuda but the possible danger from the situation to us all is so much on my mind that I intrude these ideas at this time in accordance with the spirit which has animated our full and frank exchange of views.

1. *FRUS, 1952–54,* 9:2065–73.

CHURCHILL TO EISENHOWER

June 12, 1953

My dear friend,

I look forward to a good talk about Egypt when we meet in Bermuda. Meanwhile, I think I must send you at once my first reactions to the new formula suggested in the message which I have just had from you.

In the hope of reaching agreement with you and your predecessor we went over all this ground before and agreed to make a number of concessions to the Egyptian point of view. Our object in these discussions was not to obtain military or financial aid from the United States, but only their moral support in what we hoped would be a joint approach to the Egyptian dictatorship. However, you decided to defer to Egyptian objections to your representatives, including General Hull, taking part in the discussions. Since then we have been disappointed not to receive more support particularly in Cairo from your Government in spite of the numerous far-reaching concessions which we made in our joint discussions with you.

We went forward alone, having made clear to you that we did not seek United States mediation or arbitration. The Egyptian dictatorship presently "washed their hands" of the discussions, timing it no doubt to fit in with Mr. Foster Dulles' visit. We are quite ready to resume the talks if they should intimate a wish to do so. This could be no humiliation to them as the meeting place is under their roof. Nothing however has happened: the campaign of threats and abuse of the most violent character to which we have been for many months subjected has not been followed by any action except a few murders. Latterly there has been a decline in the campaign of threats and abuse, and this no doubt is due to the fact that the Egyptian people have lost faith in its sincerity and consider it all bluff for political purposes, or are hoping for some help from the United States. We propose to await developments with patience and composure. If a further approach is made to us to resume discussions, we shall comply without, however, any change in principle in the terms on which we had decided and to which we understood you had in the main agreed. I should have no objection to your advising the Egyptians to resume the talks, provided of course they were not led to believe that you were whittling us down, or prepared to intervene in a matter in which the whole burden, not nineteen-twentieths but repeat the whole burden, falls on us, and about which I thought we were agreed. After all there are other bases conceded for mutual security in other countries not even established by formal treaty—for instance yours in the United Kingdom.

If at the present time the United States indicated divergence from us in spite of the measure of agreement we had reached after making so many concessions, we should not think we had been treated fairly by our great Ally, with whom we are working in so many parts of the globe for the causes which we both espouse. If as a result of American encouragement at this juncture or a promise or delivery of arms, Dictator Naguib is emboldened to translate his threats into action, bloodshed on a scale difficult to measure beforehand might well result, and for this we should feel no responsibility, having acted throughout in a sincere spirit for the defence not of British but of international or inter-Allied interests of a high order.

As I have said I look forward to talking these matters over with you in Bermuda. Meanwhile I watch the progress of events with the closest attention.

I asked General Robertson, who with our Ambassador has been conducting the negotiations and is now in London, for his opinion. My immediately following telegram contains the note he has written.[1] I send it to you although it was not drafted for your eye, and I wrote my own cable before seeing it.

I am sending you a separate message about other events.

Kindest regards, Winston

1. Note by General Robertson, PREM 11 1074, June 12, 1953.

CHURCHILL TO EISENHOWER

June 12, 1953

My dear friend,

Our Egyptian correspondence seems to add a greater urgency to our meeting at Bermuda. On the other hand the French vacuum continues and our Ambassador in Paris reports that we may well have to wait for a fully functioning French Government until the 22nd, and I suppose they would like to have some discussion among themselves after that. Then there is the Fourth of July which I presume would require your presence at home. I will come any time but it seems doubtful whether the Big Three including the one who perhaps ought to be called the Unknown Quantity can meet before the end of the first week in July or perhaps even later. In the meantime there is this controversy about Egypt, the developments in the Far East and Adenauer's fortunes at the German elections,[1] on all of which it is urgent that you and I should reach agreement.

I really think we should both make it clear to the French that we are going to meet as proposed on the 29th for which all arrangements have been made. Might this not be a spur to the French or at least teach them a lesson?

Winston

1. Election in the Federal Republic of West Germany, September 6, 1953.

EISENHOWER TO CHURCHILL

June 13, 1953

I am concerned about the continuing French Cabinet crisis. According to the best guess of my people and assuming that he will get his vote of investiture, Andre Marie cannot be expected to have his cabinet formed and functioning before the end of next week at best.[1] This would give our French friends only a short week to take stock of their situation and to review their policies before joining us at Bermuda. I do not believe that this would contribute to the general lines of agreement which I hope will result from our talks. I therefore suggest that our Ambassadors inform the French Government that we fully appreciate their difficulties and propose to postpone our meeting at Bermuda by two weeks to give them ample time to settle their internal problem and to prepare for our meeting.

I believe the French would appreciate this initiative on our part and that it should yield dividends when we meet.

When one takes into account the possibility that Andre Marie may fail in his attempt to form a government, the above course of action seems even more advisable.

Ike

1. André Marie was one of several French political leaders who unsuccessfully attempted to form a government in May–June 1953.

CHURCHILL TO EISENHOWER

June 14, 1953

We are certainly prepared to help in transporting Indian troops to Korea. Nehru[1] will I am sure be very willing to help. I have told him it would mean 5,000 men. He said he had passed this to his Commander-in-Chief in India. I do not know whether he would choose Cariappa[2] but I am confident he will do his best to find a good man.

1. Pandit Jawaharlal Nehru, prime minister of India.
2. General K. M. Cariappa, commander in chief of the Indian army.

CHURCHILL TO EISENHOWER

June 16, 1953

My dear Friend,

I have just had a long talk with Winthrop Aldrich and I was delighted to hear from him all the friendly things you said about me and our close relationship in the face of so many baffling problems.

About Bermuda. Our telegrams of the 12th and the 13th evidently crossed and I suppose we were both waiting to hear from each other. André Marie has accepted and my information from our Embassy in Paris is that he may well be accepted by the Chamber on Thursday the 18th; that Bidault would be his Foreign Secretary; that the foreign policy would be very much what Mayer and he were pursuing and that therefore there would still be time for them to make the 29th, as you proposed to me when the 15th failed. I am told that the Quai d'Orsay have not received any suggestion from the United States that the date should be again put off, and that they have not made any request themselves, and also that they are going on with the arrangements for the journey of the French representatives to Bermuda. I hope therefore we may await what happens in Paris on the 18th and 19th before offering a further delay.

It seems to me that the imminence of this date, the 29th, will help André Marie to get his vote because there is deep concern in French circles lest their failure to form a Government should prevent their formal recognition by our two countries as being one of the Big Three.

Of course if they fail again or if the new Premier asks for a little more time you and I could consider that together. I hope however that we should not go beyond an extra week, say Tuesday, July 7th. I have my problems too and Parliament rises on July 31. It would leave me very little time to get back after the conference and put the case resulting from our decisions to them if we did not meet before the 15th. Moreover the world anxiously awaits the result of our mission and no one is more worried than Dr. Adenauer, with his elections pending in the last days of August.

I am still hoping for the 29th and all my plans and also arrangements in Bermuda have been made for the 29th. I trust therefore we can keep our options open till we see what happens in Paris on Thursday the 18th.[1] Please let me know your wishes at your earliest convenience.

> With kindest regards,
> Winston

1. A vote in the French National Assembly was scheduled for June 18, 1953, on Marie's attempt to form a new government.

EISENHOWER TO CHURCHILL

June 17, 1953

Dear Winston,

Thank you very much for your prompt response to my recent message on Egypt. There are certain passages in your reply which I fail to understand but I believe it more profitable to leave these for the personal talks we anticipate in Bermuda.

I was interested to note that Robertson feels that agreement might be reached which would retain the essentials of Case A, providing there is reasonably prompt resumption of discussions and that some adjustments are made to meet Egyptian sensibilities. As you know, I personally believe that the best interests of all of us will be served if friendly discussions are promptly resumed in Cairo. Obviously, however, it would be worse than futile to resume those talks unless you and I are absolutely clear as to the minimum objectives we hope to attain, and have some reason to believe that these would not be rejected out of hand by the Egyptians. Perhaps our March agreement on the type of base arrangement to be sought, which you mention, would serve the purpose. If my memory serves me correctly, the negotiators were to have flexibility between arrangements which would insure a working Base in peace which would be immediately operable in event of war, and one which would require 60 days for reactivation. Won't you please dismiss any thoughts of us, here, seeming to desert any agreed position or exhibiting weakness. Foster's statements in Cairo[1] and his notification to the Egyptians that they cannot get arms as long as you and they are disagreed should reassure you on this.

With warm personal regard, Ike

1. Dulles's statements to the British ambassador to Egypt in Cairo, May 12–13, 1953, *FRUS, 1952–54*, 9:2065–73.

CHURCHILL TO EISENHOWER

June 19, 1953

My dear Friend,

I was very glad to get your message of the 18th about Egypt. I look forward to a good talk with you about the problems at Bermuda. Thank you especially for your final paragraph. I did not mean to suggest anything to the contrary in my cable, as I have absolute confidence in American goodwill and fair play.

The French and Bermuda. Marie has failed. These recurring delays are very painful to me and very bad for world affairs. You and I have quite a lot of things which concern us both on which our public agreement would be helpful all round. Could we not both tell the French that we two shall be meeting on July 8, and hope they will join us?

This would enable me to receive you at any time convenient to yourself on the 7th with the Guard of Honour of the Welch Regiment which I have brought from Jamaica. The Conference could start the next day, the 8th. Such a message would, I believe, help to clinch matters in the French Chamber. Every day's delay before we meet is unfortunate and it would be a disaster if our meeting did not take place. Uncertainty and bewilderment are growing in Europe every day, and Adenauer's election draws near.

I was very glad to read Foster Dulles' statement about Syngman Rhee's violation of the United Nations agreement.[1] I shall do all I can to keep Parliament in step with you on these lines. There will be a lot of trouble if the war goes on while Syngman Rhee remains in office.

I shall be grateful if you would let me know about Bermuda at the earliest moment, and also let me know when you receive this.

With kindest regards,
Winston

1. Following Rhee's release of twenty-five thousand prisoners on June 18, Dulles warned him that he must abide by United Nations authority in ending the war or "another arrangement" (unspecified) would be necessary.

EISENHOWER TO CHURCHILL

June 19, 1953

Dear Winston,

I have put off attempting a definitive reply to you regarding a date for our Bermuda talks, because of the uncertainty of the French situation. I know that Foster has kept you advised of our thinking through Roger Makins. Now the latest effort to form a French Government under Marie has failed and I suppose we cannot anticipate a government before the latter part of next week, which would be only a day or two before the Prime Minister and Foreign Minister would presumably have to leave if we hold to the 29th. It seems to me unrealistic to think that under these circumstances we can have a responsible and authoritative French government to talk with at Bermuda on the 29th. I am reluctant to proceed without them or with only token French representation, because many of the matters on which we should reach an understanding involve the French. I have particularly in mind such matters as firming up on EDC and also arriving at some clear understanding of how the French propose to deal with the situation in Indochina. This touches both of us deeply—you because of your Malayan problem[1]—us because we are already footing much of the bill, and because what happens there has a great bearing on the offshore position, including the Philippines and Japan.

Under the circumstances, I suggest we should advise the French Government that we are postponing our Bermuda Conference until

July 13. I am very reluctant to do this, as I know you are, but I really see no practical alternative.

Another consideration is the extremely awkward turn that Rhee has given the Korean situation. We do not know yet what this may portend—whether it is a single gesture of defiance, following which he will go along in efforts to repair if possible the damage and make an armistice possible or whether he is determined to prevent any armistice. I fear the latter.

Foster and I must give this matter close attention for a few days and from that standpoint a little delay on Bermuda could be put to good advantage by us in relation to Korea. Please let me know as soon as convenient how your own thoughts are running on this matter.

Faithfully yours,
Ike

1. Communist guerrilla forces engaged in terrorist activities against the British colonial authorities in Malaya.

EISENHOWER TO CHURCHILL

June 19, 1953

Dear Winston,

Your message just reached my office.

First, with respect to Bermuda. This morning I sent you a message suggesting the 13th, but I can easily make the 8th, if that is more convenient for you. Consequently, we shall count on arriving there on the 7th, with work to start on the 8th, and will notify the French of this intent. This, however, does not preclude the possibility that either you or I may be faced with some circumstance that again will require modification of our plans. I hope that will not be the case, because I quite agree with you that we should have a meeting, and I sincerely trust that the fixing of this kind of date may put some pressure on the French.

The Korean business is indeed difficult. There can be no question as to the soundness of your observation about the trouble we shall have if the war goes on and Syngman Rhee remains in his present office. It is remarkable how little concern men seem to have for logic, statistics, and even, indeed, survival; we live by emotion, prejudice and pride.

With warm regard,
Ike

CHURCHILL TO EISENHOWER

June 20, 1953

Thank you so much for your latest telegram. I shall sail in the Vanguard to arrive Bermuda on the 6th and welcome you on the 7th. The more we can make it clear this date is a fixture the better will be the chances of a French Government. I must again emphasize my own difficulties in further indefinite delay.

You may like to see the directive about E.D.C. which I have sent to our Conservative delegates at Strasbourg.[1]

Clemmie and I are looking forward so much to meeting you and your family party. All good wishes in these troublous times.

Winston

1. Churchill enclosed a directive to Conservative delegates to the Council of Europe in Strasbourg pledging British support of, though not membership in, EDC.

CHURCHILL TO EISENHOWER

June 21, 1953

I have received the following message from Sir Oliver Harvey[1] in reply to a "buck-up" telegram I sent him about the Bermuda rendez-vous.

Begins. "I conveyed your message to Parodi this morning. French authorities had received similar communication from Washington. M. Bidault has replied that they agree." Ends.

I am therefore making all arrangements to leave here in the "Van-guard" on the night of June 30 and look forward to receiving you on the 7th in Bermuda. My projected movements will be published here tomorrow Monday.

As military questions are sure to crop up between us I should like to bring Alex with me and, as I wish to talk over with you atomic matters and a document I showed you when we met last January, to bring the Prof., i.e. Lord Cherwell.[2] He explains things to me I cannot otherwise understand. I do not suppose you have any objection to this addition to my party. It would not in any way impede our separate private talks.

W.S.C.

1. Sir Oliver Harvey, British ambassador to France.
2. Lord Cherwell, Churchill's scientific adviser.

EISENHOWER TO CHURCHILL

June 22, 1953

Dear Winston,

Thank you very much for your several messages. I am particularly delighted to read the instructions that you have sent to your delegation at Strasbourg. I have always felt certain that an emphatically stated British position on this point would be most effective. At different times you have given all of the assurances that seemed to be necessary or appropriate, but many people have doubted British enthusiasm.

I shall be looking forward to seeing you on the 7th.

Ike

EISENHOWER TO CHURCHILL

June 23, 1953

I should like you to know that I have personally approved the proposal which I have asked Foster to make to Roger Makins that the United States, British and French Governments invite Pug Ismay[1] to come to Bermuda in his capacity as Secretary General of NATO. This step would demonstrate to the world the solidarity of the North Atlantic Alliance in a highly effective and dramatic way. Furthermore, I am sure you will agree that Pug's informal advice, counsel and comradeship will be of great value to us.

1. Lord Hastings Lionel Ismay, NATO secretary-general, 1953–57.

EISENHOWER TO CHURCHILL

June 23, 1953

Dear Winston,

Circumstances have arisen which make it inadvisable for me to bring Mamie and her mother to Bermuda. This I regret very much but it cannot be helped. Mamie is very disappointed to miss this fine opportunity to visit with Clemmie.

Warm personal regard. Ike

CHURCHILL TO EISENHOWER

June 23, 1953

I am very sorry about Mamie but Clemmie will come all the same in a private capacity.

I am bringing Alex and the Prof with me. We all hope to have a good rest during the voyage although we shall be in full contact both ways.

I am holding three battalions and an artillery regiment at short notice in Hong Kong "to reinforce General Mark Clark's army in any action that may be required of them by the United Nations." Let me know whether you would like this made public. I did not quite understand what "gainsaying" meant, but presume you meant it would stave off adverse criticism in the U.S.A.[1]

Am looking forward so much to seeing you.

Kindest regards,
Winston

1. Reference to "gainsaying" puzzled Eisenhower, as indicated in the following telegram. The quotation is from an unidentified telegram, not written by Eisenhower.

EISENHOWER TO CHURCHILL

June 25, 1953

Dear Winston,

I am still chasing the word "gainsaying" back and forth across the ether waves of the Atlantic. Certainly I have never been guilty of using such a ten shilling monstrosity.

Ike

Churchill's Stroke

On the evening of June 23, 1953, Churchill suffered a stroke. The nature of his ailment, however, was disguised from the public and from most of his colleagues. A vague, bland medical report regarding the prime minister's illness was issued to explain the postponement of the Bermuda Conference. The public did not learn that the illness was a stroke until Churchill referred to the matter in a speech in the House of Commons on March 2, 1955.

The possibility of an immediate resignation was complicated by the serious illness at the same time of the heir apparent, Anthony Eden. Churchill had talked of retirement since 1952, but he was very reluctant to go, so that Eden's illness provided him with a convenient excuse to stay on in the summer of 1953. In any event, he made a relatively strong recovery, just as he had recovered from a previous stroke in 1949 and from other similar ailments. In October 1953 he made an effective leader's speech at the annual Conservative party conference, and this convinced him that he could continue in office for some time longer. His physical condition increasingly showed signs of old age and the effects of strokes. At some times he was perfectly normal. At other times he was very feeble and his mind wandered, which, combined with his growing deafness and unwillingness to use a hearing aid, made him appear a pathetic figure and a painful embarrassment in company. But he was not senile. In short spasms, on topics of particular interest to him, he was more or less his old self in his conduct of affairs.

CHURCHILL TO EISENHOWER

June 26, 1953

You will see from the attached medical report the reasons why I cannot come to Bermuda. I am as bad as the French, thinking that the conference should be postponed. Meanwhile Lord Salisbury could fly to Washington at any time convenient to you in the next fortnight and would put our point of view and establish the intimate Anglo-American contact which is the keystone of our policy.[1]

Let me know your reaction. No announcement will be made till tomorrow.

Thanks for your gainsaying telegram.

Every good wish.
Winston

Medical Report (Communique)

The Prime Minister has had no respite for a long time from his very arduous duties and is in need of a complete rest. We have therefore advised him to abandon his journey to Bermuda and to lighten his duties for at least a month.

Moran. Russell Brain.[2]

1. The Marquess of Salisbury was acting foreign secretary, June–October 1953.
2. Lord Moran, Churchill's personal physician; Dr. Russell Brain, a leading specialist on strokes.

EISENHOWER TO CHURCHILL

June 26, 1953

Dear Winston,

I am deeply distressed to learn that your physicians have advised you to lighten your duties at this time and that consequently you will be unable to come to Bermuda for our talks.

I look upon this only as a temporary deferment of our meeting. Your health is of great concern to all the world and you must, therefore, bow to the advice of your physicians.

With best wishes from your friend.

Ike

CHURCHILL TO EISENHOWER

July 1, 1953

My dear Ike,

It was indeed kind of you to send me such a nice letter. I am so sorry to be the cause of upsetting so many plans. I had a sudden stroke which as it developed completely paralysed my left side and affected my speech. I therefore had no choice as I could not have walked with you along the Guard of Honour of the Welch Regiment, complete with their beautiful white goat, whose salute you would I am sure have acknowledged.[1] Four years ago in 1949, I had another similar attack and was for a good many days unable to sign my name. As I was out of Office I kept this secret and have managed to work through two General Elections and a lot of other business since. I am therefore not without hope of pursuing my theme a little longer but it will be a few weeks before any opinion can be formed. I am glad to say I have already made progress. I have not told anybody these details which are for your eyes alone.

Meanwhile I am sure you and Foster will like Salisbury. He holds all my views on Egypt and the Sudan very strongly and I think his idea of bringing General Robertson with him next week is a very good one. I still hope that he and Hull and our two Ambassadors may jointly meet the Egyptian Dictator and that Agreement may be reached on the general basis of Case A. If we could say that you are satisfied with the arrangements for security of the Base and with the discharge of our international duty, it would make a solution easier and better looking. I wish I could have talked to you about all this and could convince you that we are only doing our duty. However I have great confidence that Salisbury, whom I have known for so many years and admired ever since he resigned from Chamberlain's Government with Anthony Eden, will put our case to you in firm but agreeable terms.[2]

I had never thought of a Four Power meeting taking place till after E.D.C. was either ratified or discarded by the French and I thought November would be the sort of time. Adenauer and Bonn seem to be moving towards a united Germany and now they speak of a Four Power Conference with approval.

I thought Senator Wiley's[3] assumption that the Russian change of policy is only due to fear among a trembling remnane [*sic*] of gangsters and felons "cringing in the Kremlin" goes too far in assessing a situation where these "cringing" people could at any moment march to the Rhine in a month and to the sea in two months, and where if they do not wish to play the full stake themselves they can stir, bribe and arm the Chinese to throw Indo-China, Siam and Burma into immense disturbance. It is this feeling that makes me so anxious that before we reject all hope of a Soviet change of heart we should convince our peoples that we have done our best. After all, ten years of easement plus productive science might make a different world. I have no more intention than I had at Fulton or in 1945 of being fooled by the Russians. I think however there is a change in the world balance, largely through American action and re-armament, but also through the ebb of Communist philosophy, which justifies a cold-blooded, factual study by the free nations while keeping united and strong.

I am venturing to send you some papers about the Duke of Windsor which I hope you will find time to consider.[4] Also I am today sending Bedell the chapters in my last volume which refer to you and to some divergencies of view between us. They will probably be published in October though whether I shall still remain in office is unpredictable.

Clemmie sends greetings to you and Mamie. She was much looking forward to our excursion.

With all good wishes.
W.S.C.

1. The goat was the regimental mascot of the Welch Regiment.

2. Eden resigned as foreign secretary and Salisbury (then Lord Cranbourne) as under secretary in February 1938 over Prime Minister Neville Chamberlain's policy of appeasement.

3. Senator Alexander Wiley (R-Wisconsin), chairman, Senate Committee on Foreign Relations, 1953–54.

4. A three-page letter from Churchill to Eisenhower on this matter, June 27, 1953, with a three-page enclosure, and a one-page reply from Eisenhower to Churchill, July 2, 1953, remain classified.

EISENHOWER TO CHURCHILL

July 6, 1953

Dear Winston,

I shall, of course, keep completely secret the character of your illness. I am cheered to note that you are very hopeful, but of course I agree that your doctors must make the final judgment on the question of your return to full duty. My prayers are with you.

While I have met Lord Salisbury only once or twice—and then very briefly—I am quite sure that I shall come to share your high opinion of him. Everything I have ever heard about him leads me to such a conclusion. Foster knows him and has the highest regard for him.

In the Egyptian affair we, of course, always have wanted to obtain a solution that would conform as nearly as possible to Case A. However, we have recognized the probability that some concessions would have to be made to Egyptian pride and spirit of nationalism. And so, in our thinking we established Case B as representative of a minimum position, and have hoped for an agreement that would be somewhere in between these two cases—as near, of course, to Case A as possible.

We shall certainly be ready to talk to Lord Salisbury about the matter. In laying out a program looking toward a settlement, we earnestly believe it would be a grave error to ignore the intensity of Egyptian popular feeling. Dictators can never afford to cease striving for popularity: I think that the methods by which they normally come to power inspire them with a feeling of great personal insecurity. In Egypt, if Naguib thought that the population wanted him to be conservative and reasonable, we would have no trouble whatsoever. As it is, I think he feels he is sitting on a lid that covers a seething desire to throw out every foreigner in the country. In other words, he believes that any formula found for the solution of this problem must have appealing features for the Egyptian population—otherwise he will find himself happy indeed to join another Egyptian exile, now in Italy.[1]

It is possible that whatever difference there may be in our respective approaches to this whole Egyptian affair springs out of our differing estimates of the flexibility that Naguib feels is available to him in negotiation. We believe that he is very definitely a prisoner of local circumstances of which the most important is Egyptian nationalism, and consequently he will act and react in accordance with them.

I note with interest your thought about a four power meeting and French action on the EDC. If the French Parliament should reject it, I cannot possibly over-emphasize the adverse effect such action would have on public opinion in this country. Our people and our Congress are getting exceedingly tired of aid programs that seem to them to produce no good results. They believe earnestly that only closer union among the nations of Western Europe, including Western Germany, can produce a political, economic and military climate in which the common security can be assured. Personally I think our people are right on this point—but the important fact is that they most earnestly believe they are right. As a consequence, if they find their judgments and convictions completely ignored by the principal NATO country in Western Europe, it will indeed take genius to keep our people from washing their hands of the whole affair. To my mind that kind of a result would be catastrophic for us all.

Not for one moment do I believe that I am overstating the adverse results in this country that would follow failure of the EDC to achieve French and other Western European endorsement. On the contrary, we are already suffering because of dilatory tactics heretofore pursued in the region. Soon we are to present to the Congress a request for appropriations to support the Mutual Security arrangements in Western Europe, and we are going to have a lot of trouble with those who believe that Europe has no intention of unifying or of adopting EDC.

I have sent messages both to Holland and Belgium urging early ratification so as to bring additional pressure on France. I have done this not because I want to interfere in anybody else's business, but because I know what it means in this country. This also is the reason why I continue to ask every personal and official friend that I think I have in Europe to get in and help. Possible alternatives to NATO's and EDC's success are too alarming to contemplate. If this country should return, no matter how reluctantly, to a policy of almost complete isolationism, or at the very least, to a "Western hemisphere only" philosophy of security and interest, then Heaven help us all.

As to your comments on some of our Senatorial speeches, you

should be no more disturbed by what some of our extremists say from the public platforms of this country, than we are by what your Mr. Bevan occasionally directs at us or at the world situation. Both Foster and I are determined to give the Soviets every possible opportunity to convince the world they have had a change of heart. Moreover, we do not believe you are fooled by the Russians. Finally, no one would be more anxious than we to develop any practical arrangement that would lead toward easing of tensions and a measurable degree of disarmament. But such arrangement must, above all else, carry its own guarantee of good faith and fulfillment.

Some days ago I replied to your question about the Windsor papers. I brought the matter to the attention of Bedell, who, as you will recall, was with me when I first came into contact with the affair. He shares my convictions expressed in my former letter, and I am hopeful that the matter will be settled with decency, justice and finality.

Again my assurances that we are looking forward to our talks with Salisbury, while we continue to hope for your early return to health and vigor.[2]

As ever,
Ike

1. Former king Farouk of Egypt.
2. A meeting at foreign minister level between the United States, Britain, and France was held in Washington, July 10–14, 1953.

CHURCHILL TO EISENHOWER

July 17, 1953

My dear Friend,

Please consider at your leisure whether it might not be better for the Four-Power Meeting to begin, as Salisbury urged, with a preliminary survey by the Heads of Governments of all our troubles in an informal spirit. I am sure that gives a much better chance than if we only come in after a vast new network of detail has been erected. Moreover, Bidault made it pretty clear he wanted this meeting to break down in order to make a better case for E.D.C. before the French Chamber, whereas it would have been a great advantage to go plus E.D.C. with friendly hands in strong array. Above all, I thought that you and I might have formed our own impression of Malenkov, who has never seen anybody outside Russia. After this preliminary meeting we might have been able to set our State Secretaries to work along less ambitious, if more hopeful, easier lines than we now propose. I am very sorry I was not able to make this appeal to you personally as I had hoped.

I have made a great deal of progress and can walk about. The doctors think that I may be well enough to appear in public by September. Meanwhile, I am still conducting business. It was a great disappointment to me not to have my chance of seeing you.

Kindest regards,
Winston

EISENHOWER TO CHURCHILL

July 20, 1953

Dear Winston,

Many thanks for your letter of July 17. First of all, let me say how greatly I rejoiced at the report of your improved health. Your own country, and indeed the world, can hardly spare you even in semi-retirement. Therefore, I am delighted that you expect to emerge in full vigor by September.

With regard to the Foreign Ministers meeting, I had, through Foster, kept in close touch with it and I gained the impression that the programming of a 4-Power meeting was along the lines agreeable to you. Indeed, this was the program which I would have presented to you at Bermuda had we been able to meet there. I have the feeling that it could be somewhat dangerous for us to meet with the Russians and talk generalities, at least unless and until it became apparent, through action in relation to Germany and Austria, that they seriously want to get on to a dependable basis with us.

I like to meet on a very informal basis with those whom I can trust as friends. That is why I was so glad at the prospect of a Bermuda meeting. But it is a different matter to meet informally with those who may use a meeting only to embarrass and to entrap. I would prefer to have our Foreign Ministers be the ones to make the first exploration on a limited and specific basis. Furthermore, as President I am very restricted by our Constitution when it comes to leaving the country because I cannot in my absence appoint an Acting President. I have to carry with me all of the paraphernalia of government.

I was very glad to get acquainted with Salisbury when he was here and I have the impression our Foreign Ministers got along well together. Their final communiqué surely showed that close unity and friendship prevail between our countries.

Again, I say, I eagerly look forward to your public reappearance.

With warm personal regard,
Ike

CHURCHILL TO EISENHOWER

August 3, 1953

My dear Friend,

Winthrop Aldrich brought me your very kind messages and enquiries last week when he visited me. I am making continual progress and have almost got back my full mobility. By the end of August I hope to be in fairly good condition bar accidents.

Winthrop conveyed to me the great news that you might perhaps find it possible to come to London for a talk about things with me. This would indeed be a memorable event and the enthusiasm which it would incite would make us all the stronger amid the difficulties which lie around and ahead.

I told the Queen about this yesterday and Her Majesty was very pleased indeed and would return from Balmoral to welcome you at Buckingham Palace during your stay. Would some time in the last week in September or the first week in October be convenient to you and Mrs. Eisenhower? If so, the procedure for the visits of Heads of States will be set in motion.

We have not had the honour of a visit from the President of the United States since Woodrow Wilson came in 1918, thirty-five years ago, and this new proof of Anglo-American friendship and goodwill would make a profound impression all over the world.

Kindest regards,
Winston

EISENHOWER TO CHURCHILL

August 8, 1953

Dear Winston,

I am afraid either that Winthrop misinterpreted a little wishful thinking on my part, growing out of disappointment at not being able to see you in Bermuda, or that you may have misunderstood him. The fact is that I am scheduled for a number of inescapable commitments during the foreseeable future and it would be impossible for me to leave the country. I am trying to get a partial vacation during the coming weeks, but even this will be heavily interspersed with business.

It was very gracious of the Queen to respond as she did to the idea of a possible visit by Mrs. Eisenhower and me. We both appreciate this most sincerely and we are equally grateful for the warmth of the welcome you promised me.

I am delighted that your progress toward complete recovery continues rapidly and without interruption.

With warm personal regards, as ever,

Ike

CHURCHILL TO EISENHOWER

October 7, 1953

My dear Friend,

I have not troubled you with telegrams lately although there are so many things I should like to talk over with you. I feel it would be a great advantage if we could meet especially now I have Anthony back.[1] The idea has occurred to me of a meeting at Azores which is not much further away for you than for us. I am sure the Portuguese would help in every way. Also I could send a ship. It would have to be next week as our Parliament meets on 20th October. If you could spare a couple of days between 15th October and 18th October inclusive (say 15th October and 16th October) we might be able to clear up a great many things. I would bring Anthony with me and hope you would bring Foster. This would be much easier for me and Anthony, who are both convalescent, than for us to fly to Washington with all the business and publicity that would involve. About the French, we should have a much better talk together alone as most topics concern our two countries. But if you wished them to come, and they could and would come to the Azores, that would be all right. In this case it would be a good thing if Laniel came along with Bidault.

I hope you will not mind my putting this suggestion to you. If you find it impossible, Eden and I will be at British Embassy, Washington, within dates mentioned.

Winston

1. Eden returned to the Foreign Office, October 5, 1953.

EISENHOWER TO CHURCHILL

October 8, 1953

Dear Winston,

It is good to know that you have Anthony back with you. I hope both of you are feeling fit.

As for the suggested talk, you have picked a week that is completely impossible for me. I leave Washington on the night of the fourteenth and have five public engagements between that time and early morning of the twentieth, when I plan to be back here. So it is not only impossible for me to go to the Azores but likewise I cannot be in Washington during the period you mention.

While Foster had planned to be with me in Texas on the nineteenth when I meet the President of Mexico, it would be possible for him to break that engagement and, consequently, could be here for the week end of the seventeenth-eighteenth if you and Anthony could fit this into your program. If you could stay through the twentieth, I could personally participate in the discussion on that day, but not earlier.

So far as the French are concerned, it seems to me quite clear that, if we meet any place, an invitation to them would be inescapable. We believe that Laniel is doing a good job, and I think it would be best for both you and us to make the gesture of an invitation. If they accept, there would still be plenty of opportunity at such a meeting for bipartisan talks between us, while if the French would find it impossible to attend, they would still be complimented by our thought of them.

All of these suggestions, of course, have no point in the event that my personal situation destroys whatever value you might see in the visit. Possibly you would want to send Anthony here by himself from the fifteenth to eighteenth because of this circumstance. Foster and his associates would welcome him.

I would appreciate hearing from you on this as soon as possible since if you can come, I would give the French as much advanced notice as possible.

With warm personal regard,

Ike

CHURCHILL TO EISENHOWER

October 9, 1953

My dear Friend,

Thank you so much for all the thought you have given this matter.

In view of your engagements, it does not look as if the meeting I had hoped for with you can be arranged immediately. I am very sorry, as there are so many things I would like to talk over with you quietly and at leisure. I earnestly hope a chance may come in the not too distant future.

Anthony has another suggestion, namely, that Foster should come over here for a tripartite talk with us and Bidault. We feel that this could be most useful, for Far Eastern as well as for European affairs. Anthony is cabling direct to Foster.

> Every good wish and kindest regards,
> Winston

EISENHOWER TO CHURCHILL

October 10, 1953

Dear Winston,

Foster has gone away for the week end but, as soon as he can be contacted, you will hear further from us. I am sure he will be most sympathetic, but I do not know what are the detailed commitments on his calendar for the near future.[1]

> With warm regard,
> Ike

1. A three-power foreign ministers meeting was arranged to be held in London on October 16–18, 1953.

EISENHOWER TO CHURCHILL

October 16, 1953

Dear Winston,

I am most happy to learn that you have been awarded the Nobel Prize for Literature.[1] The Swedish Academy could have made no more fitting choice. Congratulations on yet another deserved tribute to your magnificent career.

> Ike

1. Churchill was awarded the 1953 Nobel Prize for literature for *The Second World War*.

EISENHOWER TO CHURCHILL

October 22, 1953

Dear Winston,

Foster tells me that you are seriously considering coming over here to join your old friend Bernie for a week in South Carolina.[1] Of course, if you come I want very much to have a good talk with you. I assume that you would land initially in New York and from there would proceed to South Carolina either by train or plane. In either case I think the earliest and most convenient opportunity we would have for a talk would be for you to stop off with me for a day. If you could arrive in Washington so as to give us a full afternoon and evening together, we could start you on your way again at a reasonable hour the next morning. Of course I should want you to spend the night at the White House and I could also put up a staff officer if one should accompany you. Quite naturally, we should hope that Mrs. Churchill would be with you.

This I think would be better than having me attempt to come to South Carolina. You are familiar with the sometimes awkward arrangements that the security people make when the President goes to a strange place. In Washington, however, all this is routine and unobtrusive.

Since our visit would be merely incidental to your longer stay in Carolina, I think it would be assumed by all our friends to be perfectly normal procedure and would awaken no particular comment or feeling of being left out.

If you think there is any possibility of making such a visit, would you give me early indication of the approximate date you might consider so that I could keep my calendar completely free of other commitments.

I was delighted at Foster's report of your almost miraculously quick and complete recovery. Also he brought a very gratifying report of how well the three Foreign Ministers had worked together.

With warm regard,

As ever,
Ike

1. Dulles met Churchill on his visit to London for the Anglo-American-French foreign ministers meeting, October 16–18, 1953.

CHURCHILL TO EISENHOWER

October 23, 1953

My dear Friend,

Thank you so much for your message. I have no plans at present and a lot is going on here. I quite understand all your difficulties and will not fail to let you know in plenty of time if anything comes into the sphere of possibility. I have never suggested the matter to Bernie.

Winston

CHURCHILL TO EISENHOWER

November 5, 1953

My dear Friend,

The Soviet answer[1] puts us back to where we were when Bermuda broke down through my misfortune. We are confronted with a deadlock. So why not let us try Bermuda again? I suggest four or five days during the first fortnight in December. We could then take stock of the whole position and I think quite a lot of people will be pleased that we are doing so. If you want the French, I am quite agreeable and it would be a good opportunity of talking to them about E.D.C., which surely we ought to get settled now. I hope you would bring Foster. Anthony would be all for it and would come with me. It would be worth trying to make Laniel come with Bidault.

All arrangements were very carefully worked out last time, and it only takes a word of command to put them all on again.

Let me know how this strikes you. I really think there will be serious criticism if we are all left gaping at a void.

Winston

1. The Soviet note of November 3, 1953, was negative in tone, resisting the proposal of a four-power meeting on Germany and proposing a five-power meeting, including Communist China, on a broad range of international issues.

EISENHOWER TO CHURCHILL

November 6, 1953

Dear Winston,

I am temporarily out of touch with Foster but I assume that within limits he could arrange his schedule to conform to whatever plans you and I might make.

Because of the negative character of the Soviet reply, there may be considerable value in a good talk between us and the French in order to survey the situation in which we now find ourselves. It would be necessary of course to avoid creating a false impression that our purpose in meeting is to issue another invitation to the Soviets. There is nothing to be gained by showing too much concern over their intransigence and bad deportment and I believe that instead of relating our meeting to any Soviet word or act, past or future, we should merely announce that we are meeting to discuss matters of common interest. I feel that the presence of the French is almost an essential because of EDC, Indochina, and NATO problems in general, in which both you and we have had such a great stake. My only reservation about our meeting would be if it were some way seized upon as a pretext by opponents of EDC in France to delay ratification. This would be a tragedy for us all. Also, in view of the French presidential elections now scheduled for about mid-December, I do not know whether the French would find it possible to attend such a meeting in early December. Of course if Laniel could not come, Bidault might attend. I assume you, as head of the host government, would issue the invitation to the French and inquire whether they could attend such a meeting.

In the event the French accept, my calendar does not leave me much leeway in choice of dates. I could reach Bermuda on the morning of December 4 and stay through the 7th, returning here on the morning of the 8th. It is also possible that I myself could arrive on the morning of the 11th returning on the 15th but in this case, Foster would be unable to come with me as the North Atlantic Council Ministers meet in Paris on December 14–16 and Foster must leave Washington not later than December 12. I give you these possibilities only tentatively because I have yet to discuss it with Foster.

Foster should be back here by Monday morning, by which time you may be able to inform me as to the suitability of the periods I suggest before making any approach to the French. I think then we would have to agree quickly as to timing of the announcement so that danger of leaks can be eliminated.

With warm regards, As ever, Ike

CHURCHILL TO EISENHOWER

November 7, 1953

My dear Friend,
  I am delighted you will come to Bermuda from December 4 till the morning of the 8th. Anthony and I will be there to receive you. If there are troubles in Trieste or elsewhere we shall probably be able to deal with them better all together than we could apart. The moment you clinch this I will invite the French. I am told the French Presidential election does not take place till the 16th or 18th and that anyhow they will not ratify E.D.C. before it happens. Thus there would be no delay of E.D.C. through our meeting on the dates fixed. By all means let us merely announce that we are meeting to discuss matters of common interest. There are quite a lot of things I want so much to talk over with you and I thought we might both brace the French up on E.D.C. Time is short. I should be most grateful if you would give me the O.K. and we can settle it all with an agreed communique for Tuesday's newspapers.

Every good wish,
Winston

EISENHOWER TO CHURCHILL

November 7, 1953

Dear Winston,
  If the French agree, and barring some consideration unknown to me which may occur to Foster, I am prepared to go ahead with the meeting on December 4th at Bermuda.
  However, Foster will not return to Washington until the afternoon of Sunday, November 8th, at the earliest. I beg of you to allow no whisper of our meeting to get out before 12:00 noon, Tuesday, November 10th, Washington time. This will give me opportunity to consult with Foster. I agree that we should then merely announce that the three of us are meeting to discuss matters of common interest.
  In the meantime I would appreciate your ideas on the specific terms in which the announcement of the meeting would be framed. If the three of us are in agreement we could each make a simple statement to the above effect at any convenient time after 12:00 noon, November 10th, Washington time.
  I think it is most important that we should all set the same tone and

that the announcement should not be misconstrued by world opinion, particularly in view of the conditions imposed by the last Russian note.

With warmest regards, Ike

CHURCHILL TO EISENHOWER

November 8, 1953

My dear friend,

I am so glad that it is all fixed. I have telegraphed to the French emphasising secrecy. I will be host at the banquet and elsewhere but you must preside at any formal conference. I send you a draft announcement which I have also sent to the French. Let me know if you want any alterations. I will announce it as you suggest at 12 noon Washington time on Tuesday, November 10th.

I am bringing my paint-box with me as I cannot take you on at golf. They say the water is 67 degrees which is too cold for me.

Winston

EISENHOWER TO CHURCHILL

November 9, 1953

Dear Winston,

This morning I was informed that the French have accepted the invitation sent to them by you. This apparently clinches the whole matter, and tomorrow at twelve noon we shall release from the White House the announcement that you suggested. However, I have just learned that there is some possibility that all of us may be pressed for an earlier release because the story has already apparently leaked in France. To us, this is a matter of indifference except that we want to be coordinated with you.

I do not know that I shall bring along my golf clubs, but I do hope that the entire period will not be one of such exhausting work that we shall be denied time for any recreation, to say nothing of a bit of thinking.

I should say that our meeting will in a sense be of itself an answer to one point in the latest Soviet note, which seriously objects to this kind of meeting between us. In any event, I am delighted that the earlier of the two periods I suggested is suitable for all because this will enable Foster to be with me at the party.

With warm regard,

As ever,
Ike

CHURCHILL TO EISENHOWER

November 12, 1953

I am very glad it is all settled about Bermuda and I share your hope that we shall not spend all our time on parade. The table I presume should be round.

I agree with you that there is no point in Soviet complaints about "collusion." I always thought allies were expected to "collude" and I have always had a great dislike for the expression "ganging up" which has several times got seriously in my way. All the same, I am, as I said last time in Parliament, hoping that we may build bridges, and not barriers.[1]

I should like to bring Lord Cherwell with me as I want to talk over with you our "collusion" on atoms, etc. Indeed, it might strengthen the impression to which I gathered you were favourable, that our meeting was not simply an incident in recent correspondence with the Soviets. He can always slip across to Washington after we have had talks if you thought it convenient for him to see more of your people.

I plan to fly with Anthony, the night of the first via Gander to Bermuda and we shall have a whole day to recuperate before receiving you on the fourth. The Welch Fusiliers with their goat will form your guard of honour. The barbed wire to protect us from the assassin or the journalists still stands as it was.

For your eyes only: I was delighted to read what you said to the press about Harry Truman.[2] He is rather a friend of mine.

Anthony sends his regards. With all my good wishes.

Winston

1. Speech in the House of Commons, May 11, 1953.
2. Eisenhower was, in fact, equivocal in his remarks at his press conference on November 11, 1953, on Truman's rejection of a subpoena to appear before the House Un-American Affairs Committee.

EISENHOWER TO CHURCHILL

November 12, 1953

Dear Winston,

Your cable came just as I was leaving for Canada. By all means bring Lord Cherwell and I shall probably bring Admiral Strauss[1] with me. The two of them can have a good talk and then give you and me a briefing. I rather think it might be a good idea to have Ismay come out with us for a day if that could be arranged. Again his presence would serve a useful purpose both for us and for the public.

Warm regard, As ever, Ike

1. Admiral Lewis Strauss, chairman, U.S. Atomic Energy Commission.

CHURCHILL TO EISENHOWER

November 14, 1953

My dear Friend,

Pug will arrive on the 6th. We are keeping it quiet till nearer the date. He was much complimented that you wanted to talk to him.

I am taking a stiff line in the House on Monday about the two year military service.[1]

With all my good wishes,
Winston

1. The length of national service in Britain was increased from eighteen months to two years in 1950. A Labour motion in the House of Commons on November 16, 1953, called for an annual review of the length of service. Churchill rejected this as creating uncertainty in military planning.

CHURCHILL TO EISENHOWER

November 26, 1953

My dear Friend,

Do you think it would be a good thing if I asked Bernie Baruch to come and spend the night of the 8th with me at Bermuda as a personal guest? He is a wise friend of both of us and I should like to pay him a courtesy and return his hospitality. I will be guided entirely by you.

Looking forward so much to seeing you.

Winston

EISENHOWER TO CHURCHILL

November 27, 1953

Dear Winston,

Of course you should ask Bernie Baruch to be your personal guest if you so desire. I do not see how his coming there could be interpreted as having anything to do with the general meeting which will have terminated prior to his arrival. I personally must leave Bermuda no later than early morning of the 8th, possibly even the evening of the 7th.

With warm personal regard,
Ike

EISENHOWER TO CHURCHILL

November 29, 1953

Heartiest congratulations on your birthday.[1] My best wishes for a cheerful celebration, and many more years of happiness and contentment. Looking forward to seeing you soon.

D.E.

1. Churchill celebrated his seventy-ninth birthday on November 30, 1953.

CHURCHILL TO EISENHOWER

December 1, 1953

Thank you so much my dear friend for your very kind telegram. I look forward much to seeing you.

Winston

The two comrades-in-arms confer in Rheims in northern France on March 4, 1944, as plans were made for the crossing of the Rhine. Churchill and Eisenhower came to know each other very well during World War II. (British War Office photo, courtesy Churchill Archives Centre)

Churchill listens as Eisenhower makes a point to Bernard Baruch, American elder statesman and financier, at a meeting between Churchill and Eisenhower in Baruch's apartment in New York, January 5, 1953. (United Press photo, courtesy Churchill Archives Centre)

French Prime Minister Joseph Laniel joins Churchill and Eisenhower for a photo session at the opening of the Big Three conference in Bermuda, December 4, 1953. (Associated Press photo, courtesy Churchill Archives Centre)

Churchill gives his famous "V for Victory" sign, which he made his hallmark in World War II, to cheering crowds along his route to the White House following his arrival at National Airport, Washington, D.C., June 25, 1954. (Associated Press photo, courtesy Churchill Archives Centre)

Churchill is welcomed to the White House by Eisenhower, June 25, 1954. Eisenhower's wife, Mamie, is at the center, and British Foreign Secretary Anthony Eden is at the right. (United Press photo, courtesy Churchill Archives Centre)

Churchill and Eisenhower enjoy the surroundings of the White House garden along with Anthony Eden (right) and U.S. Secretary of State John Foster Dulles (left), June 26, 1954. (U.S. National Park Service photo, courtesy Churchill Archives Centre)

Eisenhower bids farewell to Churchill at the end of their White House talks,
June 29, 1954. Eisenhower did not see Churchill again as prime minister.
(United Press photo, courtesy Churchill Archives Centre)

This portrait of Churchill was painted by Eisenhower in 1955 and a copy now hangs in the President's Suite of the Walter Reed Army Hospital in Bethesda, Maryland. Eisenhower and Churchill were both keen and reasonably talented amateur painters. (U.S. Navy photo, courtesy Dwight D. Eisenhower Library)

THREE

Bermuda, H-Bombs, Indochina
December 6, 1953–June 23, 1954

The Bermuda Conference, December 4–7, 1953, gave Churchill and Eisenhower the opportunity to discuss the issues which had been raised in their correspondence, especially relations with the Soviet Union, atomic energy, and Egypt. Eisenhower's attention was concentrated on a speech which he delivered at the United Nations on December 8, 1953, immediately after the Bermuda Conference, on cooperation on atomic energy for peaceful purposes, his so-called Atoms for Peace proposal. Correspondence on this matter took place both at Bermuda, where Eisenhower sent Churchill a draft of his speech for comment, and in the weeks following.

Churchill was disappointed at Bermuda when it was decided that there should be a four-power foreign ministers' meeting on the specific subjects of Germany and Austria, rather than a heads of government summit with the Soviet Union with an open agenda. As Churchill anticipated, the foreign ministers' conference at Berlin in January–February 1954 degenerated into recriminations with no progress. There was less correspondence exchanged between Churchill and Eisenhower in January and February 1954 than in almost any other two-month period in the time when they both held office.

Churchill then became very concerned about the issues of the hydrogen bomb. He was also disturbed by issues on East-West trade. Moreover, at the end of the Berlin Conference it was agreed that a five-power conference, including Communist China as well as the United States, Britain, France, and the Soviet Union, should be held in Geneva in the spring of 1954 to discuss Korea and Indochina. The Korean issue was soon relegated into the background when the conference opened in April 1954, but, with French forces facing defeat at Dien Bien Phu, Indochina became a matter of central importance. Anglo-American differences of viewpoint on Indochina were frankly expressed in the letters between Churchill and Eisenhower.

The rift over Indochina was part of the reason, along with a desire to clear the air on other matters and to improve personal contacts in general, for Churchill's suggestion of a visit to the United States. Eisenhower was quite willing to agree, and Churchill visited Washington, D.C., June 25–29, 1954.

CHURCHILL TO EISENHOWER

December 6, 1953

My dear Ike,
I think it is a very fine speech[1] and tackles the terrible problems which confront us with your usual courage and candour. I think it will help towards the "easement" of which I have sometimes spoken, and it may well be that the contacts which may develop will be useful. It is a great pronouncement and will resound through the anxious and bewildered world.

Naturally I do not like what appears on page 11. History will, I am sure, make a different appraisement.[2]

About page 7. I hope we may have some further talk, for I know you understand the reservations I have to make in the light of our exposed position.[3] Circumstances, proportion and the fate of friends and allies would never, I am sure, be absent from your mind.

I am sending you privately a short note about the proposed international Atomic Energy Administration which Cherwell prepared for my eye.

Yours sincerely,
Winston S.C.

P.S. It is nice to see you and talk freely, amid all our terrible problems.

1. Draft of Eisenhower's "Atoms for Peace" speech.
2. Eisenhower referred to the "obsolete colonial mould." In response to Churchill's objections, the phrase was removed.
3. In place of a phrase asserting that the United States was "free to use the atomic bomb," Eisenhower substituted a phrase with regard to the United States "reserving the right to use the atomic bomb."

CHURCHILL TO EISENHOWER

December 7, 1953

My dear Friend,
Thank you so much for your kind consideration of the points I felt it

is my duty to make. I have one more, bearing on page 7. The last part of your speech will of course thrill the world and dominate opinion. Do you need to take the emphasis off it by a sentence or a phrase which will undoubtedly be fastened on by all the enemies of America and Britain at home or abroad?

Whatever you decide to say it should be made clear that it is your speech and your inspiration and that you take full responsibility for it. The fact that you have shown it to me and some of your friends beforehand is only an example of the intimate terms on which we work.

I have in my letter expressed to you my association with the spirit and mood of your new message about atomic material; but whereas your speech is the result of long consideration and study I and Anthony have only had a brief opportunity to examine the problem which your courtesy allowed us.

You ought to see if you have not already done so the front page of today's WASHINGTON POST.[1] We live under a system of Cabinet Government and not one of our colleagues has even dreamed of the departure that you are going to make.

I am looking forward to half-an-hour with you around 10.00 a.m. tomorrow or any other time you send for me.

Yours very sincerely,
Winston

1. A front-page article in the *Washington Post*, December 7, 1953, gave an outline of the important points which Eisenhower would make in his Atoms for Peace speech at the United Nations on December 8.

CHURCHILL TO EISENHOWER

December 7, 1953

We agreed, did we not, that Admiral Strauss and Lord Cherwell should compile a White Paper of the documents, and their linking together, which constitute the story of Anglo-American relations about the Atomic Bomb. You and I will then consider and discuss whether it will be helpful or not to publish. Personally I think it will be. We both desire a fuller interchange of intelligence and the fact that secrecy is evaporating through growth of knowledge between us, and alas between both of us and Soviet Russia, makes it desirable that we two should make the best joint progress we can. Your speech will, I think, encourage the new atmosphere. Cherwell and Strauss, I understand, take it that they should prepare the White Paper.

EISENHOWER TO CHURCHILL

December 8, 1953

Dear Winston,

As I depart from this lovely spot, I leave this note behind to thank you once again for acting as our host for a very interesting and, I hope, profitable conference. While my disposition has not always been equal to the pressures of some of the lectures, I think that I came through my first international conference—in a political role—in fairly good shape.

Give my love to Clemmie and all your nice family.

With warm personal regard,

As ever,
Ike E.

CHURCHILL TO EISENHOWER

December 8, 1953

I feel bound to let you know that the Goat's explanation for refusing the cigarette is that he thought he was forbidden to use tobacco on parade.[1]

Winston

1. As a joke, Eisenhower, a very heavy smoker, offered a cigarette to the goat, the regimental mascot of the Welch Fusiliers, who provided the guard of honor at Bermuda.

EISENHOWER TO CHURCHILL

December 9, 1953

Dear Winston,

The Goat's soldierly deportment puts me to shame—you would suppose that after some forty years in the Army, I would not have embarrassed him so sadly.

With best wishes,

As ever,
Ike

CHURCHILL TO EISENHOWER

December 14, 1953

My dear friend,
I am so glad that the Russians seem to be ready to give your far reaching scheme more reasonable consideration than first appeared.[1] Thank you for your letter, it was very pleasant seeing you again.

All good wishes
Winston

1. December 9, 1953, Moscow Radio denounced "the warmongering speech of President Eisenhower."

CHURCHILL TO EISENHOWER

December 16, 1953

My dear Friend,
I have to tell the House of Commons tomorrow about our meeting and I send you a draft of what I have prepared on atomic affairs.[1] I hope that you only need to send me an O.K. as time is so very short before I speak at 3.30 p.m. G.M.T. tomorrow Thursday.
I have included nothing of what I shall say about our talks and interchanges upon your U.N.O. speech as I am giving full support to your inspiring lead and trying to persuade the bear to stop growling. I shall make it clear that I no more write your speeches than you write mine and I expect to stave off questions about the untruthful press rumours of which there have certainly been no lack.
I shall defend Foster for speaking frankly to the French in Paris about E.D.C.[2] Anthony and I both believe the secondary reaction may be favourable.

Kindest regards,
Winston

1. Draft in *FRUS, 1952–54*, 2:1301–2; Churchill's speech, *Parliamentary Debates* (Hansard), 5th ser., vol. 522, House of Commons, cols. 577–86, December 17, 1953.
2. At a North Atlantic Council meeting in Paris, December 14, 1953, Dulles warned of an "agonizing re-appraisal" of American commitments to Europe if EDC was not ratified.

December 16, 1953

Dear Sir Winston,

Just this minute I received your cable and immediately consulted with Admiral Strauss. He points out that the last sentence of your first paragraph is somewhat in error because the agreement on this point was firmed and announced here several weeks before the Bermuda talks took place.[1]

Admiral Strauss also suggests that before you make your talk you consult again with Lord Cherwell about the final two sentences. He feels that Lord Cherwell might want you to be very general and indefinite in talking about a possible white paper.[2]

Having said all the above, I assure you that we have no objection to the paper.

With warm regard,
Ike

1. In his speech in the House of Commons, December 17, 1953, Churchill clarified that agreement was reached before Bermuda.
2. In his House of Commons speech Churchill referred specifically to the White Paper but was vague as to whether it would be published.

CHURCHILL TO EISENHOWER

December 19, 1953

My dear Friend,

I am very much worried at the idea of the grant of American economic aid to Egypt at a time when our differences with them are so acute. It would, I am sure, have a grave effect in this country on Anglo-American relations. The Socialist Opposition would use it to urge us to press for the inclusion of Red China in UNO and might class it with trade to that country upon which subject McCarthy's unjust charges are already much resented.[1] The frontier of the Suez Canal Zone shows very much the same conditions of unrest and potential warfare as does the frontier in Korea. So much for the Opposition. On our Conservative side too we have a disturbed and increasingly angered section who could at any time cancel our modest majority.[2] They would not, I think, do that but the fact ought not to be ignored.

Whether in your policies and immense responsibilities you would get much help from a Socialist Government, I shall not attempt to predict, and it would not be my business anyhow. What I fear, however, is that the offended Conservatives might add their voices to that section of the Socialist Party who criticize the United States. In fact I think there would be a considerable outpouring which of course would be used in America by all who are hostile to the unity of action of the English-speaking World. This would make more difficult the solving of those large problems which occupy your mind and in which I do all I can to help. I ask you to think over this particular proposal about Egypt with due regard to its setting in the general picture, which may be out of proportion to your interest or ours. We have not the slightest intention of making any more concessions to Egypt after all we have done in these long negotiations, and fighting might easily occur at any moment.

I have had a nice message from Foster about the support which I gave to his blunt but salutory [*sic*] statement in Paris about the agonising re-appraisal. If E.D.C. is repudiated by the French, I still think some variant of N.A.T.O. will be necessary. After all, this meets the French objection to being in a European association alone or almost alone with a much more powerful Germany. I think you would find it very difficult to make and get a good plan on the "empty chair" basis.[3]

Kindest regards,
Winston

1. Senator Joseph McCarthy (R-Wisconsin) vociferously condemned Britain's continuing trade with China during the Korean War.
2. The Conservatives held a majority of seventeen in the House of Commons.
3. One proposal in the event of French rejection of EDC was to proceed with EDC with a chair left empty for France to fill in the course of time.

EISENHOWER TO CHURCHILL

December 20, 1953

My dear Winston,
You are so well aware of my convictions as to the necessity for sound and friendly Anglo-American relations that you must keenly realize the concern I feel over the somber tone of your cabled message.

Because it is a personal communication, I am answering in the same fashion, without waiting to call together the State Department staffs which will be, of course, deeply interested in what you have to say. I shall hope to get this cable off to you the first thing Monday morning so that I may have your further observations on certain delicate phases of this matter.

In considering our common interests in various areas, I am, of course, anxious to take into consideration your particular political problems and to adjust our activities so as best to accommodate your position so long as this leads towards a satisfactory solution. We likewise have our political problems. For example, our aid program for the Mid-East was drawn up and was approved by the Congress on the basis that there would be a reasonable division of aid between Israel and Arab countries.

Since we have already made allocations to Israel, we have little excuse to avoid moving in the case of the Arab countries, but as you know, at your request we have not only withheld military aid from Egypt, but have likewise postponed several times the initiation of economic aid.

You state that the Socialist Opposition would be bitterly resentful of American economic aid to Egypt because of the American objection to trade with Communist China. It has been my understanding that Britain has continued to carry on trade in economic non-strategic items with Red China, and we do not now propose more with respect to Egypt than beginning to help develop its economy. Consequently, I am at a loss to understand the basis on which the Socialists could make a logical attack. You likewise mention that the Opposition would resent any economic aid to Egypt so bitterly that they would urge you to press for inclusion of Red China in the UN. By implication this would seem to mean that if we do not extend economic aid to Egypt, you are prepared to stand firm with us in opposing the inclusion of the bloody Chinese aggressor into the council of peaceful nations, at least until Red China withdraws her invading armies, ceases supporting the Indo-China war and begins to act like a civilized government.[1] Could you confirm this to me?

I assume, of course, that you are genuinely anxious to arrange a truce with Egypt and that the only remaining obstacles are the two points you mentioned to me at Bermuda, namely, availability and uniforms.[2] Now if we continue to press Egypt to accept your conditions on these two points, can we do so with the assurance that they can count on a settlement if they accept your position? You can understand my anxiety to avoid asking our people to do everything in their power to bring about a settlement of this situation, including another postponement of economic aid, and then discover that we have been operating on a complete misunderstanding.

As I told you at Bermuda, I am most deeply sympathetic with your whole problem in the area, even though at times I have believed that different methods might have been more effective. I repeat that in our actual dealings with Egypt, we have gone to great lengths to meet your convictions and opinions. We certainly want to continue to do so. We think we proved that in Persia, and I hope we shall together make that effort seem worthwhile.

I know that you realize that there are in this country many people who believe that the United States has treated the Arab countries shabbily and, because parts of the Arab holdings are vital to the Western world, this segment of our citizenry asserts that we should work to improve our relationships with the Arab countries. But this government has always refused to do this at the cost of anything we believed detrimental to Anglo-American best interests. In spite of outrageous and irresponsible criticism of each other on both sides of the Atlantic, American governmental policy and popular sentiment recognize the great value to the free world of keeping Anglo-American relationships coordinated with respect to the rest of the world and friendly as between themselves.

Now a word about EDC. I appreciate what you say about the "empty chair" idea, and I am quick to agree. But I re-state my conviction that any, and I repeat any, projected alternative to EDC will present problems no less acute and difficult to solve. All the treaties made with West Germany and ratified in that country on the so-called contractual theory are based upon the premise that EDC will come into being. To scrap that work and to start again, particularly at a time when some dissatisfaction seems to be growing in West Germany and while increased Russian pressures are constantly exerted against our European friends, would be dangerous in the extreme. On the other hand, I believe that if we, and by we I mean you and I and the governments we head, continue to press earnestly, sincerely and constantly for the enactment of EDC, we shall get it. I shall make another public statement on this matter as soon as France elects a President, and I shall continue to do so as opportunity presents itself.[3]

I hope that you can find it possible to answer this personal cable promptly so that I can assemble the necessary staffs and go over this whole matter in detail. I assure you that I am prepared to meet locally any political difficulty in carrying out whatever arrangements we may make between ourselves for the common good of our two countries.

I realize that this is a long and possibly a tedious cablegram. But it is quite necessary that there be the clearest kind of understanding between us if we are at one and the same time to operate together in some of these critical situations abroad and still be able to withstand any kind of political problem and criticism that can arise in our respective countries.

I shall look forward to early receipt of your comments.

With warm personal regard.

As ever,
Ike

1. In January 1950 Britain recognized Communist China and supported the admission of Communist China into the United Nations. In April 1951 Britain agreed to an American suggestion of a moratorium on support for Chinese admission to the United Nations while hostilities continued in the Far East.

2. Two terms which Britain sought in negotiations with Egypt were the reactivation of the base by Britain in certain conditions after withdrawal and the right of British troops in Egypt to wear British uniforms.

3. December 23, 1953, René Coty was elected president of France. Eisenhower's next statement on EDC was in his State of the Union message, January 7, 1954.

EISENHOWER TO CHURCHILL

December 23, 1953

Dear Winston,

I have your reply to my message. We shall study it and you will hear further from us, probably through the State Department. Foster knows that I am anxious to find a way for us to conform as far as possible to your views on Egypt. Of course you know of our conviction that if we can together reach a prompt and completely successful arrangement with Iran, this will immeasurably strengthen our hands here at home against any opponent seeking to weaken our support of the efforts you are making to reaching a proper arrangement in Egypt.

Merry Christmas to you and yours,

As ever,
Ike

CHURCHILL TO EISENHOWER

December 25, 1953

Many thanks for your reply of 23rd December.

I saw Malik yesterday before his return to Moscow.[1] I impressed two things on him. Firstly that your atomic proposal was not a mere propaganda move but a sincere attempt to break the deadlock and, though on a small scale, might well achieve invaluable results and also open fruitful contacts. Secondly, there was no chance of splitting the English-speaking world, though we use our common language to argue about a lot of things.

Coty has for long been a keen supporter of European movements and has frequently spoken in favour of the European Defence Community. I think we might easily have got someone worse. Anyhow no one can now say that Foster's outspoken warning, which I supported, has done any harm. It seems that in France in order to get on you have to be unknown. It is different in our two democracies where a certain amount of publicity is not necessarily always a drawback.

Clemmie and I send our best wishes to you both for a Happy Christmas.

Winston

1. Yakov Malik, Soviet ambassador to Britain.

CHURCHILL TO EISENHOWER

January 1, 1954

All good wishes to you both for the new year.

Winston and Clemmie Churchill

EISENHOWER TO CHURCHILL

January 25, 1954

Dear Winston,

Your American publishers have just sent me a copy of "Triumph and Tragedy" with your inscription and good wishes.

I am more than delighted to have this final volume of your masterful history of World War II. On the personal side, of course, there is much of intense interest to me. Thank you for your thoughtfulness in seeing that a copy reached me.

With warm personal regard,

As ever,
Ike E.

EISENHOWER TO CHURCHILL

February 9, 1954

Dear Winston,

Recent reports that you have been on the firing range personally testing the merits of the new Belgian rifle would indicate that you are again in the very best of health. Needless to say, your friends here greet such indications with great joy.

My official reports from Berlin[1] are not quite so discouraging as would be expected after reading some of the Molotov outbursts in the daily press. I grow weary of bad manners in international relationships. When abuse grows so flagrant as to include insult, false charges and outright vituperation, I sometimes wonder whether we help our own cause by allowing the world to believe us so meekly ready to sit quietly under such attacks for no other apparent reason than a desperate hope for a crumb of concession out of the propaganda feast the enemy enjoys at our expense.

The free nations' case must be better understood by the entire world—including ourselves. More and more I come to the conclusion that the salvation of liberty rests upon the unremitting effort of all of us to establish a solidarity among ourselves that in major objectives and purposes will remain firm against any assault. Such an association of free nations must be expanded as widely as possible, even to include very weak nations when those weak nations are exposed directly or indirectly to the threats and blandishments of the Soviets. We are deeply concerned of course with Indo-China, Iran and Egypt. But the entire Moslem World, India and Southeast Asia, as well as our European friends, are all important to us!

Such an association of nations must have clear political, economic and military objectives of its own; while avoiding all belligerence in its attitude, it must still be so firmly confident of its own security that it will have no reason to worry about the possibility that the stupid and savage individuals in the Kremlin will move against us in any vital way.

At the very best, of course, to produce such an association of nations will require the finest of leadership. To this we, the larger nations, must contribute. We must be generous, understanding, determined, and always faithful to our pledges. Tactics will vary. In some areas and on some subjects, we will have to use cajolery; in others, firmness. In some situations, some particular one of the principal countries of the coalition should take the lead in the conduct of negotiations; in others, another will have to assume the burden.

Of one thing I am certain. If we could get real unity of understanding and basic purpose among a few of the principal nations of the free world—including, of course, West Germany—it would not be long until the common security of all of us was vastly improved and the material fortunes of our countries would be advanced markedly and continuously.

The problem, of course, is to achieve much more than mere paper agreement. Our consortion [*sic*] must rest solidly upon a common understanding of the Russian menace and in the clear conviction that only through unity, stubbornly maintained in the face of every inconsequential point of argument and difference among us, can these great things be achieved.

Of course there is no real reason for writing you such a letter as this. Not only do you understand these things better than I—in many instances I have absorbed my ideas from you. But I've been thinking a bit of the future. I am sure that when history looks back upon us of today it will not long remember any one of this era who was merely a distinguished war leader whether on the battlefield or in the council chamber. It will remember and salute those people who succeed, out of the greatness of their understanding and the skill of their leadership, in establishing ties among the independent nations of the world that will throw back the Russian threat and allow civilization, as we have known it, to continue its progress. Indeed, unless individuals and nations of our times are successful—soon—in this effort, there will be no history of any kind, as we know it. There will be only a concocted story made up by the Communist conquerors of the world.

It is only when one allows his mind to contemplate momentarily such a disaster for the world and attempts to picture an atheistic materialism in complete domination of all human life, that he fully appreciates how necessary it is to seek renewed faith and strength from his God, and sharpen up his sword for the struggle that cannot possibly be escaped.

Destiny has given priceless opportunity to some of this epoch. You are one of them. Perhaps I am also one of the company on whom this great responsibility has fallen.

With warm personal regard,

As ever,
Ike E.

1. The Berlin Conference on Germany and Austria, January 25–February 18, 1954.

CHURCHILL TO EISENHOWER

February 12, 1954

I will think deeply over all you say. All good wishes.

Winston

CHURCHILL TO EISENHOWER

February 27, 1954

Dear Mr. President,
I have not yet answered your letter of February 9 but do not think that it is not always in the forefront of my thoughts.

Winston

EISENHOWER TO CHURCHILL

March 1, 1954

Dear Winston,
Thank you for your note. Please do not trouble yourself about any need for replying to my letter of February ninth. I meant it as only an item in a friendly exchange of ideas that has extended now over a period of a dozen years. I think that possibly I was merely testing my thoughts against yours to determine whether we are as basically in agreement as I think we are.
With warm regard,

As ever,
Ike

CHURCHILL TO EISENHOWER

March 9, 1954

Thank you for your letter. I am honoured by the kind personal things you say.
There is no difference between us upon the major issues which overhang the world, namely, resistance to Communism, the unity of the free nations, the concentration of the English-speaking world,

United Europe and NATO. All these will and must increase if we are to come through the anxious years and perhaps decades which lie ahead of hopeful but puzzled mankind.

On the day that the Soviets discovered and developed the Atomic Bomb the consequences of war became far more terrible. But that brief tremendous phase now lies in the past.

An incomparably graver situation is presented by the public statements of Mr. Sterling Cole[1] at Chicago on February 17. I have discussed these with my expert advisers. They tell me that the 175ft displacement of the ocean bed at Eniwetok Atoll may well have involved a pulverisation of the earth's surface three or four times as deep. This in practice would of course make all protection except for small Staff groups, impossible. You can imagine what my thoughts are about London. I am told that several million people would certainly be obliterated by four or five of the latest H Bombs. In a few years these could be delivered by rocket without even hazarding the life of the pilot. New York and your other great cities have immeasurable perils too, though distance is a valuable advantage at least as long as pilots are used.

Another ugly idea has been put in my head, namely, the dropping of an H Bomb in the sea to windward of the Island or any other seaborne country, in suitable weather, by rocket or airplane, or perhaps released by submarine. The explosion would generate an enormous radio-active cloud, many square miles in extent, which would drift over the land attacked and extinguish human life over very large areas. Our smallness and density of population emphasizes this danger to us.

Mr. Cole further stated that Soviet Russia, though perhaps a year behind the United States, possessed the know-how and was increasing its production and power of delivery (or words to that effect). Moreover after a certain quantity have been produced on either side the factor of "over-taking", "superiority", etc., loses much of its meaning. If one side has five hundred and the other two hundred both might be destroyed. A powerful incentive to achieve surprise would be given to the weaker—what about Pearl Harbour? His natural fears would prey upon his moral and spiritual inhibitions (if indeed he was so encumbered).

When I read Mr. Cole's widely reported speech, I was surprised that its searing statements attracted so little comment. The reason is that human minds recoil from the realization of such facts. The people, including the well-informed, can only gape and console themselves with the reflection that death comes to all anyhow, sometime. This merciful numbness cannot be enjoyed by the few men upon whom the supreme responsibility falls. They have to drive their minds forward into these hideous and deadly spheres of thought. All the things that are happening now put together, added to all the material things that ever happened, are scarcely more important to the human race. I consider that you and, if my strength lasts, I, cannot flinch from the mental exertions involved.

I wondered, pondering on your letter, whether this was the background which had forced you to express yourself with such intense earnestness. I understand of course that in speaking of the faith that must inspire us in the struggle against atheistic materialism, you are referring to the spiritual struggle, and that like me, you still believe that War is not inevitable. I am glad to think that in your spirit, as in mine, resolve to find a way out of this agony of peril transcends all else.

I entirely agree with Mr. Cole's remark that in this matter "It is more sinful to conceal the power of the atom than it is to reveal it." This would not of course mean one-sided imparting of secret knowledge. But perhaps we have now reached, or are reaching, the moment when both sides know enough to outline the doom-laden facts to each other.

Of course I recur to my earlier proposal of a personal meeting between Three. Men have to settle with men, no matter how vast, and in part beyond their comprehension, the business in hand may be. I can even imagine that a few simple words, spoken in the awe which may at once oppress and inspire the speakers might lift this nuclear monster from our world.

It might be that the proposals which you made at Bermuda and which are accepted by the Soviets for parleys on this subject, could without raising the issue formally give a better chance of survival than any yet mentioned. The advantage of the process you have set in motion is that it might probe the chances of settlement to the heart without at the same time bringing nearer the explosion we seek to escape.

Yours ever,
Winston S. Churchill

1. Congressman W. Sterling Cole (R-New York), chairman of the Joint Committee on Atomic Energy.

EISENHOWER TO CHURCHILL

March 11, 1954

Dear Winston,
   My grateful thanks for your thoughtful letter. I shall be answering
within a few days.

Ike E.

EISENHOWER TO CHURCHILL

March 19, 1954

Dear Winston,
   I have pondered over your letter. You are quite right in your estimate of my grave concern at the steady increase in methods of mass
destruction. Whether or not the specific possibilities of devastation
that you mention are indeed demonstrated capabilities, the prospects
are truly appalling. Ways of lessening or, if possible, of eliminating the
danger must be found. That has been my principal preoccupation
throughout the last year.
   It was after many weeks of thinking and study with political and
technical advisers that I finally reached the conclusion which we
talked over at Bermuda and which was embodied in my eighth of
December address to the United Nations Assembly. As you are well
aware, that plan was designed primarily as a means of opening the
door of world-wide discussion—with some confidence on both sides
—rather than as a substantive foundation of an international plan for
the control or elimination of nuclear weapons. But honest, open technical discussions on an internationally supported plan to promote
peaceful uses of this new science might lead to something much more
comprehensive.
   Since last December, we have been following up this matter as
actively as its technical character permits. Foster had two or more talks
with Molotov when they were at Berlin. We have a draft plan which,
after consultation with your people and those of two or three other
countries, will, I expect, be transmitted to the Soviet Union through
diplomatic channels, as agreed, probably next week.
   While there have been some indications that the Soviets might want
to confuse the issues with extraneous political matters, on the whole it
is encouraging that they so far seem prepared to accept businesslike
procedures. In its entirety the problem is one of immensity and diffi-

culty, as you so graphically stated. But I repeat that I deem it important to make a beginning in an exchange of views, which, as you suggest, could open up new and more hopeful vistas for the future.

I doubt whether the project on which we are engaged would, at this moment, be advanced by a meeting of heads of government. In fact, I can see that such a meeting might inject complications. From our side, there is the question of France, which is very delicate at the moment. The Soviets have indicated that, if there were oral conversations, they would want to bring in the Chinese Communists.

My impression is that matters are in a reasonably good way, but that they require constant concern and vigilance and, I hope, frequent and intimate personal exchanges of views between the two of us.

With warm regard,

As ever,
Ike

East-West Trade

From the late 1940s Britain and the United States adopted a somewhat different approach with regard to trade with the Soviet bloc. There was agreement on a ban on the sale of weapons and materials of obvious strategic significance. But whereas the United States wished to impose a ban on a very wide range of goods, Britain favored a much more liberal policy. Britain felt that trading links were not without importance in establishing contacts with the Soviet Union, while they were at the same time of useful economic value. Britain faced chronic balance of payments crises in the postwar years and was consequently interested in any possible export markets. American aid through the Marshall Plan eased Britain's economic difficulties in the late 1940s. With the end of Marshall aid in December 1950, Britain received aid from the United States through the military assistance program and through various means such as "off-shore purchases," that is, the purchase by American forces in Europe of military equipment from Britain. In the early 1950s, however, American aid was insufficient to enable Britain to avert serious balance of payments crises, while at the same time American policy imposed restrictions on British trade with Communist countries.

In 1951 COCOM (the Co-ordinating Committee of the Consultative Group of Nations) was formed in Paris as a means through which the West European nations and Japan agreed on items which should be restricted in trade with the Soviet bloc. Lists were drawn up, namely,

International List I (Embargo), II (Quantitative Control), and III (Surveillance). The United States wished the list of restricted goods to be lengthened, and in 1951 Congress passed the Mutual Defense Assistance Control Act, popularly known as the Battle Act after its sponsor, Congressman Lucius D. Battle, which drew up long lists of goods prohibited from trade with the Soviet bloc and barred American aid to nations which engaged in trade in such goods with Communist countries. The issue became emotive in public opinion in Britain and in the United States. Talks between British and American officials in November 1953 made little progress. On February 25, 1954, Churchill made a speech in the House of Commons on East-West trade outlining the proposals submitted to the United States on March 1, 1954, that List I be drastically reduced and Lists II and III be eliminated altogether. The United States was prepared to accept only a gradual and moderate shortening of the lists. A visit to Britain by Harold Stassen for talks with Churchill and other British officials, March 29–31, 1954, resulted in a reasonably satisfactory compromise.

EISENHOWER TO CHURCHILL

March 19, 1954

Dear Winston,

I have studied carefully the proposals for relaxation of East-West trade controls which officials of your Government gave to our Embassy in London on March 1. I understand that these proposals have been personally approved by you.

As you no doubt realize, the United States Government has for some time been conducting a searching review of all aspects of East-West trade controls. I can assure you that the United States is prepared to go a significant distance toward the contraction and simplification of those controls—objectives which we both share.

However, we do not believe we should go a great distance and so suddenly as the United Kingdom proposals suggest. To do so would be, I think, to go beyond what is immediately safe or in the common interest of the free world.

I appreciate the weight that must be given to the strong views in favor of decontrol that are held by the British public and by the British business community. I assume, however, that you equally realize the weight of public and Congressional opinion in the United States and the problems arising out of the Battle Act. It would be most unfortunate if pressures in either of our countries produced reactions adversely affecting Anglo-American relations—political, economic, and military—as well as the strength of the Nato coalition.

Ordinarily, I would not insert into our correspondence any matter of detail that properly belongs to our respective diplomatic services. But because your recent speech indicates that you have personally considered some of the included questions of the broad general subject, I feel a slight deviation from our normal practice is justified.

I feel strongly that the control system must continue to include equipment and raw materials of high war-potential significance, whether or not they have wide civilian use, where the Soviet bloc has a serious deficiency which it cannot overcome in a short time. However, there is room for discussion as to the scope and severity of the controls which should be applied under this principle.

Whereas the United Kingdom proposals would appear to eliminate International Lists II and III, I am convinced that there is an area in which quantitative restrictions are the most appropriate control mechanism. Of course, I recognize that it may be desirable to narrow substantially the area to which such controls need be applied, but I do not think we can scrap them altogether.

These seem to me to be the main difference between us. Although the gap appears to be wide, we have resolved greater differences before this to our mutual advantage and will do so again. I suggest, then, that we ask our responsible officials to meet together very soon, presumably with their French counterparts, and try to find the common ground on which we can continue jointly to provide constructive leadership to the Consultative Group.

Finally, I have two other suggestions to make. For one thing, I think it would be very useful if our representatives and subsequently the members of the Consultative Group, were jointly to examine and assess the meaning and direction of the Russians' new trade policy, including the much-publicized Russian profession of interest in consumer goods. Secondly, I think it would be advantageous for our representatives to explore ways and means by which the free world might exploit, in its relations with the Soviet bloc, any decision to relax existing controls.

As ever,
D.E.

CHURCHILL TO EISENHOWER

March 24, 1954

My dear Friend,

Thank you for your message of March 19 about the relaxation of East/West trade controls. We shall be very glad to talk over with your representatives the points set out in your message and I would urge that the talks should take place as soon as possible. I agree that French representatives should also take part. I suggest that if possible our officials should be informed before the discussions begin what variations in terms of items your Government would wish to make to the revised list we have proposed.

Winston

CHURCHILL TO EISENHOWER

March 24, 1954

My dear Friend,

Thank you very much for your letter about East/West Trade. As consultation and discussion between our two countries were urgent, I sent you my telegram of today's date. I now venture to put before you some of the wider considerations that have influenced my thought.

While doing all that is possible to increase our joint strength and unity, I am anxious to promote an easement of relations with Soviet Russia and to encourage and aid any development of Russian life which leads to a wider enjoyment by the Russian masses of the consumer goods of which you speak and modern popular amenities and diversions which play so large a part in British and American life. I hope that this process will lead to some relaxation of the grim discipline of the peoples of this vast land ocean of Russia and its satellites. Moreover, trade means contacts and probably involves a good deal of friendly infiltration which I think would be to our advantage from every point of view, including the military.

I am, of course, opposed to exportation to Russia of weapons or military equipment in a direct form, but I do not think this principle should be used to ban so many items because they might be used for military purposes in a secondary or subsequent stage. Any advantage given by this would only be on a small and almost trivial proportion of Russian armaments, for the whole scale of East/West Trade is small and we should be dealing only with a percentage of a percentage. I do not think this ought to stand in the way of the widening of commercial intercourse so long as only conventional forms of equipment are concerned. On the contrary I believe that even in this limited military sphere we should, I think, gain as much or almost as much as we should lose.

Over and beyond that there are those hopes of a broadening of Russian life and relaxation of international tension which may lead to the reestablishment of a peaceful foundation for the tormented and burdened world.

How minute do all these military considerations, arising out of trade as limited, appear compared to the Hydrogen bomb and the rapid progress the Soviets are said to be making with it. There is the peril which marches toward us and is nearer and more deadly to us than to you. We may be sure that whatever raw materials or equipment is available to the Russians, whether from their own resources or from imports, the first priority will be given to nuclear expansion, just as at a former stage in Germany guns counted before butter. I fear, therefore, that even a total prohibition of all East/West trade would not impede the physical progress of these fearful forces. On the other hand there is the hope that the inspiring conceptions of which you told me at Bermuda and with which your letter of March 19, which I received yesterday and to which I will reply later, also so pregnantly deals.

I have not hampered this expression of my most anxious thought by expatiating on the well known arguments about British trade in the present economic phase. I will merely mention the headings. If the United States will not let us pay for her goods by rendering reciprocal services and make a reasonable proportion of things your people want or might be attracted by, as is our deep desire, the present deadlock must continue. As the old tag says, those who do not import cannot export. I have learned all about these difficulties from my political youth up and am making no complaint. "Off shore" purchase is a Godsend, but you are still in the position of having to give away on a vast scale with generosity and human patriotism what we should like to earn by hard work and mental exertion. The arrival of Germany and Japan in the world market make it necessary that we should open out our trade in every possible direction for we have to keep 50 million people alive in this small island as well as maintaining the greatest armaments next to your own in the free world.

As the proportion of our trade with Russia must in any case be on a minor scale for many years, I cannot rate the commercial aspect so highly as I do those I have mentioned above.

I enclose a copy of the telegram which I have agreed with my colleagues and which will by now have reached you.

With all good wishes,
Yours ever,
Winston S. Churchill

EISENHOWER TO CHURCHILL

March 27, 1954

Your letter of March 24th only reached me Saturday afternoon; the plane which brought it having been delayed. Consequently I did not have an opportunity to go over it with Harold Stassen before he left for London. However, Harold is fully informed of my views on this difficult and important matter. As I indicated in my earlier letter your proposals in this field seem to go a bit further than seems wise or necessary. However, it remains my hope that after Harold has explained the lines along which our thoughts are running, and when we pass from general to the concrete we shall be able to reach agreement.

With warm regard,
Ike

CHURCHILL TO EISENHOWER

March 29, 1954

My dear Friend,
There is widespread anxiety here about the H-bomb and I am facing a barrage of questions tomorrow about the March 1 explosion. Our instruments here record a second explosion in the series mentioned in our private talks at Bermuda on 26 instant.[1]

I am well aware of all your difficulties in view of the McMahon Act, etc., and of the efforts you are making to obtain greater freedom to give us the information and I shall do my utmost to safeguard our common interests as they are developing. It would be a great help to me if I could say that in return for the facilities we accorded to American aircraft at the Australian experiments the American authorities had agreed to our sending aircraft to collect samples of debris at very great heights.[2]

I should also like to say that apart from this act of reciprocity we have no information as yet of the results of the experiment but we hope it may be possible within the limits of existing United States legislation to give us a report of what occurred.

I shall of course repulse all suggestions—and there are many—that we should protest against the continuance of your experiments. I have to speak at 3.30 p.m. G.M.T. Tuesday 30. The Prof is also telegraphing to the Admiral.

Winston

1. March 1, 1954, a U.S. H-bomb test in the Pacific, code-named BRAVO, resulted in radiation sickness suffered by twenty-three Japanese fishermen. A test on March 26, 1954, had no fallout incident, but public apprehension over radioactive fallout from H-bomb tests was rising in Britain and in the United States.

2. Britain allowed the United States to observe and collect intelligence from British atomic tests at Woomera, Australia.

EISENHOWER TO CHURCHILL

March 29, 1954

Dear Winston,

Greatly appreciate your message. Admiral Strauss has just returned from the Pacific and I shall not see him until tomorrow. I understand however that he has been in touch with your Ambassador and that the first two points you raise have been covered to your satisfaction.

With warm personal regard,
Ike E.

CHURCHILL TO EISENHOWER

April 1, 1954

My dear Friend,

I am grateful to you for permission to speak about the aircraft in reply to a Question. As we are going to have a full dress Debate on Monday the Question has been postponed. I send you herewith the Answer I was going to give which I think meets most of Strauss's misgivings.[1] I shall now weave it into my argument. Meanwhile any topical comments upon it will be welcome.

Another matter far more important presses upon me. The foundation of my argument is that the United States Government is bound by the McMahon Act and cannot disclose forbidden information even to their closest friends. You are appealing to Congress for more flexibility in view of our own knowledge on this subject. Our Opposition, especially its anti-American Left Wing, are trying to put the blame for the present restriction of information on to me and this increases my difficulty in defending, as I have done and will do, your claim to keep your secrets as agreed with the late Socialist Government. I am also supporting, as you will have seen, your continued experiments.

In view of the attacks, however, I am sure you will agree that the only course open to me is to quote and publish the text of my agreement with F.D.R. in 1943, which completely vindicates my own care of British interests. You will remember I showed it to you in Bernie's flat before you had assumed power, on my way to Jamaica in January, 1953. It will prove decisively that the Opposition, not I, are responsible for our present position, and how great is the difference between the situation which I handed over when I was thrown out by the Election of 1945 from the new position which I inherited from the Socialists in 1951.

The fourth clause of this document about commercial possibilities contains a prediction by me that I was content to leave the future of commercial atomics to the President of the United States, "as he considered to be fair and just and in harmony with the economic welfare of the world." This has now been vindicated in a striking manner by your scheme announced in U.N.O. on December 8, 1953.

I feel I have the right to disclose this document which I signed with your predecessor eleven years ago, and which had since been superseded by other Treaties agreed between Great Britain and the Truman Administration. I am nevertheless explaining my position and intentions to you because of our personal friendship and our various talks about the document. It would be an encouragement to me to hear from you that you are content with the course I am taking.

Our talks with Stassen went off very well and will I am sure produce fruitful and harmless results.

With kindest regards,
Winston

1. Churchill enclosed a draft of the answer to a parliamentary question on atomic energy.

EISENHOWER TO CHURCHILL

April 2, 1954

Dear Winston,

I have your letter received today.

I give you quickly my reaction which on both counts is affirmative. The proposed text referred to in paragraph 1 is quite in order from our standpoint. With reference to the matters dealt with in your second, third and fourth paragraphs I can only say that I am, to use your word, "content" with the course you plan. Of course some of this history is not fully known to me but I certainly would not feel disposed to interpose any objection. I am confident you have weighed this matter with the wisdom which you always bring to bear on these momentous matters.

Harold Stassen has just told me of his talks and I share your judgment of the outcome.

With warm regard,
Ike

CHURCHILL TO EISENHOWER

April 4, 1954

My dear Friend,

Thank you so much for your most kind and considerate telegram. I hope you will be "content" with the way I am dealing with the problem in my speech tomorrow.

With all good wishes,
Winston

Southeast Asia

At the end of the Second World War, Britain took the lead in ensuring that France regained her colonial possessions in Vietnam, Laos, and Cambodia. The United States was very critical of the French colonial record in Indochina and acquiesced with misgivings in the restoration of French colonial rule. With the growing Communist threat worldwide, however, and Communist Chinese aid to the insurgent Vietminh in Indochina, the United States began in 1950 to give aid to the

French in Indochina, and by 1954 80 percent of French military costs in the war was borne by the United States. Britain, on the other hand, despaired of France's position in Indochina and was skeptical of the degree of influence of the Chinese over the Vietminh. Britain wished to avoid the extension of the war in Indochina into a wider war in Asia involving Communist China, which, aside from other dangers, would threaten Britain's colony in Hong Kong.

In the spring of 1954 the situation in the Indochina War became critical, with a French garrison cut off and surrounded by the Vietminh in the fortress of Dien Bien Phu in Vietnam. At the same time the Geneva Conference on Korea and Indochina was due to begin on April 26, 1954. Eisenhower favored "united action" by means of the formation of a coalition of France, the Associated States of Vietnam, Laos and Cambodia, the United States, Britain, Australia, New Zealand, Thailand, and the Philippines. The establishment of such a coalition, it was hoped, would stiffen the French will to resist and act as a deterrent against the Communists, especially the Chinese. The proposal on "united action," spelled out in a speech by Dulles in New York on March 29, involved a commitment to military intervention if necessary, but Eisenhower felt that the commitment in itself by this group of nations would provide the necessary deterrent so that intervention would not be required in practice. When Dulles met Eden in London on April 13, 1954, he felt that he had secured Britain's agreement to "united action." Within a few days, however, it became clear that Britain did not accept the proposal, fearing a wider war in Asia and feeling that France should settle for the best terms available. Some Americans, especially Admiral Arthur Radford, chairman of the Joint Chiefs of Staff, advocated unilateral military intervention on the part of the United States, but Eisenhower was unwilling to ask Congress for authority for American intervention in Indochina unless support was given by America's allies, among whom Britain was crucial. Following the fall of Dien Bien Phu on May 7, the Indochina phase of the Geneva Conference opened on May 8. In July the Geneva Convention was signed, with French withdrawal and the division of Vietnam at the 17th parallel. Britain agreed to united action only in its later form of participation in SEATO, which came into being in September 1954 and which included the non-Communist parts of Indochina in the area under its security guarantee.

EISENHOWER TO CHURCHILL

April 4, 1954

Dear Winston,

I am sure that like me you are following with the deepest interest and anxiety the daily reports of the gallant fight being put up by the French at Dien Bien Phu. Today, the situation there does not seem hopeless.

But regardless of the outcome of this particular battle, I fear that the French cannot alone see this thing through, this despite the very substantial assistance in money and material that we are giving them. It is no solution simply to urge the French to intensify their efforts, and if they do not see it through, and Indochina passes into the hands of the Communists, the ultimate effect on our and your global strategic position with the consequent shift in the power ratio throughout Asia and the Pacific could be disastrous and, I know, unacceptable to you and me. It is difficult to see how Thailand, Burma and Indonesia could be kept out of Communist hands. This we cannot afford. The threat to Malaya, Australia and New Zealand would be direct. The offshore island chain would be broken. The economic pressure on Japan which would be deprived of non-Communist markets and sources of food and raw material would be such, over a period of time, that it is difficult to see how Japan could be prevented from reaching an accommodation with the Communist world which would combine the manpower and natural resources of Asia with the industrial potential of Japan. This has led us to the hard conclusion that the situation in Southeast Asia requires us urgently to take serious and far-reaching decisions.

Geneva is less than four weeks away. There the possibility of the Communists driving a wedge between us will, given the state of mind in France, be infinitely greater than at Berlin. I can understand the very natural desire of the French to seek an end to this war which has been bleeding them for eight years. But our painstaking search for a way out of the impasse has reluctantly forced us to the conclusion that there is no negotiated solution of the Indochina problem which in its essence would not be either a face-saving device to cover a French surrender or a face-saving device to cover a Communist retirement. The first alternative is too serious in its broad strategic implications for us and for you to be acceptable. Apart from its effects in Southeast Asia itself, where you and the Commonwealth have direct and vital interests, it would have the most serious repercussions in North Africa, in Europe and elsewhere. Here at home it would cause a widespread loss of confidence in the cooperative system. I think it is not too much to say that the future of France as a great power would be fatally affected. Perhaps France will never again be the great power it was, but a sudden vacuum wherever French power is, would be difficult for us to cope with.

Somehow we must contrive to bring about the second alternative. The preliminary lines of our thinking were sketched out by Foster in his speech last Monday night when he said that under the conditions of today the imposition on Southeast Asia of the political system of Communist Russia and its Chinese Communist ally, by whatever means, would be a grave threat to the whole free community, and that in our view this possibility should now be met by united action and not passively accepted. He has also talked intimately with Roger Makins.

I believe that the best way to put teeth in this concept and to bring greater moral and material resources to the support of the French effort is through the establishment of a new ad hoc grouping or coalition composed of nations which have a vital concern in the checking of Communist expansion in the area. I have in mind in addition to our two countries, France, the Associated States, Australia, New Zealand, Thailand and the Philippines. The United States Government would expect to play its full part in such a coalition. The coalition we have in mind would not be directed against Communist China. But if, contrary to our belief, our efforts to save Indochina and the British Commonwealth position to the south should in any way increase the jeopardy to Hong Kong, we would expect to be with you there. I suppose that the United Nations should somewhere be recognized, but I am not confident that, given the Soviet veto, it could act with needed speed and vigor.

I would contemplate no role for Formosa or the Republic of Korea in the political construction of this coalition.

The important thing is that the coalition must be strong and it must be willing to join the fight if necessary. I do not envisage the need of any appreciable ground forces on your or our part. If the members of the alliance are sufficiently resolute it should be able to make clear to the Chinese Communists that the continuation of their material support to the Viet Minh will inevitably lead to the growing power of the forces arrayed against them.

My colleagues and I are deeply aware of the risks which this proposal may involve but in the situation which confronts us there is no course of action or inaction devoid of dangers and I know of no man who has firmly grasped more nettles than you. If we grasp this one together I believe that we will enormously increase our chances of bringing the Chinese to believe that their interests lie in the direction of a discreet disengagement. In such a contingency we could approach the Geneva conference with the position of the free world not only unimpaired but strengthened.

Today we face the hard situation of contemplating a disaster brought on by French weakness and the necessity of dealing with it before it develops. This means frank talk with the French. In many ways the situation corresponds to that which you describe so brilliantly in the second chapter of "Their Finest Hour", when history made clear that the French strategy and dispositions before the 1940 breakthrough should have been challenged before the blow fell.

I regret adding to your problems. But in fact it is not I, but our enemies who add to them. I have faith that by another act of fellowship in the face of peril we shall find a spiritual vigor which will prevent our slipping into the quagmire of distrust.

If I may refer again to history, we failed to halt Hirohito, Mussolini and Hitler by not acting in unity and in time. That marked the beginning of many years of stark tragedy and desperate peril. May it not be that our nations have learned something from the lesson?

So profoundly do I believe that the effectiveness of the coalition principle is at stake that I am prepared to send Foster or Bedell to visit you this week, at the earliest date convenient to you. Whoever comes would spend a day in Paris to avoid French pique. The cover would be preparation for Geneva.

With warm regard,
Ike

CHURCHILL TO EISENHOWER

April 6, 1954

My dear friend,
I have received your most important message of April 4. We are giving it earnest Cabinet consideration.

Winston

CHURCHILL TO EISENHOWER

April 7, 1954

My dear Friend,

We discussed your proposal about Indo-China in the Cabinet this morning and we are certainly giving it a great deal of thought. It is however a topic which raises many problems for us and I am sure you will not expect us to give a hurried decision. We shall be very glad to see Foster here and talk the matter over with him. If Monday next, April 12, were convenient to him it would suit us well to open the talks that day.

Every good wish,
Winston

CHURCHILL TO EISENHOWER

April 22, 1954

My Dear Friend,

I am told that you will be in Washington between May 20 and 24, before you receive the Emperor of Abyssinia. I should very much like to have some talks with you. I would stay at the Embassy and probably a night or two with Bernie. We shall know more than we know now about several things—mostly tiresome. I should keep the plan secret till the last moment. Do you like the idea?

All good wishes,
Winston

EISENHOWER TO CHURCHILL

April 23, 1954

Dear Winston,

Of course you will be welcome. I agree with you that it is high time that we make certain of our common understanding of current and impending events that affect both our countries intimately. I am temporarily out of Washington but will be back there Monday, at which time I shall cable you again as to exact dates.

With warm regard,
Ike

EISENHOWER TO CHURCHILL

April 26, 1954

Dear Winston,

Please let me refer again to your suggestion that we have a meeting to talk over things of great significance to our two countries. I am continually impressed by the drastic critical changes in the world situation that each day seems to bring us in this obviously critical period. Likewise, I am deeply concerned by the seemingly wide differences in the conclusions developed in our respective governments, especially as these conclusions relate to such events as the war in Indo-China and to the impending conference at Geneva.

In order that our talks may have the maximum fruitfulness, I think it best to await the return of Foster to Washington before you and I try to work out firm details as to timing and subjects of our conversations. Foster will bring back to me valuable impressions and conclusions that I should study before you and I meet to explore why we seem to reach drastically differing answers to problems involving the same sets of basic facts. Certainly I agree with the thought, implicit in your suggestion, that we must reach a true meeting of minds so that we may work more in concert as we attack the critical questions of the day.

I assure you that I am anxious, as I have always been, to reach a common understanding that will be squarely based upon existing fact and to which both governments can logically adhere to their mutual advantage.

With warm regard, As ever, Ike

EISENHOWER TO CHURCHILL

May 12, 1954

Dear Winston,

In my message of April 26 I promised you a further reply after I had an opportunity to talk with Foster concerning the timing of your visit to Washington. I have now had the opportunity to discuss it with him and we are agreed that some time in June would be best from our point of view. By then Geneva will have unfolded further and we will both better know where we stand in the matter of IndoChina, where I think a greater show of unity is essential. In addition to this consideration, the present series of our tests will not have been evaluated until the early days of June and it would be useful for progress on that front if I had the results of those before me when we talked.

Let me know how your schedule looks for June and we can then agree on the most convenient date for both of us.

> With warm regard,
> Ike

CHURCHILL TO EISENHOWER

May 13, 1954

My dear Friend,

How would Friday June 18 suit you or will you be going away for the week-end? I could stay for four or five days at your convenience at the Embassy. I am most anxious to survey with you the whole question of sharing information about the bomb, etc. It will be most valuable to learn your evaluation of the latest series of tests. I should also welcome a talk with you about the Indo-China imbroglio. If you preferred weekdays I could start Sunday June 20.

> Kindest regards,
> Winston

EISENHOWER TO CHURCHILL

May 15, 1954

Dear Winston,

Friday, June 18th, suits me very well. It will give us a good weekend for talks. I hope very much you are counting on bringing Anthony with you also that he may talk with Foster. The two of them could help us keep our talks related to the many delicate aspects of the world situation. Moreover their presence should be helpful to them in understanding any ideas we might agree upon.

My thought is that we should see that social affairs are kept at a minimum or totally eliminated so that we could have the maximum time for leisurely discussions. Do you agree with this or would you like to make some different suggestions?

The matter of announcements, so far as I am concerned, can be determined by Foster and Anthony, but if you have any particular thought on this point, I will be glad to have it.

With warm regard,

> As ever,
> Ike

CHURCHILL TO EISENHOWER

May 16, 1954

My dear Friend,

So many thanks for your telegram of May 15. Of course I should like to bring Anthony with me. I agree that social affairs should be eliminated though probably I should be urged as on all previous occasions to lunch with the Washington Press Club where the proceedings have always been confidential.[1]

I did not think any announcement was urgent. We might discuss this at the end of May when perhaps Geneva will be over.

Kindest regards,

Yours always,
Winston

1. As Makins noted to Eisenhower, Churchill meant this as a joke.

CHURCHILL TO EISENHOWER

May 24, 1954

My Dear Friend,

I am planning to leave for Washington on the 17th arriving 18th as outlined in our telegrams of May 13 and 15, and shall be at your convenience at the British Embassy for a few days thereafter. I think the announcement might be fitted in with Geneva as soon as possible, perhaps even this week. If you still like the idea, I will suggest the text of the communique.

The main and obvious topic is interchange of information about atomics, etc., and the progress of your great design to develop its harmless side. Apart from that we will talk over anything that crops up. For instance, I should like to reinforce Malaya, and Egypt is my first reserve. With your support a sound and dignified arrangement should be possible. I sincerely hope you will be able to postpone sending the Egyptians any aid until you and I have had our talks.

Anthony would like very much to come as you suggested, though perhaps he could not be there the whole time. I agree with you that it is essential to have him and Foster together and with us.

It seems to me that our meetings in the easy informal manner that we both desire may be a help in brushing away this chatter about an Anglo-American rift which can benefit no one but our common foes.

Every good wish,
Winston

EISENHOWER TO CHURCHILL

May 24, 1954

Dear Winston,
    Many thanks for your letter to which I promptly reply. Please suggest announcement and timing as soon as convenient. Am desirous that you stay with me at least for the weekend upon your arrival, and I can also put up an aide-de-camp at the White House. Looking forward to a good talk, I am,

As ever,
Ike

CHURCHILL TO EISENHOWER

May 26, 1954

My Dear Friend,
    I shall be delighted to come to you at the White House on June 18 for the week-end. I hope Anthony will come over at the same time.
    I see no hurry for the announcement until things are clearer at Geneva. Anthony thinks that we should postpone it for perhaps ten days.

Yours always,
Winston

EISENHOWER TO CHURCHILL

May 27, 1954

Dear Winston,
    I shall be more than happy if Anthony also will be my guest at the White House during your stay there. This should provide maximum convenience for you both. Won't you please inform him as soon as

possible that I should be pleased and complimented by his acceptance?

I shall wait to hear from you with regard to the announcement. I
agree that there is no hurry about it.

With warm regard,

As ever,
Ike

CHURCHILL TO EISENHOWER

May 29, 1954

My Dear Friend,

Thank you so much for your message and invitation. We shall both
be delighted to stay with you for the week-end.

With every good wish,

Winston

CHURCHILL TO EISENHOWER

June 10, 1954

My dear Friend,

I was very glad to hear through our Ambassador that your invitation to me and Anthony to spend the week-end with you might be
postponed for one week, namely from the 18th to the 25th without
causing you any inconvenience. This probably resolves the puzzle
about whether Anthony could leave Geneva in time. He feels that it is
his first duty to play the hand through at the Conference and not to
incur reproach for breaking it up by his sudden departure.

Like you I feel that the sooner an announcement can be made
without complicating Geneva the better and I will suggest a draft for
your consideration in my next.

I look forward to those talks between you and me which we had
always considered an essential part of the vital cooperation of the
English-speaking world. I feel that we have reached a serious crisis in
which the whole policy of peace through strength may be involved.

EISENHOWER TO CHURCHILL

June 11, 1954

Dear Winston,

It is easy for me to make the change of one week and I am particularly glad that this will cause less inconvenience to Anthony. I shall be waiting for your suggested draft of the necessary announcement.

It will be like old times to have a weekend with you. I know that it will be interesting and enjoyable and I am certainly hopeful that it will be profitable for both our countries.

As ever,
Ike

CHURCHILL TO EISENHOWER

June 11, 1954

My Dear Friend,

Anthony suggests the following announcement which seems to me very suitable:—

"Some weeks ago the President of the United States invited the Prime Minister and the Foreign Secretary to spend a week-end as his guests in Washington. The invitation was cordially accepted and it has been arranged for the visit to take place during the week-end beginning June 25."

As to the timing, I should prefer to make the announcement to Parliament when it meets next Tuesday. This would be at 3.30 p.m. our time, i.e. 10.30 a.m. your time. This is quite agreeable to Anthony from the Geneva point of view.

I am so glad it is all arranged and I look forward keenly to seeing you again. Please give my regards to Foster.

W.S.C.

CHURCHILL TO EISENHOWER

June 17, 1954

My Dear Friend,

Thank you so much for all the charming things you have said about our visit. The plan is greatly welcomed here. Its announcement may have healthy effects both on French and Chinese.

Would it suit your convenience if we stayed to dinner with you Sunday and slept the night at the Embassy? I thought I would stay at the Embassy day and night of 28th and fly to Ottawa for 29th and 30th, then would stay two nights with Bernie, who has a reporter-proof country house an hour from New York. But these plans are of course flexible.

Kindest regards,
Winston

EISENHOWER TO CHURCHILL

June 17, 1954

Dear Winston,

The arrangements you suggest are perfectly satisfactory. I would be delighted to have you stay with me Sunday night or at the Embassy whichever you prefer.

With warm regard,
Ike

EISENHOWER TO CHURCHILL

June 18, 1954

Dear Winston,

Do you interpret the elevation of Mendes-France[1] and the pledges he has made as evidence of a readiness on his part to surrender completely in Southeast Asia? If this is so, can you give me some idea of your solution to the resulting problems? If you have formulated any thoughts on these delicate matters, I should like to have them so that I can give them some contemplation before we meet.

I understand that you and Anthony reach here about 10 a.m. on Friday. This will be splendid, as both Foster and I are looking forward eagerly to our talks.

With warm regard,

As ever,
Ike

1. June 12, 1954, Laniel's government fell over Indochina. Pierre Mendès-France, who pledged to end the Indochina War on reasonable terms by July 20 or resign, was chosen as prime minister, June 17, 1954.

CHURCHILL TO EISENHOWER

June 21, 1954

My dear Friend,

I have always thought that if the French meant to fight for their Empire in Indo-China instead of clearing out as we did of our far greater inheritance in India, they should at least have introduced two years' service which would have made it possible for them to use the military power of their nation. They did not do this but fought on for eight years with untrustworthy local troops, with French cadre elements important to the structure of their home army and with the Foreign Legion, a very large proportion of whom were Germans. The result has thus been inevitable and personally I think Mendes-France, whom I do not know, has made up his mind to clear out on the best terms available. If that is so, I think he is right.

I have thought continually about what we ought to do in the circumstances. Here it is. There is all the more need to discuss ways and means of establishing a firm front against Communism in the Pacific sphere. We should certainly have a S.E.A.T.O. corresponding to N.A.T.O. in the Atlantic and European sphere. In this it is important to have the support of the Asian countries. This raises the question of timing in relation to Geneva.

In no foreseeable circumstances, except possibly a local rescue, could British troops be used in Indo-China, and if we were asked our opinion we should advise against United States local intervention except for rescue.

The S.E.A.T.O. front should be considered as a whole, and also in relation to our world front against Communist aggression. As the sectors of the S.E.A.T.O. front are so widely divided and different in conditions, it is better, so far as possible, to operate nationally. We garrison Hong Kong and the British Commonwealth contributes a division to Korea. But our main sector must be Malaya. Here we have twenty-three battalions formed into five brigades. You are no doubt aware of the operation contemplated in the event of a Communist invasion from Siam. I will bring detailed plan with me. Alex, who I understand is coming over in July, will discuss it with your Generals. The question is whence are we to draw reinforcements. There are none at home; our last regular reserves are deployed. It would be a pity to take the troops from Germany. On the other hand we have what are called 80,000 men in the Egyptian Canal zone, which mean 40,000 well-mounted fighting troops. Here is the obvious reserve.

Now is the time the Middle East front should be considered together by the United States and Britain. I had hoped more than a year ago that the United States would act jointly with us in negotiating an agreement with the Egyptian military dictatorship in accordance with the terms already agreed between the British and American staffs. It was, however, felt at Washington that America could not go unless invited. The negotiations therefore broke down. Since then there has been a deadlock though the area of dispute is limited.

As time has passed, the strategic aspect of the Canal Zone and base has been continually and fundamentally altered by thermo-nuclear developments and a Tito-Greek-Turco front coming into being and giving its hand to Iraq and by America carrying N.A.T.O.'s finger-tips to Pakistan. I like all this improvement in which you and the power and resources of the United States have played so vital a part.

These events greatly diminish the strategic importance of the Canal Zone and base, and what is left of it no longer justifies the expense and diversion of our troops, discharging since the war, not British but international purposes. As far as Egypt is concerned, we shall not ask you for a dollar or a marine. I am greatly obliged by the way you have so far withheld arms and money from the Egyptian dictatorship.

The general theme of completing and perfecting in a coherent structure the world front against Communist aggression, which I suppose might in current practice be described as N.A.T.O., M.E.A.T.O. and S.E.A.T.O., is of course one, but only one of the topics I am looking forward to talking over with you.

The other two have long been in my mind. One is the better sharing of information and also perhaps of resources in the thermo-nuclear sphere. I am sure you will not overlook the fact that by the Anglo-American base in East Anglia we have made ourselves for the next year or two the nearest and perhaps the only bull's eye of the target.[1] And finally I seek as you know to convince Russia that there is a thoroughly friendly and easy way out for her in which all her hard-driven peoples may gain a broader, fuller and happier life.

You know my views, already publicly expressed in October, 1953, about Germany. If E.D.C. fails, we ought to get her into N.A.T.O. or a revised form of N.A.T.O. under the best terms possible.

I would not have tried to put all this on paper but for your direct request. So if there is anything in it which you do not like, let it wait till we are together for our weekend meeting, to which I am so keenly looking forward.

With kindest regards,
Winston

1. In 1948 the first postwar American base in Britain was established in East Anglia, with B-29s, the planes used by the Americans to carry atomic bombs, stationed there.

EISENHOWER TO CHURCHILL

June 22, 1954

Dear Winston,

As you know, I had planned to keep social engagements to a minimum during your stay with me until Sunday night or Monday morning. I think we shall use luncheon and dinner periods for small business meetings, except for Friday evening when I thought a very few members of the Cabinet and their wives should come in to meet you and Anthony. At Saturday's luncheon I shall hope to bring in a few of our top legislative people to meet with you for an hour or so. None of this will be formal, but it might be nice to have a black tie for the Friday evening affair. I understand that a group of associates will accompany you and Anthony to Washington. I would be pleased if you would select three of four of them as additional guests at dinner Friday night. I would appreciate your sending me their names.

Warm regard,
Ike

CHURCHILL TO EISENHOWER

June 23, 1954

My dear Friend,

I like all your plans very much indeed. I should be grateful if you would invite the following friends of mine to dinner on Friday: Lord Cherwell, Lord Moran, Sir Edwin Plowden,[1] Sir Harold Caccia.[2]

I am a tardy riser so I think it would be better for me to leave the White House for the Embassy on Sunday night after dinner.

I have a feeling that this meeting to which I have so long looked forward is more timely now than at earlier dates. It may be that our all being together will make other people more careful.

All good wishes,
Winston

1. Sir Edwin Plowden, former Treasury chief planning officer.
2. Sir Harold Caccia, deputy under secretary of state, Foreign Office.

FOUR

EDC, West Germany, and NATO
July 7–December 27, 1954

Churchill had a very successful visit to Washington, D.C., June 25–29, 1954. He was received with great warmth by the American press, public, and Congress, and, especially in his answers to questions from the press, he was in sparkling form. His talks with Eisenhower helped to reduce the tensions in Anglo-American relations over such issues as Indochina, East-West trade, and exchange of atomic information. Above all, however, Churchill wanted to make another effort to secure Eisenhower's agreement to a summit meeting with the Soviets.

At their first talk in Washington, Eisenhower appeared to agree with Churchill's proposal of a summit, but by the end of Churchill's visit Eisenhower had reverted to his more equivocal position on the subject. Churchill then decided on his voyage home across the Atlantic on the *Queen Mary* to take the bold step of sending a telegram to Molotov without clearing the matter first with the Cabinet, to begin discussion of a possible meeting of the Soviet leadership with Churchill alone if not with Churchill and Eisenhower. Throughout July 1954 Churchill faced severe opposition within his own government to the summit proposal and to his handling of the matter, until a Soviet note of July 24, 1954, effectively ended the possibility of a summit at that time. The Churchill-Eisenhower correspondence in the summer of 1954 was therefore dominated by the aftermath of Churchill's visit to Washington and the issue of a possible meeting with the Soviets.

Eisenhower was still deeply concerned over issues in the Far East, so that letters were exchanged over Indochina and China. In August 1954 the French National Assembly vote against ratification of the EDC treaty created a major crisis which absorbed the attention of the NATO allies over the following months. The Churchill-Eisenhower letters covered the problems relating to German rearmament and NATO unity following French rejection of EDC. Churchill realized, however, that although Eden's initiatives ultimately produced a satisfactory solution to the issue of German rearmament, there was little prospect of progress toward his most highly desired objective, a summit meeting with the Soviets, until negotiations were complete on a satisfactory substitute for EDC.

CHURCHILL TO EISENHOWER

July 7, 1954

Dear Friend,

In the light of our talks and after careful thought I thought it right to send an exploratory message to Molotov to feel the ground about the possibility of a two power Meeting. This of course committed nobody except myself. The following is a summary of my message.
Begins:

After referring to my speech of May 11, 1953, for a top level Meeting of the Big Three, and to the statements I have made from time to time in the House of Commons that if this were impossible I would seek to make a contact myself with the Soviet Government, I put the question, how would they feel about it. I should like to know this, I said, before we make any official proposal, or considered such questions as the time and place. I went on, "I should be very glad if you would let me know if you would like the idea of a friendly Meeting, with no Agenda and no object but to find a reasonable way of living side by side in growing confidence, easement and prosperity. Although our Meeting, wherever held, would be simple and informal and last only a few days, it might be the prelude to a wider reunion where much might be settled. I have, however, no warrant to say this beyond my own hopes. I ask you to let me know, as soon as you can, what you and your friends think."
Ends.

This evening I received an answer from Molotov, which I send you textually. I should like to know how this strikes you.
Begins:

"I express my gratitude for your important message handed to me by Ambassador Hayter on the 4th July.

It is with interest that the Soviet Government got acquainted with this message, the importance of which is quite clear. You may be sure that your initiative will find here favourable attitude which it fully deserves especially in the present international situation in general.

Your idea about a friendly Meeting between you and Premier G. M. Malenkov as well as the considerations expressed by you regarding the aims of such a Meeting, have met with sympathetic acknowledgement in Moscow. Mr. Anthony Eden's participation in such a Meeting who is closely connected with the development of the relations between our countries, is, of course, accepted as quite natural. We feel that such a personal contact may serve to carrying out a broader Meeting on the highest level, if it is accepted by all the parties which are interested in easing the international tension and in strengthening peace.

I deem it necessary to express to you the general opinion of the leading political statesmen in Moscow. They have often recalled about our friendly relations during the war and about the outstanding role which you personally played in all that. Once again you have rightly reminded of this time. One may ask why during the years of war there existed between our countries the relations which had a positive significance not only for our peoples but for the destinies of the whole world, and why such relations cannot be developed in the same good direction now. As to us we are striving to this end and we are regarding your message from this point of view."
Ends.

We have many pleasant and enduring memories of our visit to the White House.

With my kindest regards,
Winston

EISENHOWER TO CHURCHILL

July 7, 1954

Dear Winston,

You did not let any grass grow under your feet. When you left here, I had thought, obviously erroneously, that you were in an undecided mood about this matter, and that when you had cleared your own mind I would receive some notice if you were to put your program into action. However, that is now past history, and we must hope that the steps you have started will lead to a good result.

I shall of course have to make some statement of my own when your plan is publicly announced. I hope you can give me advance notice as to the date that you will make a public statement on the subject. In this way, I will have time to prepare my own statement carefully.

I probably shall say something to the effect that while you were here the possibility of a Big Three Meeting was discussed; that I could not see how it could serve a useful purpose at this time; that I said that, if you did undertake such a mission, your plan would carry our hopes for the best but would not engage our responsibility.

The fact that your message to Moscow was sent so promptly after you left here is likely to give an impression more powerful than your cautioning words that in some way your plan was agreed at our meeting. Of course, the dating of your message may not become public. This I think would be best because it will call for less explanation from me to the American public. In any event, I think you will agree that your program should be handled with the greatest delicacy to avoid giving either the misapprehension that we are in fact party to it, or the equally dangerous misapprehension that your action in this matter reflects a sharp disagreement between our two countries. I know that you will be aware of these twin dangers and I hope that by understanding and cooperation we can surmount them.

As to the content of Molotov's message as related in your cable, I can only observe that it must be almost exactly what you would have expected in the circumstances.

I am delighted that you enjoyed your visit here. I think that one of the major advantages we may have gained from it is what seems to me an obvious drawing together of Anthony and Foster in their thinking and relationships.

With warm personal regard,

As ever,
Ike

CHURCHILL TO EISENHOWER

July 8, 1954

Dear Friend,

I hope you are not vexed with me for not submitting to you the text of my telegram to Molotov. I felt that as it was a private and personal enquiry which I had not brought officially before the Cabinet I had better bear the burden myself and not involve you in any way. I have made it clear to Molotov that you were in no way committed. I thought this would be agreeable to you, and that we could then consider the question in the light of the answer I got.

Much grass has already grown under our feet since my telegram to you of May 4, 1953. I should be grateful if you would glance again at our correspondence of that period. I have of course stated several times to Parliament my desire that a top level meeting should take place and that failing this I did not exclude a personal mission of my own. I have never varied, in the fourteen months that have passed, from my conviction that the state of the world would not be worsened and might be helped by direct contact with the Russia which has succeeded the Stalin era. However, as you say this is now past history.

I thought Molotov's reply was more cordial and forthcoming to what was after all only a personal and private enquiry than I had expected. It strengthens my view that the new government in the Kremlin are both anxious about the thermo-nuclear future and secondly, attracted by the idea of a peaceful period of domestic prosperity and external contacts. This is certainly my view of what is their self interest. I was struck by the fact that they did not suggest a meeting in Moscow but respected my wish to leave the time and place entirely unsettled. Of course it would be much better to have even the two power meeting about which I enquired in Stockholm or Vienna or Berne and if the Cabinet decide to go forward with the project a margin of six or eight weeks would be open to us for fitting the timing into the movement of events both at Geneva and in Indo-China.

It is on all this that I most earnestly seek your advice, while being willing to bear the brunt of failure on my own shoulders.

I fear that grave military events impend in the Tonkin Delta and indeed, throughout Indo-China. I have heard that General Ely[1] does not think that there is any hope of holding an effective bridgehead in the Delta. There is, I am told, no doubt which way the Viet Nam population would vote if they were freely consulted. I well understand the sense of disaster and defeat in Indo-China may produce a profound effect in the United States as well as far-reaching reactions in Siam and Malaya. It is my hope that an increasing detachment of Russia from Chinese ambitions may be a possibility, and one we should not neglect.

Meanwhile, we shall keep you most thoroughly informed and I shall not seek any decision to make an official approach until I hear from you again. All I have said to Molotov in thanking him for his telegram is that a few days will be needed before any reply can be sent. There can be no question of a public announcement before our two governments have consulted together about policy and also agreed on what it is best to say.

I have impressed on the Soviet Ambassador the importance of absolute secrecy.

With kindest regards,

Yours ever,
Winston

1. General Paul Ely, French commander in chief in Indochina.

EISENHOWER TO CHURCHILL

July 8, 1954

Dear Winston,

Thank you very much for your message, just this minute received. Of course I am not vexed. Personal trust based upon more than a dozen years of close association and valued friendship may occasionally permit room for amazement but never for suspicion. Moreover, I cannot too strongly emphasize to you my prayerful hope that your mission, if you pursue it, may be crowned with complete success. My appreciation of the acute need for peace and understanding in the world certainly far transcends any personal pride in my judgments or convictions. No one could be happier than I to find that I have been wrong in my conclusion that the men in the Kremlin are not to be trusted no matter how great the apparent solemnity and sincerity with which they might enter into an agreement or engagement.

Unfortunately I find no reason for taking a brighter view of the Tonkin Delta situation than is expressed in your fourth paragraph. This, of course, is all the more exasperating to our people because they are well aware that ever since I came into office this government has been suggesting and urging some internationalization of the Indo-China conflict so as to mark it clearly as another instance of Communist aggression against the independence of small countries. In this case I do not think it a harsh judgment to observe that the French have been wrong both from the viewpoint of world peace and of their own prestige. Again I suppose we must sadly observe that is now history.

At this moment the international question that most engages the attention of our people is the possibility that some kind of armistice in Indo-China will be used as an excuse for raising the issue of Red China's entrance into the United Nations. You, of course, put the case very succinctly when you said to me that there can be no serious consideration of this proposition as long as the United Nations is at war with China over the Korean question. On this one matter I honestly believe that American opinion is so firmly fixed that in the absence of a series of deeds that would evidence a complete reversal of Red China's attitude, the introduction of this question for debate in the United Nations would create real difficulty in this country. This is far less a matter of geography than of principle. I have heard it said that America makes a mistake in attempting to introduce moral codes into international relationships and that morals and diplomacy have nothing in common. Be that as it may, the fact remains that the American people like to think that they are being just and fair in these matters and therefore they will not be brow-beaten into accepting something that they consider completely unfair, unjust and immoral.

The bill of particulars against Red China includes, among many other things, its invasion of North Korea where its armies still are stationed. Secondly, Red China by its own admission illegally holds a number of Americans as prisoners. This outrages our entire citizenry. Third, Communist China has been the principal source of the military strength used in the illicit and unjust aggression in Indo-China. Finally, Red China has been guilty of the most atrocious deportment in her dealings with the Western World. At Geneva it excoriated the United Nations and asked for the repudiation of decisions by that body. Red China has been worse than insulting in its communications to ourselves and others, while the public statements of its officials have been characterized by vilification and hatred.

Frankly, I have no worries whatsoever about the ability of your government and this one to keep Anglo-American relationships on a sound, friendly and cooperative basis as long as this one question, which looms so importantly in the American mind, does not rise up to plague us. I pray that you and our other friends may be able, as long as Red China persists in her inexcusable conduct, to help us keep this one matter from appearing on the agenda either in the Security Council or the General Assembly of the United Nations.

With warm personal regard,

As ever,
Ike

CHURCHILL TO EISENHOWER

July 9, 1954

Dear Friend,

I am very much relieved by your kind telegram which reassures me that no serious differences will arise between our two governments on account of Russian excursion or "solitary pilgrimage" by me. I feel sure that you will do your best for me in presenting it to the United States public. I accept the full responsibility as I cannot believe that my American kinsmen will be unanimous in believing I am either anti-American or pro-Communist.

I do not intend to go to Moscow. We can only meet as equals and though Stockholm which you mentioned to me before you took office, or Vienna, are both acceptable, Anthony has proposed what I think is the best, namely, Berne. If Malenkov will come to Berne when Geneva is over, Molotov could meet him there and Anthony and I could have a few talks on the dead level.

My idea is to create conditions in which a three, or perhaps with the French, a four-power conference might be possible, perhaps, as I said to you, in London early in September. For this I feel, and I expect you will agree, that Russian deeds are necessary as well as words. I should ask then for a gesture or as better expressed, "an act of faith" after all Stalin's encroachments in Poland, Czechoslovakia, Korea, etc. which ruptured Anglo-American wartime comradeship with them, and created the world wide union of the free nations, of which N.A.T.O. is the first expression and M.E.T.O. and S.E.A.T.O. are coming along. This sort of gesture I should seek at Berne would be, as I think I mentioned to you, an undertaking to ratify the Austrian Treaty on which all their conditions have been agreed, and to liberate Austria and Vienna from Russian military domination. Surely also it would be a help if they would accept your atomic theme which you told us about at Bermuda and afterwards proposed to U.N.O.

But I am not asking any promise from you that even if the above gesture were attained you would commit yourself to the three or four power conference in London, but naturally my hopes run in that direction.

Of course all this may be moonshine. The Soviets may refuse any meeting place but Moscow. In that case all would be off for the present, or they will give nothing and merely seek, quite vainly, to split Anglo-American unity. I cherish hopes not illusions and after all I am "an expendable" and very ready to be one in so great a cause.

I should like to know your reactions to what I have set out above before I formally ask the Cabinet to propose to the Soviets the two power meeting as described.

Now let me come to the main subject of your telegram. Anthony and I were astonished on the voyage to read the press extracts and other reports, etc., about the storm in the United States about the admission of Red China to U.N.O. against American wishes. Still more were we amazed (though not suspicious) that this seemed to be in some way or other linked with our visit as if we had come over for such a purpose. In fact it was hardly discussed. A brief reference was made to it on June 27 at the Foster Anthony talks in which Anthony is recorded by us as having said the following:—

CHINA

"Mr. Eden said that he thought he knew something about the difficulties which the United States Government faced in relation to their policy towards China. But Her Majesty's Government also had their difficulties. In dealing with this problem, he wished to keep in step with the United States. But he could give no unequivocal guarantee that it would be possible to do so."

There is also a very well informed account in the Paris edition of the New York Herald Tribune of July 7. This states inter alia that Mr. Eden "according to information available here did not press his point but rather sought to reach a meeting of minds. In doing so he promised to give further thought to the question, to consult his Cabinet colleagues, and to enter into conversation with other governments which perhaps were considering favourable action on the Red China view."

The British position has in fact been defined in our absence but with our full agreement by the Foreign Office on July 5 as follows:—

"The United Kingdom policy has been constant since 1951 when Mr. Morrison, the then Foreign Secretary, stated that Her Majesty's Government believed that the Central People's Government should represent China in the United Nations. In view however of the Government's persistence in behaviour which was inconsistent with the purposes and principles of the Charter it appeared to Her Majesty's Government that consideration of this question should be postponed. That was the policy of the late Government and it has been the policy of the present government. This policy was reaffirmed in July 1953 by the Chancellor of the Exchequer who stated that the only accretion or addition which he could make was the hope and trust that the day for settling this and other problems would have been brought nearer by the Korean armistice."

I shall confirm this in the statement I am to make to the House of Commons on Monday next and also point out that since July 1953 there has been no settlement of the Korean question—the armies are still in presence—and the problem of Indo-China has assumed more serious proportions. I hope that will ease American minds. I am very sorry that this business which anyhow does not come up at U.N.O. until the third week in September should have been magnified by Knowland[1] and others into a serious difference between the United States and Great Britain on which the press on both sides of the Atlantic are having a good time. It has somewhat taken the bloom off the peach of our visit, especially as we have not yet been able to make clear by deeds and policy the full measure of our agreement on what I think are far more urgent matters.

I need not say how deeply I feel the force of the arguments you use in the latter part of your last telegram. Although we do not think that any nation could never come into U.N.O. we feel as strongly as you do that they should not come in as a result or at the time of successful and impenitent defiance of the Charter and while still persisting in this attitude. Meanwhile surely the easiest way is to postpone it? We have got enough difficulties in the world to face without it at present.

Meanwhile I cannot see why Anthony should not go on trying to persuade China to behave decently even if their conduct should make them more eligible ultimately for membership of the club. I earnestly hope that all the talk and feeling that has been aroused about the issue will not spoil the prospects of a cease-fire leading to a settlement in Indo-China. Such a settlement would in no way weaken our resolve to develop S.E.A.T.O. on the widest lines including the Colombo Powers[2] and bringing Great Britain in for the first time to A.N.Z.U.S. affairs.[3]

> With my kindest regards,
> Yours very sincerely,
> Winston

1. Senator William Knowland (R-California), right-wing, pro-Nationalist China, Anglophobic Senate majority leader.

2. At a conference in Colombo, Ceylon, in 1950, the Colombo Plan was drawn up for development aid for Asian Commonwealth countries, namely, India, Pakistan, Ceylon, and Malaya, from Britain, Canada, Australia, and New Zealand, and for political cooperation among the participating nations.

3. The ANZUS pact between Australia, New Zealand, and the United States, signed in 1951, illustrated the declining British role and the rising American role in the defense of those two Commonwealth countries.

EISENHOWER TO CHURCHILL

July 10, 1954

Dear Winston,

Thank you for your long cablegram. I shall study it over the weekend and send you a complete reply early next week.

> As ever,
> Ike

EISENHOWER TO CHURCHILL

July 12, 1954

Dear Winston,

I have given much thought to your meaty message of July 9.

You ask for my reactions to what you say about your proposed trip.

You, of course, know that never for one moment would this create any difference between two Governments which are headed by you and me, or alter in the slightest my profound confidence in your dedication to the principles which have so often united our two nations in time of peril, and which today constitute a most precious asset and the best guarantee of peace. I cannot, of course, undertake to deliver unto you what you refer to as the "United States Public." I fear that it may reflect some doubts. But I pledge you that I will do my best to minimize whatever may be the immediate and unfavorable reaction. There will, I am confident, be general acceptance of the sincerity and lofty motivations of your efforts. Probably the majority will consider it, as Hoover is supposed to have said of Prohibition, "a noble experiment."

I am glad that you will not be willing to meet except on a basis of full equality, as indeed I had always assumed. Also, I am reassured that you share the view I have often expressed that Russian deeds are necessary as well as words. Certainly, nothing but an evil purpose can prevent their liberation of Austria, where our Foreign Ministers at Berlin accepted all of the Soviet terms. The same applies to my atomic project which cannot possibly harm them and which could reestablish confidence if that be their desire.

Let me now turn to the other subject of your telegram, namely Red China. I too was amazed at the storm which was raised in the press about your presumed intentions. I cannot explain its origin. Foster's recollection is the same as Anthony's as to what he said and is as you put it in your message to me.

I have just been told of the statement on this matter which you have made today. The word came as I was writing this message to you. I am confident that what you have said will indeed ease American minds.

Already I think, as a result of what Foster and I have said, there has been a subsiding of Congressional emotion and its action now contemplated does not bear the bellicose note which was originally threatened.

Neither Foster nor I have ever used the "never, never" theme and we can only rejoice if ultimately the rulers of Red China behave as decent civilized persons. Even this, of course, would leave us the problem of loyalty to our friends on Formosa whom we cannot turn over to the untender mercies of their enemies. This, however, is a matter for the future.

Foster tells me that the talks here with reference to SEATO are going forward in good spirit and at good speed. I earnestly hope that we shall quickly create something to stop the onrush of communism in Southeast Asia. The French position is crumbling alarmingly.

I am talking now with Foster about whether we should participate in the Geneva Conference. We have agreed that he should offer to meet with Anthony and Mendes-France in Paris tomorrow evening if they desire, with a view to seeing whether in fact we can create a "united front." Our great concern is to avoid getting into a position at Geneva where we should be forced to disassociate ourselves publicly and on the basis of principle from a settlement which the French feel they had to take. This would, I feel, do much more lasting harm to Western relations than if we did not appear at a high level at Geneva.

I am glad to see that you have resumed talks with the Egyptians. It would indeed be happy if this friction could be settled and your forces in the Suez made available as a more flexible reserve.

I feel confident that in these and other ways the value of our visit together will progressively manifest itself. The memories of it remain fresh and pleasant in my mind.

With warm personal regard,

As ever, Ike

EISENHOWER TO CHURCHILL

July 22, 1954

Dear Winston,

I have been thinking over some of the conversations we had during your recent visit, particularly those dealing with our joint pronounce-ment on the principles and purposes which will guide our interna-tional behavior. I have in mind also your confidential statement that within a reasonable time you want to shift the responsibility of the Premiership to other shoulders—one reason being that you wish to give to your successor a chance to establish himself politically before the next elections.[1]

Considering these two matters together, I am certain that you must have a very deep and understandable desire to do something special and additional in your remaining period of active service that will be forever recognized as a milestone in the world's tortuous progress towards a just and lasting peace. Nothing else could provide such a fitting climax to your long and brilliant service to your sovereign, your country and the world.

I am sure that some such thought of your conscious or subconscious mind must be responsible for your desire to meet Malenkov and to explore, so far as is possible, the purposes of his heart and the designs of his brain.

As you know, while I have not been able to bring myself to believe wholeheartedly in the venture, I most earnestly pray that you may develop something good out of what seems to me the bleakest of prospects. This I say not primarily because of my deep affection and respect for an old and valued friend and the satisfaction I would take in such a personal triumph of yours, but because the world so desperately needs to be strengthened in hope and faith and confidence that anyone who would not pray for the success of your venture would indeed be wicked.

Having said this, I must also say that because of my utter lack of confidence in the reliability and integrity of the men in the Kremlin and my feelings that you may be disappointed in your present hopes, my mind has been turning toward an exploration of other possibilities by which you could still give to the world something inspiring before you lay down your official responsibilities. It should be something that would so well serve the cause in which we believe that it would indeed be considered one of your finest contributions.

Another factor to be considered is that in far too many areas the Kremlin is pre-empting the right to speak for the small nations of the world. We are falsely pictured as the exploiters of people, the Soviets as their champion.

I suggest to you a thoughtful speech on the subject of the rights to self-government, so vigorously supported in our recent joint communique.[2]

At first glance, this seems a thorny nettle to grasp. But I believe that by looking closely we can find that this is not necessarily so.

In our conversations, we agreed that in a number of areas people are not yet ready for self-rule and that any attempt to make them now responsible for their own governing would be to condemn them to lowered standards of life and probably to communistic domination. At the same time, we must never allow the world to believe that we are ready to abandon our stated purposes merely because of this obvious, negative, truth.

Colonialism is on the way out as a relationship among peoples. The sole question is one of time and method. I think we should handle it so as to win adherents to Western aims.

We know that there is abroad in the world a fierce and growing spirit of nationalism. Should we try to dam it up completely, it would, like a mighty river, burst through the barriers and could create havoc. But again, like a river, if we are intelligent enough to make constructive use of this force, then the result, far from being disastrous, could redound greatly to our advantage, particularly in our struggle against the Kremlin's power.

To make use of the spirit of nationalism, we must show for it a genuine sympathy; we must prove that the obstacles that now prevent self-government in certain regions genuinely concern the free world and engage our earnest purpose to work for their elimination. This you and I stated in our joint communique. But to make it a real and vital thing in the lives of so many peoples throughout the world, we ought, I think, to make the whole matter a subject of more detailed explanation both as to objective and as to methods for attaining them.

A speech on the matter—and no other could so well do it as you—should deal with the need for education and announce the cooperative purpose of great nations in the Western World to bring educational opportunities to all peoples we are able to reach.

The talk would not, of course, ignore the economic requirements of independent existence and would certainly dwell at length upon the advantages of voluntary agreements and associations in order to promote the freest and most fruitful kind of commerce. There would have to be discussed the burdensome responsibilities of self-rule; internal and external security; proper systems for the administration of justice, the promotion of health and the general welfare.

Finally, it seems to me that such a talk should announce a specific hope of aim in terms of the time limit for the attainment of announced objectives. Possibly it might be said that our nations plan to undertake every kind of applicable program to insure that within a space of twenty-five years (or by some other agreed upon, definite, date), all peoples will have achieved the necessary political, cultural and economic standards to permit the attainment of their goals.

If you could say that twenty-five years from now, every last one of the colonies (excepting military bases) should have been offered a right to self-government and determination, you would electrify the world. More than this, you could be certain that not a single one of them would, when the time came, take advantage of the offer of independence. Each would cling more tightly to the mother country and be a more valuable part thereof.

Equally important with this particular announcement would be the outline of the program jointly to undertake to help these nations achieve this level of progress.

The kind of talk that I am thinking of would seek to put this whole matter in such a light as to gain us friends—to be positive rather than negative. The attitude should be that we recognize great difficulties, some of which will take time to overcome, but that we know the job can be done.

Of course, in developing such a subject, one would want to contrast, if only by passing reference, this great purpose and development with the practice of the communists in Eastern Europe and wherever their evil power reaches. A good bit of cold war campaigning could be carried on in such a talk without ever making that particular objective an obvious one. For the same reason, reference could be made again to the plan for making nuclear science serve the peaceful interests of all nations, particularly in those areas where people are starved for adequate power.

I long to find a theme which is dynamic and gripping, and which our two countries can espouse together. In this way, we can exercise the world leadership to which the communists aspire. Also by working together for concrete constructive goals, we can cement our relationship in a way which is only possible if there is fellowship in deeds. We found that fellowship in war, and we must equally try to find it in peace.

The theme I outline seems to me to be the one which best fills the need. It is, however, not a theme which the United States can develop alone without seeming to put the United States into opposition to Britain, which is the very result we do not want. Therefore, I bespeak your cooperation and indeed your initiative in opening what could be a great new chapter in history.

It seems to me that to say anything more in this letter would merely be repetitive or redundant. I am sending this through the mails rather than by cable because I want no other to see it except you and me.

> With warm personal regard,
> Ike

1. A British general election was due before October 1956. It was in fact held in May 1955. Churchill told Eisenhower in Washington in June 1954 that he planned to retire in the near future.

2. Communiqué at the end of Churchill's visit to Washington, D.C., June 29, 1954.

EISENHOWER TO CHURCHILL

July 23, 1954

Dear Winston,

By this mail I am sending you a very long letter which I hope you will read when you have a bit of leisure time. I assure you that in writing it I am thinking only of our joint hope of welding among the nations of the free world bonds that will grow ever stronger and more durable.

With affectionate regard,

As ever,
Ike

CHURCHILL TO EISENHOWER

August 8, 1954

Am sending you by bag today answer to your very kind letter of the 22nd.

CHURCHILL TO EISENHOWER

August 8, 1954

My dear friend,

I have been pondering over your very kind letter of July 22nd and I am most grateful to you for this further proof of our friendship. One has to do one's duty as one sees it from day to day and, as you know, the mortal peril which overhangs the human race is never absent from my thoughts. I am not looking about for the means of making a dramatic exit or of finding a suitable Curtain. It is better to take things as they come. I am however convinced that the present method of establishing the relations between the two sides of the world by means of endless discussions between Foreign Offices, will not produce any decisive result. The more the topics of discussion are widened, the more Powers concerned, and the greater the number of officials and authorities of all kinds involved, the less may well be the chance of giving effective results in time or even of using time to the best advantage.

I have, as you know, since Stalin's death hoped that there could be a talk between you and me on the one hand, and the new Leaders of Russia, or as they might be, the Leaders of a new Russia, on the other. It will seem astonishing to future generations—such as they may be— that with all that is at stake no attempt was made by personal parley between the Heads of Government to create a union of consenting minds on broad and simple issues. This should surely be the foundation on which the vast elaborate departmental machinery should come into action, instead of the other way around.

Fancy that you and Malenkov should never have met, or that he should never have been outside Russia, when all the time in both countries appalling preparations are being made for measureless mutual destruction. Even when the power of Britain is so much less than that of the United States, I feel, old age notwithstanding, a responsibility and resolve to use any remaining influence I may have to seek, if not for a solution at any rate for an easement. Even if nothing solid or decisive was gained no harm need be done. Even if realities presented themselves more plainly, that might bring about a renewed effort for peace. After all, the interest of both sides is Survival and, as an additional attraction, measureless material prosperity of the masses. "No", it is said, "The Heads of Governments must not ever meet. Human affairs are too great for human beings. Only the Departments of State can cope with them, and meanwhile let us drift and have some more experiments and see how things feel in a year or two when they are so much nearer to us in annihilating power."

Now, I believe, is the moment for parley at the summit. All the world desires it. In two or three years a different mood may rule either with those who have their hands upon the levers or upon the multitude whose votes they require.

Forgive me bothering you like this, but I am trying to explain to you my resolve to do my best to take any small practical step in my power to bring about a sensible and serious contact.

I read with great interest all that you have written me about what is called Colonialism, namely: bringing forward backward races and opening up the jungles. I was brought up to feel proud of much that we had done. Certainly in India, with all its history, religion and ancient forms of despotic rule, Britain has a story to tell which will look quite well against the background of the coming hundred years.

As a matter of fact the sentiments and ideas which your letter expresses are in full accord with the policy now being pursued in all the Colonies of the British Empire. In this I must admit I am a laggard. I am a bit sceptical about universal suffrage for the Hottentots even if refined by proportional representation. The British and American Democracies were slowly and painfully forged and even they are not perfect yet. I shall certainly have to choose another topic for my swan song: I think I will stick to the old one "The Unity of the English-speaking peoples." With that all will work out well.

Enclosed with this private letter I send you the telegrams I have interchanged with Molotov since I sent you my last on the subject. I told the Bedell to tell you that I was "an obstinate pig." Alas, the best I can do.

Please believe me always your sincere friend,

Winston S. Churchill

EISENHOWER TO CHURCHILL

August 12, 1954

Dear Winston,

My grateful thanks for your very interesting letter. I assure you I shall keep reading it until I have absorbed it thoroughly. As ever,

Ike

EISENHOWER TO CHURCHILL

August 20, 1954

Dear Winston,

I have carefully studied your recent letter and I think I fully understand your views and position.

Right now I am wondering how you will handle the Cypress situation.[1] This, of course, is strictly one of your family problems and I am not mentioning it with any thought that my own opinions should have a bearing on such a matter. My indirect concern, though, arises out of resultant effects upon American opinion. You and I have devoted a lot of time and thought to keeping relationships between our two peoples both durable and cordial, and I am anxious to be in a position to be as helpful as possible when there appears to be any chance of damage to those relationships.

If you should like to give me a little briefing on the matter, I might be in a position to do something. Incidentally, some of our people who have been travelling recently in Greece have come back and spread stories to the effect that Greece and Cypress are quite ready to be reasonable and conciliatory—of course I do not know how accurate are their observations and their reporting. But this kind of thing does serve to give you some idea of why I am interested in the other side of the story.

[. . .][2]

I am hopeful either tomorrow or the next day that I can move the Summer White House to Denver.[3] The season has been a wearing one and I am quite tired. Nevertheless, if you want to communicate with me, your letters or cablegrams will come through in their accustomed secrecy. I shall not be separated from adequate communications.

With warm regard,

As ever,
Ike

1. A curious spelling of Cyprus. Cyprus was a British colony since 1878. The majority of its population were ethnic Greeks, the minority ethnic Turks. Britain faced varying demands from Cypriots and from the Greek government for independence for Cyprus or for the union of Cyprus with Greece.

2. Two paragraphs classified.

3. Eisenhower established a summer White House at the U.S. Air Force base at Lowry Field near Denver, convenient for golfing and for fishing in the Rockies.

West German Entry into NATO

The rejection of the EDC treaty by the French National Assembly in August 1954 created a major crisis in the Western alliance, which was, however, swiftly and satisfactorily resolved, largely as a result of energetic and imaginative diplomacy on the part of Anthony Eden. Eden sought West German rearmament and West German sovereignty, but with some limits on West German military independence. He felt that this could be achieved by West German adherence to the Brussels Pact, which had been signed by Britain, France, Holland, Belgium, and Luxembourg in 1948 and which would be renamed the Western European Union, and by subsequent West German entry into NATO. In order to gain French acceptance of West German sovereignty and rearmament without complex safeguards which would alienate Adenauer and exasperate the Americans, Eden offered to maintain indefinitely the current level of British forces in Europe, namely, four divisions. Adenauer agreed to some voluntary limits on the manufacture by West Germany of certain arms, including atomic, bacteriological, and chemical weapons.

Eden discussed matters on a tour of European capitals, September 11–17, 1954, and he arranged a conference in London, which opened on September 28, 1954. Agreement in principle was quickly reached and after final details were arranged the agreements were signed in Paris in October. Ratification procedures followed, including ratification in France in March 1955, and West Germany entered NATO in May 1955.

CHURCHILL TO EISENHOWER

September 3, 1954

I should like you to see the following message I sent to Dr. Adenauer which I believe had a fairly good reception. I will write again soon in answer to your letter of August 20. Kindest regards. Message begins.

It seems to me that at this critical juncture a great opportunity has come to Germany to take her position among the leaders of free Europe. By a voluntary act of self-abnegation she could make it clear that in any new arrangement as a substitute for E.D.C. she would not ask for a level of military strength beyond that proposed in the E.D.C. plan or to be agreed with her partners in western defence. This would invest the new Germany with a moral dignity and respect far more worth having than merely claiming the right to create as many divisions as she chose or as anybody else and plunging into an endless legalistic argument on the subject. This might well be expressed in terms in no way derogating from the equal and honourable status of the German Federal Republic and would indeed open a new chapter by the very fact that the decision was taken on the initiative of Germany herself. I beg you to think this over as coming from one who after so many years of strife has few stronger wishes than to see the German nation take her true place in the world-wide family of free nations.

Winston S. Churchill

EISENHOWER TO CHURCHILL

September 5, 1954

I think your message to Dr. Adenauer is perfect. I hope he responds favourably.

With warm regards,

Ike

CHURCHILL TO EISENHOWER

September 5, 1954

I have now received the following answer to the message which I sent to Dr. Adenauer.

Message begins. Dear Sir Winston. I thank you for the personal message which you have sent me at this critical juncture. The thoughts and sentiments which you express in it have greatly moved me.

I can assure you that nothing is further from my mind than to waste time, which is becoming even more precious, in theoretical disputes, or to slip into extreme courses, now that difficulties have arisen in the way of the well-considered solution envisaged by the E.D.C. treaty as regards the strength of the German defence contribution. The idea of a link with the allocation of forces in the E.D.C. plan had already occurred to me as well. But above all I share your view that the solution must consist in a voluntary act of self-limitation, if it is to give Germany moral dignity and respect. I therefore note with gratitude that you too consider that the solution should have a form which in no way prejudices the equal and honourable status of the German Federal Republic.

With great admiration for the historic task which you are accomplishing for Europe and the peace of the world. I am yours very sincerely, Adenauer. Message ends.

CHURCHILL TO EISENHOWER

September 9, 1954

My dear Friend,

Thank you so much for your message of September 6. Adenauer's response was good and I think his attitude is easier.

We are all agreed that an 8-power meeting of allies, plus Canada, would be the right move now and prefer it to the 16 NATO powers proposal, which might well follow it, and we should like very much to have it in London which is a big and well known place and has stood by the Thames for quite a long time without having a conference of this kind. Anthony, who knows all the continental personalities involved from long experience, feels that he could smooth out difficulties, queries and objections, of which there are no lack, better by personal contacts than by the interminable interchange of coded messages and arguments. He is, therefore, at the desire of the Cabinet, proposing to start on a flying circuit of Brussels, Bonn, Rome and Paris to see what he can do. We shall keep you and Foster fully and punctually informed.

If he succeeds, it seems to me not improbable that we might reach a considerable measure of agreement and that the NATO meeting would follow as the second stage.

Of course it is always my hope that the prospects of an improvement in our affairs, arising out of a London conference, might be so good, or the results in sight become so good, that you might be able to come yourself, at least for the finale, and make that State visit I mentioned to you at the White House. But that of course is not a matter which requires decision now.

I have read what has been disclosed to our people in Washington about the Pentagon's views on re-appraisal.[1] This, I am sure, would mean disaster if it actually came to pass. I hope, nonetheless, that if such ideas are shaping themselves in Washington, you will let the French know about them at an early stage. It might help them to do their duty.

Kindest regards,
Winston

1. The U.S. Joint Chiefs of Staff put forward various contingency plans on strategic regrouping, such as German rearmament outside of NATO, in the event of a continuing French veto on any form of German rearmament.

CHURCHILL TO EISENHOWER

September 12, 1954

My dear Friend,

I promised to keep you fully informed of Anthony's tour.

He had a successful talk yesterday with Benelux Ministers whom he found robust and realistic.

They are disturbed at the growth of nationalism in Germany and fear that the dangers which confront us all are not apprehended by Mendes-France or the French Chamber.

They are agreed on German entry into NATO with such safeguards as we can extract in the present German atmosphere. They are also attracted by the suggestion which Anthony laid before them of modifying the Brussels Treaty so as to admit Germany and Italy. We want of course to keep this idea secret until we can put it to the French.

As to procedure they consider that whilst the NATO Council must be brought in, a preliminary 9 power meeting should be held. They hoped this would take place in London as soon as possible after Anthony's tour, and be followed by a NATO meeting.

Finally they consider that we must proceed rapidly on the lines on which we are all agreed and do what we can to convince the French. But we must be ready to go ahead without France in the last resort (policy of the empty chair presumably) making clear our intentions in Paris in good time.

Kind regards,
Winston

CHURCHILL TO EISENHOWER

September 14, 1954

My dear Friend,

You will have seen the messages which Anthony sent Foster last night on his talks in Bonn. Anthony found Adenauer in fairly good health and as quick as ever, though aged since their last meeting. Adenauer much liked the Brussels Treaty idea which he described as a most happy thought and psychologically valuable as providing a focus for European policies and keeping alive German youth's faith in the European idea. It was also important he thought to devise means of saving Mendes-France's plight.

We must now see how the talks in Paris go, but on present form it looks as if there will be plenty to discuss with Foster if, as we hope, he can pay us a visit.

Kind regards,
Winston

EISENHOWER TO CHURCHILL

September 15, 1954

Dear Winston,

Your report on the progress of Anthony's tour is very helpful to us. It is encouraging to know that the Benelux people are thinking along constructive and realistic lines. We will look forward to the more detailed account of your proposals which Anthony has promised to send Foster at the end of his tour.

In the meantime, we are trying to pull together some useful ideas to contribute with respect to both the plan for German membership in NATO and a course of action in the unhappy event that the French refuse to go along. I feel that you and we should agree on this latter point as soon as possible since I am not certain that anything less drastic will bring the French to their senses.

With kindest regards, D.D.E.

CHURCHILL TO EISENHOWER

September 15, 1954

My dear Friend,

Anthony's talks in Rome went well. The Italians accepted unreservedly as a basis for discussion the ideas which had emerged from the talks in Brussels and Bonn. Piccioni[1] said that the consolidation of Europe with the association of the United Kingdom would weaken neutralist tendencies in Italy.

Anthony emphasised the part which the Italians could play in influencing the French. Piccioni said he could not guess the French reaction and expressed concern at what would happen in the event of French rejection. He enquired whether we would then be prepared to go ahead. Anthony replied that the mood of the Benelux Governments was to go ahead and leave the French to come along later, and this seemed also to be Adenauer's thought. He explained that the British Government had not yet taken a decision, but he certainly intended to make it clear in Paris that the French could not be allowed to frustrate our plans indefinitely. He added that it was unfortunate that the issues had never been explained to the French people by their public men and that the French had probably convinced themselves that American talk of reappraisal was bluff.

Piccioni agreed that the French could not be allowed to impede indefinitely and said he would try to influence the French in the right direction.

Kind regards,
Winston

1. Attilio Piccioni, Italian minister of foreign affairs.

CHURCHILL TO EISENHOWER

September 18, 1954

My dear Friend,

Thank you very much for your message of September 15. I am glad I was a good reporter. I made my living as a journalist.[1] I believe you have them in your country too.

Foster lunched with me and Anthony today and we had an agreeable and helpful talk. As you know, EDC was very different from the grand alliance theme I opened at Strasbourg in August, 1950.[2] I disliked on military grounds the Pleven European army plan which began with mixing races in companies if not platoons. At that time when I saw you in Paris[3] I was talking of it as "sludgy amalgam." However, when I came to power again I swallowed my prejudices because I was led to believe that it was the only way in which the French could be persuaded to accept the limited German army which was my desire. I do not blame the French for rejecting EDC but only for inventing it. Their harshness to Adenauer in wasting three years of his life and much of his power is a tragedy. Also I accepted the American wish to show all possible patience and not to compromise the chances of EDC by running NATO as a confusing rival.

All this time I kept one aim above all others in view, namely a German contribution to the defense of an already uniting Europe. This, I felt, was your aim too, and I am sure we both liked the plan better when the intermingling was excluded from all units lower than a division. But it was to get a German army looking eastward in the line with us that commanded my thought, and also I felt yours, with all its military authority. Although the French have rejected EDC I do hope and pray that you and I will still keep the German contribution as our No. 1 target and also to get them on our side instead of on the other.

When Anthony recently proposed taking the Brussels Treaty of 1948 turned upside down, as a model for preserving the cause of European unity, coupled with a variant of NATO to include Germany, I thought it was a first rate plan. I hope earnestly that it will commend itself to you. It may lead on as time passes to United Europe and also gain for us both what we have tried for so hard, namely, the German comradeship. Now Foster tells me that there is a widespread feeling in America that it has not got any, or at least enough, "supra-national" characteristics. I hope this will not prevent you giving it all the help you can. European federation may grow but it cannot be built. It must be a volunteer not a conscript.

After all if the realities can be achieved and if Gruenther[4] can form a front including French and German armies by whose side we and you stand, we need not worry too much about the particular theories which are favoured or rebuffed. Above all, we should not lose more time when what we have worked so long and hard to win may now be within our grasp.

I have been distressed to hear talk (not from Foster) about the withdrawal of American forces from Europe and even that a German contingent might fill the gap. If the U.S. loses, or seems to lose its interest in Europe there might well be a landslide into Communism or into a kow-towing to Soviet influence and infiltration which would reduce the continent to satellite status. I really do not see how we British could stay there by ourselves.

Forgive me burdening you with all this, but I feel it a great comfort when I am sure our thoughts are marching along the same roads. You may imagine how pleased I was by your applying the word "perfect" to my message to Adenauer.

Kindest regards,
Winston

1. Throughout most of his life Churchill wrote newspaper articles, which, along with his books, were the main source of his wealth.

2. August 11, 1950, Churchill made a speech at the Consultative Assembly of the Council of Europe in Strasbourg on cooperation on defense matters between the United States, Britain, and the continental European nations including West Germany.

3. In December 1951 Churchill met Eisenhower in Paris, when Eisenhower was SACEUR.

4. General Alfred Gruenther, SACEUR, 1953–56.

CHURCHILL TO EISENHOWER

September 18, 1954

My dear Friend,

I did not complicate my long telegram to you about Europe by referring to the isolated question of Cyprus about which you wrote to me on August 20.

A factual note is being prepared which I will send by airmail, but I understand our Embassy in Washington has already supplied the State Department with information. A simple test is to compare the conditions prevailing in Cyprus with those in the Greek Islands and particularly in Rhodes since the Greeks took them over from the Italians.[1] Cyprus has never known more rapid progress while in the others there is a grievous decline.

I feel it is my duty to tell you that the failure of the United States to support us at U.N.O. would cause deep distress over here and add greatly to my difficulties in guiding public opinion into the right channels in much larger matters.[2]

It cannot be disputed that our claim against the inscription of this question affecting our own external affairs is justified by the statutes and spirit of U.N.O. If any such item were discussed by the Assembly, we would of course walk out. Injury would be done to that institution of which the United States and Britain and her Commonwealth are the main pillars. Cyprus would acquire utterly disproportionate publicity and be magnified by the enemies of the English Speaking world on both sides of the ocean into a marked difference between us. I do trust therefore that we shall not be confronted with American abstention.

Kindest regards, as ever,
Winston

1. Greece regained Rhodes and other Aegean islands from Italy after World War II.
2. Britain opposed discussion by the United Nations General Assembly of an internal colonial matter. The United States equivocated, considered abstention, but ultimately supported Britain.

EISENHOWER TO CHURCHILL

September 30, 1954

Dear Winston,

Foster has kept me informed on the progress of the talks now going forward in the Nine Power Conference. Both officially and personally I am most deeply appreciative of the contribution that Britain has offered to make to advance European unity.

Of course I understand fully your reluctance to move without parallel commitment by us. However, our constitutional processes do not permit this, but I am certain that so long as Europe is moving towards unified action, you can always be sure of our effective cooperation on the continent. In this statement I know I speak for the tremendous majority of the citizens of our country.

In this often confused world, it is encouraging to witness the enlightened and courageous statesmanship exhibited by you and Anthony. In this instance, as in so many others, I have the greatest admiration for your judgments and actions.

Please give my warm regard to Anthony, and, as always the best to yourself.

As ever,
Ike

EISENHOWER TO CHURCHILL

November 28, 1954

Dear Winston,

I know I speak for my fellow countrymen, as I enthusiastically do for myself, in sending you warmest congratulations on reaching a new landmark in a life that is in itself a series of landmarks.[1]

We Americans have known you and of you over the years—as roving war reporter, as adventurous soldier, as administrator and parliamentarian and, increasingly with each passing year, as statesman and defender of freedom.

We have seen the great Anglo-American partnership grow and flourish, with you as one of the staunch advocates. In the dark times of war, and the anxious ones of uncertain peace, this partnership has sustained us all and given us strength.

Now, as you reach four score, we Americans salute you as world statesman, an unconquerable warrior in the cause of freedom, as our proven friend of many valiant years.

With warm personal regard,

As ever,
Dwight D. Eisenhower

1. On November 30, 1954, Churchill became eighty years old.

CHURCHILL TO EISENHOWER

November 29, 1954

Thank you so much for your letter which I greatly value. I am writing.

W.

EISENHOWER TO CHURCHILL

November 29, 1954

Dear Winston,

You will be deluged, I know, with messages of felicitation on your eightieth birthday from all over the world. I have myself sent one through our State Department. But I want to add to that deeply felt but somewhat official note, a sense of my appreciation of the privilege that has been mine to call you friend—in the truest meaning of the word—for these many years. Mamie and I join in warmest affection and admiration for you.

Ike E.

CHURCHILL TO EISENHOWER

December 1, 1954

My dear Ike,
I am most grateful for your personal message. I am writing when I can get my head above water.

W.

CHURCHILL TO EISENHOWER

December 7, 1954

My dear Friend,
I am so sorry that the pressure upon me of events both large and small has been so unceasing that I have not replied other than by telegrams to your last three most kind letters, including the two about my birthday. I am so grateful to you for all that you wrote. Our comradeship and friendship were forged under hard conditions, and stood the test of war and aftermath. They always remain for me a possession of inestimable value. Thank you so much.

About the present and future. I think our two countries are working together even more closely than I can ever remember. They certainly need to do so. I greatly admired your speech on Thursday last about China in the teeth of the brutal maltreatment of your airmen.[1] In my view China is not important enough to be a cause of major hazards. Many people over here exaggerate the power and importance of China as a military factor, and talk about six hundred million Chinese who, as we are told, have all become Communists.

I am old-fashioned enough to look to Steel as a rather decisive index of conventional military power, and of manufacturing and communication capacity. Crude steel output in 1953 of the non-Soviet world was 182.2 million tons, and that of the total Soviet bloc was 51.5 million tons. Of this China contributed 1.7 million tons. I have had a number of other principal metals examined from this viewpoint and enclose a list, (A).[2]

These figures seem to me to deserve taking into account when thinking about the power to conduct modern war of the six hundred million Chinese now said to exist. It may be a different picture in a decade. When I was young I used to hear much talk about "the Yellow Peril."

I am thinking of course only on a "conventional" basis. But you have no reason to be worried about the nuclear balance. It is Soviet Russia that ought to dominate our minds. That is one of the reasons for my pleasure at your speech and the profound sense of proportion which it revealed.

I still hope we may reach a top level meeting with the new regime in Russia and that you and I may both be present. We can only contemplate this on the basis of the London Agreement and a united NATO. In spite of the tyrannical weakness of the French Chamber I still hope for ratification of all Powers in the first few months of the New Year. It is in the hope of helping forward such a meeting that I am remaining in harness longer than I wished or planned. I hope you will continue to look to it as a goal in seeking which we could not lose anything and might gain an easier and safer co-existence—which is a lot. When I had my last Audience with The Queen she spoke of the pleasure with which she would welcome a State visit by you to London. This might be combined in any way convenient with a top level meeting. Anyhow please keep it high in your mind among your many cares and hopes.

With kindest regards to you and Mrs. Eisenhower,

Believe me,
Yours sincerely, Winston

1. At a press conference on December 2, 1954, Eisenhower condemned China's decision to continue to imprison as spies thirteen American airmen captured in the Korean War rather than to release them as prisoners of war, but Eisenhower warned against allowing the issue to be a provocation of hostilities against China.

2. List of figures on Chinese metal production, PREM 11 1074, PRO.

EISENHOWER TO CHURCHILL

December 14, 1954

Dear Winston,

You have given a flawless exposition of Red China's relative weakness if we have under consideration only the possibility that she might launch aggressive war against either of our two countries. However, it is clear that our vital interests can be seriously damaged by operations that she is capable of carrying out against weaker areas lying along the boundaries of her territory. We saw what she tried to do in Korea and was foiled only by the intervention of strong allied forces, and we likewise saw what gains she made in the Indo-China region due to the political and military weakness of one of our allies. She can pay any price in manpower, with complete indifference to the amount. Consequently, she is a distinct threat to the peace of the world as long as she may be sufficiently irresponsible to launch an attack against peoples and areas of tremendous importance to us. This imposes on us the burden of supporting native forces in the region and of supplementing these with some of our own units.

Here I shall not outline the importance to the Western world of Japan and the island chain extending on to the southward, as well as the bits of mainland on the Pacific that still remain in the possession of the free world. The moral, political and military consequences that could follow upon the loss of important parts of this great chain are obvious to both of us and to the staffs that work for us in the military, economic and diplomatic fields. So I think it dangerous to dismiss too complacently the risks that the bad faith, bad deportment and greed of Red China pose to our world. Some of our citizens are particularly sensitive to this threat and openly argue that it would be a mistake to allow this threat to endure and extend until the day comes when Red China may actually achieve the capacity to endanger us directly. I know that neither of us is blind to this possibility, even though we consider that such a development is somewhat doubtful and in any event its attainment would involve such a long time that world conditions and balances of power could well have been radically changed in the meantime. But, of course, I agree with you that our attention and watchfulness should be directed mainly to Moscow.

Incidentally, I was interested in your renewed suggestion of a top-level meeting with the regime in Russia. I have always felt, as you know, that it would be a mistake for you and me to participate in a meeting which was either essentially social or exploratory. A social meeting would merely give a false impression of accord which, in our free countries, would probably make it more difficult to get parliamentary support for needed defense appropriations. Within the captive world it would give the impression that we condone the present state of affairs. And if these are to be exploratory talks, should they not be carried out by our Foreign Ministers, so that Heads of Government would come in only if some really worthwhile agreement is in likely prospect?

The latter, I fear, is not an early possibility. There are still several months to go before we shall know where we are on the London and Paris Accords and all the indications are that if they go through, the Russians will probably "play tough", at least for some little time. Therefore, I do not see the likelihood of our Foreign Ministers usefully meeting for some considerable period. So, I am bound to say that, while I would like to be more optimistic, I cannot see that a top-level meeting is anything which I can inscribe on my schedule for any predictable date. I regret this the more because if a top-level meeting were to take place and if it led to a personal visit to London, I would indeed be very happy.

I hope you will find some way of letting the Queen know how deeply I appreciate her gracious reference to the possibility of such a visit.

Foster and I have just had luncheon together and now he starts immediately for the NATO meeting. We discussed a number of matters including a series of urgent requests that in our view practically amount to demands received from Mendes-France. He wants us to make public pronouncements supporting his statements affecting the Saar,[1] Morocco[2] and commitments of American troops to Europe. Important as French cooperation is to the great NATO Plan, Mendes-France seems to forget that the safety, security and welfare of France are far more directly and intimately involved in the projects now under discussion than is the future of this country or of yours. One of the virtues of EDC was that it contained an acceptable solution of the Saar problem and it was French desertion of that plan that insured its defeat.

I see no good reason for this government to re-state its intentions about the stationing of American troops in Europe or take a position as to the Saar arrangement at least until the French Parliament has by some positive action shown itself capable of making decisions in keeping with the responsibilities of a great European power. I have asked Foster to confer with Anthony on these matters. Likewise, I have asked him to avoid any rigid position of refusal in considering the seemingly unreasonable requests of Mendes-France, but I am determined that we shall begin to realize some dividends on the constant pledges and pronouncements that seem to be expected of us.

I like your phrase "tyrannical weakness." It sharply defines the situation.

As you know, I occasionally flatter myself by attempting to paint likenesses of friends. I would be tremendously intrigued by the effort to paint one of you. Would it be an intolerable burden on you to allow an artist friend of mine to visit you long enough to take a few photographs and draw a few hasty color sketches that I could use in such an attempt?

The final result would, of course, not be good, but also it might not be so bad as to be unendurable. If you feel this would not make an unjustified demand upon your time, I could send my artist friend over soon after the first of the year. I should think that something about thirty minutes to an hour would be sufficient for what I would need from him.

This is just an idea and I shall not be at all offended by your inability to entertain it.

With warm personal regard,

As ever,
Ike

1. The Saar, on the border of France and Germany, was rich in coal. Its mines were operated by France after 1919 as part of reparations until in a referendum in 1935 the Saar reverted to Germany. In 1946 France made the Saar a separate entity in economic union with France. The issue was a bitter irritant in Franco-German relations, and an agreement was drawn up to be ratified along with the EDC treaty. After rejection of EDC a new agreement was drawn up by which, following a referendum in 1955, Saarland became a land in the Federal Republic of West Germany.

2. The French government was attempting to hold at bay the pressure for independence in French Morocco.

EISENHOWER TO CHURCHILL

December 27, 1954

Dear Winston,

You may be sure that we feel as you do.

Both Foster and I have made clear how seriously we view the situation.[1] If we have done so in different words it may be even more effective.

Christmas greetings.

As ever,
Ike

1. On December 24, Eisenhower was sent the text of a Foreign Office statement expressing the British government's deep concern over French delay in ratifying the Paris and London agreements of October 1954.

FIVE

Quemoy and the Matsus
January 11–April 7, 1955

In his last months in office, Churchill was under pressure to retire, which, to Eden's exasperation, he continued to delay. Having celebrated his eightieth birthday in November 1954, Churchill realized that his time in office was at last drawing to a close. Hence, issues were covered in the Churchill-Eisenhower correspondence in these months on which Churchill felt deeply, such as atomic weapons, German rearmament, and a summit meeting with the Soviets. The most immediate issue, however, was the perilous crisis over Quemoy and the Matsus, the Nationalist Chinese islands close to the Communist Chinese mainland which the Communists began to shell. Because Churchill and Eisenhower were very far apart on the issue, the correspondence in its final part dealt not with an issue likely to create Anglo-American accord, such as a European matter, but with an issue in the Far East on which Britain and the United States were in profound disagreement.

CHURCHILL TO EISENHOWER

January 11, 1955

Should be delighted to see your artist friend and am much honoured at the prospect. Am writing at length about other matters. Kindest regards,

W.

CHURCHILL TO EISENHOWER

January 12, 1955

My dear Friend,

I waited to answer your letter of December 15[1] until the vote had been taken in the French Chamber[2] and after that our Governments were in such complete accord that I let the day slip by. There are still opportunities open to the French obstructors for making serious delays. Anthony and I are in full agreement with you that there can be no Four Power Conference of any kind until ratification is complete, and we feel of course that everything reasonable in our power should be done to press for a definite decision. I suppose they could, if they chose, spread the whole process out for four or five months. I am sure you will agree that this would be a most improvident way of wasting the ever-shortening interval of time before the Soviets have developed their nuclear strength, including delivery, though not to anything approaching equality with you, to what is called "saturation point," namely the power to inflict mortal injury upon the civilized structure of the free world.

Britain will, of course, be stronger in two or three years in nuclear weapons. I visited some of our secret establishments last week, and was struck by their progress and prospects, both in the atomic and in the hydrogen sphere ("sphere" is apposite in more senses than one). We are making atomic bombs on a steadily increasing scale, and we and our experts are confident that we have the secret, perhaps even with some improvements, of the hydrogen bomb. I am very glad that the difficulties about the "fittings" which you promised me at Bermuda have been solved, and that your officers have been over here talking to ours.[3] Thank you very much.

Looking back and knowing your views throughout the story, I cannot but regret that you had not the power at the time the McMahon Act was under discussion. If the agreement signed between me and F.D.R. had not been shelved we should probably already have been able to add a substantial reinforcement to your vast and formidable deterrent power. We have, however, through Attlee's somewhat unconstitutional exertions in making vast sums available for nuclear development without disclosing the fact to Parliament, mastered the problems both of the atomic and hydrogen weapons by our own science independently. The inevitable delay must, however, be regarded as a severe misfortune to our common cause from which your convictions would have saved it.

I enclose a paper which I wrote for my colleagues before the recent NATO Meeting in Paris.[4] This secured a very large measure of agreement between them and in several cases the same opinion had been spontaneously reached. I feel pretty sure that you and I were thinking separately on the same or similar lines—as we have done before.

I cabled you on Monday about your artist friend. I need hardly say I shall be greatly honoured to be one of your subjects in an artistic sense. Although my experiences as a model have not been altogether agreeable lately I submit myself with great confidence to your well-balanced love of truth and mercy.

With every good wish,

Believe me always your sincere friend,
WSC

1. Eisenhower to Churchill, December 14, 1954, received by Churchill on December 15.

2. On December 28, 1954, the French National Assembly voted in favor of ratification of the Paris and London agreements. Formal ratification was also required by the Council of the Republic.

3. In 1954, as part of the increase in atomic information to Britain, the United States provided information on external fittings of atomic bombs.

4. C(54) 390, Cabinet Papers, PRO. The document is classified.

EISENHOWER TO CHURCHILL

January 25, 1955

Permit me to refer to paragraph eight, page two, of your top secret memorandum on tube alloys.[1] Our conclusions here on the particular subject of that paragraph do not fully conform to yours. We believe that consequences would not be so far reaching as you describe.

On the other hand, your paper seems to me to under-emphasize a point of such moment that it constitutes almost a new element in warfare. I refer to the extraordinary increase in the value of tactical or strategic surprise, brought about by the enormous destructive power of the new weapons and the probability that they could be delivered over targets with little or no warning. Surprise has always been one of the most important factors in achieving victory. And now, even as we contemplate the grim picture depicted in your memorandum, we gain only a glimmering of the paralysis that could be inflicted on an unready fighting force, or indeed upon a whole nation, by some sudden foray that would place a dozen or more of these terrible weapons accurately on target.

I personally believe that many of our old conceptions of the time that would be available to governments for making of decisions in the event of attack are no longer tenable. I think it possible that the very life of a nation, perhaps even of Western civilization, could, for example, come to depend on instantaneous reaction to news of an approaching air fleet; victory or defeat could hang upon minutes and

seconds used decisively at top speed or tragically wasted in indecision.

I completely agree with all that you say about deterrents. The principal weakness of this policy is that it offers, of itself, no defense against
the losses that we incur through the enemy's political and military
nibbling. So long as he abstains from doing anything that he believes
would provoke the free world to an open declaration of major war, he
need not fear the "deterrent." Since he knows that we, in our democracies, are honestly devoted to peace and by instinct and training
abhor the thought of mass destruction and attacks that would necessarily involve helpless people, he knows that there is a great area of
fruitful opportunity open to him lying between the excitation of a
global war on the one hand and passive acceptance of the status quo
on the other. At this moment, the Kremlin and Peiping are driving
forward with their plans and purposes in this realm of relative safety.

The theory of the deterrent should, at the very least, logically be
backed up by the most careful studies on our part to decide upon the
conditions under which we would find it necessary to react explo-
sively. A concomitant problem would be how we could inform the
enemy of the first decision so that he would not, through miscalcula-
tion, push us to the point that global war would result. However,
there can be local as well as global deterrents.

I share your feelings of satisfaction in the process of your country
toward nuclear stockpile; I share your regret that through unfortunate
circumstances of the past, that development is not further advanced.

In Europe we must now wait final action in the French and German
Parliaments on our latest plans for military cooperation in that area,
particularly between these two ancient enemies. Nothing must be
done that could give a reason or excuse for delay in this work. Just as
you deplore the delays that were experienced in your country in the
initiation of your atomic project, so I bitterly regret that all of us did
not put our shoulders to the wheel some three years ago when the
prospects for the approval of EDC looked bright. All the free world
could breathe easier today had that venture been a success.

Respecting the Far East—yesterday I sent a message to the Congress
to clarify the intention of this nation in the region of the Formosa
straits. It would be a pity if the Communists misinterpreted our fore-
bearance [*sic*] to mean indecision and precipitated a crisis that could
bring on a nasty situation.

I note that in the memorandum accompanying your letter, your
Government fears that during the next two or three years the United
States may, through impulsiveness or lack of perspective, be drawn
into a Chinese war.

I trust that my message to the Congress reassured you as to our basic attitudes and sober approach to critical problems.

It is probably difficult for you, in your geographical position, to understand how concerned this country is with the solidarity of the Island Barrier in the Western Pacific. Moreover, we are convinced that the psychological effect in the Far East of deserting our friends on Formosa would risk a collapse of Asiatic resistance to the Communists. Such possibilities cannot be lightly dismissed; in our view they are almost as important, in the long term, to you as they are to us.

I am certain there is nothing to be gained in that situation by meekness and weakness. God knows I have been working hard in the exploration of every avenue that seems to lead toward the preservation and strengthening of the peace. But I am positive that the free world is surely building trouble for itself unless it is united in basic purpose, is clear and emphatic in its declared determination to resist all forceful Communist advance, and keeps itself ready to act on a moment's notice, if necessary.

Thank you very much for your nice reply concerning my artist friend. Right now I have put in some odd moments in attempting to copy a photograph I have of a portrait painted of you some years ago. It shows you sitting down, in semi-formal attire, with a cigar in your right hand.[2] But I would far rather work on something that was not a mere slavish copy.

I have earnestly instructed my artist friend to be as sparing of your time as possible. Incidentally he was born, raised and trained in Britain. He has been an American citizen for only three or four years. His name is Thomas E. Stephens. I think it best that he makes contact with you through the American Embassy, and I am asking Winthrop to contact your secretary at the proper time. If present plans go through, Mr. Stephens will be in Britain next week.

With my continuing warm regard, and with my sincere wishes for your health, strength and happiness,

Ike

1. C(54) 390, Cabinet Papers, PRO. Tube alloys was the code name for atomic weapons.

2. This was the basis of the portrait of Churchill painted by Eisenhower in March 1955, which was sent to Walter Reed Army Hospital in August 1957 to be hung in the President's Suite. The original was later given to Mrs. Eisenhower but was replaced by a copy which still hangs in the President's Suite in Walter Reed Army Hospital.

CHURCHILL TO EISENHOWER

February 5, 1955

I had a very agreeable meeting with Stephens and Chambliss to-day.[1] I hope the results will inspire you.

1. The artist and photographer who took photographs of Churchill for a painting by Eisenhower.

EISENHOWER TO CHURCHILL

February 8, 1955

My dear Sir Winston,
My grateful thanks. The inspiration is guaranteed; the big question mark is the result. With warm regard. As ever.

Ike

Quemoy and the Matsus

When Chiang Kai-shek and the Nationalists fled from the Chinese mainland to Formosa in 1949, they retained control over the Pescadores, close to Formosa, nearly a hundred miles from the mainland, and some offshore islands less than ten miles from the mainland, namely, the Tachens, Quemoy (the island of Quemoy and the neighboring Little Quemoy), and the Matsus (a group of nineteen islands often referred to as Matsu, though Churchill and Eisenhower used the plural form).

Britain had had misgivings with regard to American policy toward Formosa since the American commitment to Formosa's defense at the outbreak of the Korean War in June 1950. Britain came to acquiesce in America's policy of the defense of Formosa, which was formalized in the U.S. security treaty with Formosa signed in 1954, but Britain saw no sensible purpose whatever in U.S. support of the Nationalists in the offshore islands, which Britain felt were much too difficult to defend. In September 1954 the Communist Chinese began to shell the offshore islands, and in January 1955 the shelling was stepped up and threats of invasion were made. The Nationalists evacuated the Tachens, but they were determined to hold on to Quemoy and the Matsus. Eisenhower supported the Nationalist stand. On January 24, 1955, Eisenhower sent a message to Congress requesting passage of the Formosa Resolution, which Congress passed on January 29, authorizing the president to take whatever action was necessary to defend Formosa while deliberately leaving ambiguous whether the resolution also covered Quemoy and the Matsus. Churchill vehemently argued that the offshore islands should be evacuated and a defensive line drawn in the Formosa straits to protect Formosa and the Pescadores. In early 1955 the situation reached a critical level, with Eisenhower threatening the use of atomic bombs against China if Quemoy and the Matsus were ever invaded. By May 1955 the crisis passed and the offshore islands remained in Nationalist hands. Eisenhower felt that the resolute stand had been justified, while the British felt that an extremely dangerous risk had been taken for no good purpose.

EISENHOWER TO CHURCHILL

February 10, 1955

Dear Winston,

I have heard how earnestly you supported throughout the Conference of Prime Ministers[1] the proposition that nothing must create a serious rift in British-American relationships. Not only do I applaud that sentiment, but I am most deeply grateful to you for your successful efforts.

I realize that it has been difficult, at times, for you to back us up in the Formosa question and, for this reason, I want to give you a very brief account of our general attitude toward the various factors that have dictated the course we have taken. You understand, of course, that we have certain groups that are violent in their efforts to get us to take a much stronger, even a truculent position. The number that would like to see us clear out of Formosa is negligible. I know that on your side of the water you have the exact opposite of this situation.

Because the Communists know these facts, there is no question in my mind that one of the principal reasons for their constant pressing on the Asian frontier is the hope of dividing our two countries. I am sure that we, on both sides of the water, can make quite clear that, no matter what may be our differences in approach or even sometimes our differences in important convictions, nothing is ever going to separate us or destroy our unity in opposing Communist aggression.

We believe that if international Communism should penetrate the island barrier in the Western Pacific and thus be in a position to threaten the Philippines and Indonesia immediately and directly, all of us, including the free countries of Europe, would soon be in far worse trouble than we are now. Certainly that whole region would soon go.

To defend Formosa the United States has been engaged in a long and costly program of arming and sustaining the Nationalist troops on that island. Those troops, however, and Chiang himself, are not content, now, to accept irrevocably and permanently the status of "prisoners" on the island. They are held together by a conviction that some day they will go back to the mainland.

As a consequence, their attitude toward Quemoy and the Matsus, which they deem the stepping stones between the two hostile regions, is that the surrender of those islands would destroy the reason for the existence of the Nationalist forces on Formosa. This, then, would mean the almost immediate conversion of that asset into a deadly danger, because the Communists would immediately take it over.

The Formosa Resolution, as passed by the Congress, is our publicly stated position; the problem now is how to make it work. The morale of the Chinese Nationalists is important to us, so for the moment, and under existing conditions, we feel they must have certain assurances with respect to the offshore islands. But these must be less binding on us than the terms of the Chino-American Treaty, which was over-whelmingly passed yesterday by the Senate.[2] We must remain ready, until some better solution can be found, to move promptly against any Communist force that is manifestly preparing to attack Formosa. And we must make a distinction—(this is a difficult one)—between an attack that has only as its objective the capture of an off-shore island and one that is primarily a preliminary movement to an all-out attack on Formosa.

Whatever now is to happen, I know that nothing could be worse than global war.

I do not believe that Russia wants war at this time—in fact, I do not believe that even if we became engaged in a serious fight along the coast of China, Russia would want to intervene with her own forces. She would, of course, pour supplies into China in an effort to exhaust us and certainly would exploit the opportunity to separate us from your country. But I am convinced that Russia does not want, at this moment, to experiment with means of defense against the bombing that we could conduct against her mainland. At the same time, I assume that Russia's treaty with Red China comprehends a true military alliance, which she would either have to repudiate or take the plunge. She would probably be in a considerable dilemma if we got into war with China. It would not be an easy decision for the men in the Kremlin, in my opinion. But all this is no excuse for fighting China. We believe our policy is the best that we can design for staying out of such a fight.

In any event, we have got to do what we believe to be right—if we can figure out the right—and we must show no lack of firmness in a world where our political enemies exploit every sign of weakness, and are constantly attempting to disrupt the solidarity of the free world's intentions to oppose their aggressive practices.

Though thus sketchily presented, this has been the background of our thinking leading up to the present day. I devoutly hope that history's inflexible yardstick will show that we have done everything in our power, and everything that is right, to prevent the awful catastrophe of another major war.

I am sending you this note, not merely because of my realization that you, as our great and trusted ally, are entitled to have our thoughts on these vital matters, but because I so value, on the more personal side, the opportunity to learn of your own approach to these critical problems.

Again my thanks to you for giving Thomas Stephens so much of your valuable time, and my apologies that he appeared in London in what was, I know, a most difficult and exhausting week for you.

With warm regard,

Your devoted friend,
Ike

1. Commonwealth Prime Ministers Conference, January 31–February 8, 1955.
2. The U.S. mutual security treaty with Nationalist China, signed in December 1954, was ratified by the U.S. Senate, February 9, 1955.

CHURCHILL TO EISENHOWER

February 15, 1955

My dear Friend,

We have all here been watching with the closest attention your decisions and moves in the Formosan crisis. For the last three weeks I have been wanting to write to you. Your most kind letter of February 10 has reached me and I find that much I had already put on paper still represents my steadily growing theme. Anthony and I, who have composed this message together, wish to do our utmost to sustain you and help you lead world opinion. There is wide recognition of the efforts you have made to keep out of war with China in spite of gross provocation. As you know, I feel strongly that it is a matter of honour for the United States not to allow Chiang Kai-shek and his adherents, with whom the United States have worked as Allies for so many years, to be liquidated and massacred by Communist China, who are alleged to have already executed in cold blood between two and three millions of their opponents in their civil war. Our feeling is that this is the prime and vital point. According to our lights we feel that this could and should be disentangled from holding the offshore islands as bridgeheads for a Nationalist invasion of Communist China. Besides this we do not think that Formosa itself, while protected by the United States, ought to wage sporadic war against the mainland.

So the problem before us at this stage centres on what should be done about the offshore islands, which we here have to admit are legally part of China and which nobody here considers a just cause of war. You know how hard Anthony and I have tried to keep in step with you and how much we wish to continue to do so. But a war to keep the coastal islands for Chiang would not be defensible here.

I had understood that the United States Government had so far been resolved to resist Chiang's pressure to give assurances about these islands, even in return for Chinese Nationalist evacuation of the Tachens, and had succeeded in doing so. I hope your last sentence on page 2 does not conflict with this.

I cannot see any decisive relationship between the offshore islands and an invasion of Formosa. It would surely be quite easy for the United States to drown any Chinese would-be invaders of Formosa whether they started from Quemoy or elsewhere. If ever there was an operation which may be deemed impossible it would be the passage of about a hundred miles of sea in the teeth of overwhelming naval and air superiority and without any tank and other special landing-craft. You and I have already studied and indeed lived through such a problem both ways.

Guessing at the other side's intentions is, as you say, often difficult. In this case of Quemoy, etc., the Communists have an obvious national and military purpose, namely, to get rid of a bridgehead admirably suited to the invasion of the mainland of China. This seems simple.

Diplomatically their motives are more fanciful. It may be, as your third paragraph suggests, that the absurd Chinese boastings about invading Formosa are inspired by the Soviet desire to cause division between the Allies in the far more important issues which confront us in Europe. It costs very little to say, as the Chinese are now reported to be doing, that "the possession of the Tachens will help the liberation of Formosa." It adds to the pretence of Communist China's might and is intended to provoke the United States into actions and declarations which would embarrass many of us, and add influence to Communist propaganda.

I have already expressed my convictions about your duty to Chiang whom you rightly called your "brave Ally." But I do not think it would be right or wise for America to encourage him to keep alive the reconquest of the mainland in order to inspirit his faithful followers. He deserves the protection of your shield but not the use of your sword. ("Sword" in this case is a rather comprehensive term). The hope of Chiang subduing Communist China surely died six years ago when Truman on Marshall's advice gave up the struggle on the mainland and helped Chiang into the shelter of Formosa.

We were of course glad to see your decision, now bloodlessly carried out, to evacuate the Tachen islands, but we still feel very anxious about what may happen at the Matsus and Quemoy. The operation of evacuating 50,000 Nationalist troops might present serious dangers, especially to the rearguard. On the other hand to linger on indefinitely in the present uncertainty might well reach the same conclusion by a slower process.

Before I got your message I had been wondering whether the following threefold policy would be acceptable and I send it now for your consideration.

(a) To defend Formosa and the Pescadores as a declared resolve.

(b) To announce the United States intention to evacuate all the offshore islands including Quemoy in the same way as the Tachens, and to declare that they will do this at their convenience within (say) three months.

(c) To intimate also by whatever channel or method is thought best that the United States will treat any proved major attempt to hamper this withdrawal as justification for using whatever conventional force is required.

This would avoid the unbearable situation of your overwhelming forces having to look on while Chiang's 50,000 men on Quemoy and any other detachment elsewhere on the offshore coastline were being scuppered. To me at this distance the plan seems to have the merit of being simple, clear, and above all resolute. It would I believe command a firm majority of support over here. It puts an end to a state of affairs where unforeseeable or unpreventable incidents and growing exasperation may bring about very grave consequences.

To sum up, we feel that the coastal islands must not be used as stepping stones either by Communists towards the conquest of Formosa or the Nationalists towards the conquest of China. But they might all too easily become the occasion of an incident which would place the United States before the dilemma of either standing by while their allies were butchered or becoming embroiled in a war for no strategic or political purpose.

If this is so, the right course must be to make sure that the United States are not put in the position of having to make such a decision over the coastal islands. This can only be done by taking advantage of the present lull to remove the Nationalists from Quemoy and the Matsus—as they have already been removed from the Tachens—before they become the occasion of further dangers. Opinion in this country, and so far as can be judged in the Commonwealth, would regard such a decision as right in law, in morals and in worldly wisdom.

Our long friendship made me wish to put these thoughts before you and now I have the generous invitation of your closing paragraph. Anthony and I deeply desire to do our utmost to help you and our strongest resolve is to keep our two countries bound together in their sacred brotherhood.

With kindest regards,

Your sincere friend,
Winston

EISENHOWER TO CHURCHILL

February 18, 1955

Dear Winston,

I greatly appreciate the message from you and Anthony. I have studied it long and carefully, as has Foster. Quite naturally, it distresses us whenever we find ourselves in even partial disagreement with the conclusions that you two may reach on any important subject. It is probable that these differences frequently reflect dissimilar psychological and political situations in our two countries more than they do differences in personal convictions based upon theoretical analysis. Nevertheless we clearly recognize the great importance to the security of the free world of our two governments achieving a step by step progress both in policy and in action.

Diplomatically it would indeed be a great relief to us if the line between the Nationalists and the Communists was actually the broad Strait of Formosa instead of the narrow Straits between Quemoy and Matsu and the mainland. However, there are about 55,000 of the Nationalist troops on these coastal islands and the problem created thereby cannot, I fear, be solved by us merely announcing a desire to transplant them to Formosa.

Foster and I have been working very hard over recent months, and he has been in close touch with Anthony, in the attempt to lay a basis for what we have hoped may prove a gradual but steady solution.

There are two important points that must be considered at every step of any analysis of this exceedingly difficult situation. The first is that this country does not have decisive power in respect of the off-shore islands. We believe that Chiang would even choose to stand alone and die if we should attempt now to coerce him into the abandonment of those islands. Possibly we may convince him in the future of the wisdom of this course, but to attempt to do more at this time would bring us to the second major point, which is: We must not lose Chiang's army and we must maintain its strength, efficiency and morale. Only a few months back we had both Chiang and a strong, well-equipped French Army to support the free world's position in Southeast Asia. The French are gone—making it clearer than ever that we cannot afford the loss of Chiang unless all of us are to get completely out of that corner of the globe. This is unthinkable to us—I feel it must be to you.

In order to make an express or tacit cease-fire likely, we have, with difficulties perhaps greater than you realize, done, through our diplomacy, many things.

1. We rounded out the far Pacific security chain by a Treaty with the Nationalists which, however, only covered specifically Formosa and the Pescadores, thus making it clear to Chiang and to all the world that we were not prepared to defend the coastal positions as Treaty territory.

2. We obtained from Chiang his agreement that he would not conduct any offensive operations against the mainland either from Formosa or from his coastal positions, except in agreement with us. Thus we are in a position to preclude what you refer to as the use of these offshore islands as "bridgeheads" for a Nationalist invasion of Communist China, or as a base for "sporadic war against the mainland" or "the invasion of the mainland of China." Under present practice we do not give agreement to any such attacks unless they are retaliatory to related, prior, Communist attacks. In these reports we have done much more than seems generally realized.

3. Furthermore, we obtained an agreement from the Nationalists closely limiting their right to take away from Formosa military elements, material or human, to which we had contributed if this would weaken the defense of Formosa itself.

4. We made possible the voluntary evacuation of the Tachens and two other islands.

5. Finally, we secured the acquiescence of the Chinese Nationalists to United Nations proceedings for a cease-fire, although the Chinese Nationalists were extremely suspicious of this move and felt that it could permanently blight their hopes.

All of this was done, as I say, in consultation between Anthony and Foster and in the hope that this would provide a basis for a cease-fire.

However, what we have done has apparently been interpreted by the Chinese Communists merely as a sign of weakness. They have intensified their threats against Formosa and their expression of determination to take it by force. Also, they continue to hold, in durance vile, our airmen who were captured by them in the Korean War and who should have been freed by the Korean Armistice.

There comes a point where constantly giving in only encourages further belligerency. I think we must be careful not to pass that point in our dealings with Communist China. In such a case, further retreat becomes worse than a Munich because at Munich there were at least promises on the part of the aggressor to cease expansion and to keep the peace. In this case the Chinese Communists have promised nothing and have not contributed one iota toward peace in the Formosa area. Indeed, they treat the suggestion of peace there as an insult.

I am increasingly led to feel it would be dangerous to predicate our thinking and planning on the assumption that when the Chinese Communists talk about their resolve to take Formosa, this is just "talk", and that they really would be satisfied with the coastal islands. I suspect that it is the other way round. What they are really interested in is Formosa—and later on Japan—and the coastal islands are marginal. They do not want to have another Chinese Government in their neighborhood, particularly one which has military power and which poses a threat to their center if ever they attack on their flanks.

Therefore, I think that if the Chinese Nationalists got out of Quemoy and the Matsus, they would not be solving the real problem, which is far more basic. I repeat that it would more likely mean that this retreat, and the coercion we would have to exert to bring it about, would so undermine the morale and the loyalty of the non-Communist forces on Formosa that they could not be counted on. Some, at least, might defect to the Communists or provide such a weak element in the defense of Formosa that an amphibious operation could give the Communists a strong foothold on Formosa.

You speak about our capacity to "drown" anybody who tried to cross the Formosa Straits. However, we do not and cannot maintain at that spot at all times sufficient force to cope with an attack which might come at any time both by sea and air and which would presumably operate from several different points and be directed against several different points on what is a very considerable body of land. It took us two days to assemble the force necessary to insure the safety of the Chinese Nationalists evacuating from the Tachens. Now most of that force has returned to its normal bases which are the Philippines,

Japan and Okinawa. The Chinese are past masters at the art of camouflage and, as bitter experience in Korea taught us, they can strike in force without detectable preparations. We must rely upon a loyal and dependable force of Nationalists on Formosa to deal with any who, for the reasons indicated, we might be unable to "drown" before the attackers reached the island.

And if perchance there should be any serious defection on Formosa, that would be a situation which we could not possibly meet by landing Marines or the like to fight the Chinese Nationalist defectors on the Island. Such a development would undermine the whole situation.

All of the non-Communist nations of the Western Pacific—particularly Korea, Japan, the Philippines, and, of course, Formosa itself, are watching nervously to see what we do next. I fear that, if we appear strong and coercive only toward our friends, and should attempt to compel Chiang to make further retreats, the conclusion of these Asian peoples will be that they had better plan to make the best terms they can with the Communists.

I know that your government's intelligence forces are very good. But this is a situation which we have worked with and lived with very intimately. We do have considerable knowledge, and the responsibility. Surely all that we have done not only here, but in Korea with Rhee, amply demonstrates that we are not careless in letting others get us into a major war. I devoutly hope that when judgments of this kind have to be made, each could, in the last analysis, trust the other in the areas where they have special knowledge and the greatest responsibility.

It would surely not be popular in this country if we became involved in possible hostilities on account of Hong Kong or Malaya, which our people look upon as "colonies"—which to us is a naughty word. Nevertheless, I do not doubt that, if the issue were ever framed in this way, we would be at your side.

We are doing everything possible to work this situation out in a way which, on the one hand, will avoid the risk of war, and, on the other hand, preserve the non-Communist position in the Western Pacific, a position which, by the way, is vital to Australia and New Zealand. However, if the Chinese Communists are determined to have a war to gain Formosa, then there will be trouble.

I see I have made this as long, and perhaps as complicated, as a diplomatic note. For that I apologize!

With warm regard,

As ever,
Ike

CHURCHILL TO EISENHOWER

March 4, 1955

My dear Friend,

I have been, as you may have noticed from the newspapers, rather hunted lately by politics[1] and have not found the time or the strength to answer your deeply interesting letter of February 19.[2] I was very glad to see from reports of your interviews with the Press that we are in such good agreement about the H Bomb and all that.[3] All went very well in the House of Commons. Considering we only have a majority of sixteen,[4] the fact that the Opposition vote of censure was rejected by 107 votes was a remarkable event and entitles me to say that our policy of "Defence through deterrents" commands support of the nation. I will be writing to you again soon in more detail.

With all my warmest regards,

I remain,
Yours always,
Winston

1. The Defence White Paper, proposing development of a British hydrogen bomb, aroused controversy culminating in a Commons debate on the matter on March 2, 1955.

2. Dated February 18, received by Churchill on February 19, 1955.

3. At a press conference, March 2, 1955, Eisenhower spoke in favor of the policy of nuclear deterrence.

4. The Conservative majority of seventeen in the general election of 1951 had been lowered to sixteen by 1955 as the result of a net loss of one seat in by-elections.

EISENHOWER TO CHURCHILL

March 4, 1955

Dear Winston,

I send you this purely personal note to thank you once again for your courtesy in seeing Mr. Thomas E. Stephens. Because of the pressure we have been under here—and lately it has seemed heavier than usual—I have not yet had a chance to see Mr. Stephens' sketches, but I look forward eagerly to seeing how his artist's eye has captured your spirit and personality. I am certain no artist can ever do it to my complete satisfaction.

Please give my affectionate regard to Clementine and, as always, the very best to yourself.

As ever,
Ike

CHURCHILL TO EISENHOWER

March 18, 1955

My dear Friend,

I am so glad you disclaimed responsibility for the issue of the Yalta papers.[1] Personally I do not at all mind their publication though I feel a strong line should be drawn by Governments between formal and plenary sessions on the one hand and after dinner conversations on the other. Also I think people should know whether they are being reported by Interpreter Bohlen or not.[2] Otherwise so far as I am concerned I am very content with the tale. What worries me is whether its publication at this moment may not endanger the French ratification of the London and Paris agreements.

I thought your letter to me and the other N.A.T.O. Prime Ministers was a splendid declaration which doubles our strength and halves our risks.[3] I am sorry we shall never meet on a Top Level confrontation of our would-be friends, but I hope indeed this applies to political occasions only.

With my sincere good wishes,

Yours always,
Winston

P.S. How are you getting on with the portrait? I hope you will show it to me when it is finished and I warn you I shall claim full rights of retaliation.

1. Owing to the controversy over the Yalta Conference of February 1945, the documents of the conference were published by the State Department in 1955.
2. Charles E. Bohlen was the American interpreter at Yalta, later U.S. ambassador to the Soviet Union, 1953–56.
3. Message by Eisenhower to the prime ministers of Belgium, Holland, Luxembourg, France, West Germany, Italy, and Britain regarding Western European union, March 10, 1955.

EISENHOWER TO CHURCHILL

March 22, 1955

Dear Winston,

The last sentence of your letter, with its implication that you are soon to withdraw from active political life, started, in my memories, a parade of critical incidents and great days that you and I experienced together, beginning at the moment we first met in Washington, December, 1941. Since reading it I have been suffering from an acute case of nostalgia.

First I recall those late days of 1941, when this country was still shuddering from the shock of Pearl Harbor. I think of those occasions during the succeeding months when I was fortunate enough to talk over with you some of the problems of the war, and I especially think of that Washington visit of yours in June of '42, when we had to face the bitter reality of the Tobruk disaster.

Somewhere along about that time must have marked the low point in Allied war fortunes. Yet I still remember with great admiration the fact that never once did you quail at the grim prospect ahead of us; never did I hear you utter a discouraged word nor a doubt as to the final and certain outcome.

Later, of course, we were often together as we planned the TORCH Operation, the Sicilian venture, the move into Italy and the campaign through Normandy. Then, in these later years, starting with my return to Europe in January of '51, I have valued beyond calculation my opportunities to meet with you, especially when those meetings were concerned with the military and diplomatic problems of the free world and our struggle against the evil conspiracy centering in the Kremlin. Because I do so highly value this long association and friendship with you, I echo your hope that the impending divergence of our lives will apply to political occasions only. Indeed, I entertain the further hope that with greater leisure, you will more often find it possible to visit us in this country—after all, we do have a fifty percent share in your blood lines, if not in your political allegiance.[1]

Of course both Foster and I have been unhappy about the affair of the Yalta papers. Actually we had hoped that we had made adequate arrangement for an indefinite postponement of the appearance of the documents; an unexplained leak finally put the State Department in the position that it had either to release the papers publicly or to allow one lone periodical a complete scoop in the matter.

As for myself, you know how earnestly I have argued that no matter what else might happen, really good international friends cannot ever afford to be guilty of bad faith, one toward the other. I pray that you do not consider that any such thing was intended in this case.

Ever since 1945, I have argued for the declassification of war records in order that our countries could profit from past mistakes. But I have also insisted that where documents touch upon our combined alliances and arrangements of the late war, published accounts should be limited to a recitation of fact and decision—they should not include mere conversation or gossip.

I think the entire subject is one to which we should give some attention because I am certain that future political battles will create, in some instances, irresistible demands for the publication of particular papers. At least I suspect that this will be true in this country and consequently I think we should prepare as intelligently as possible for this eventuality.

Foster has just returned from Canada where he had a series of very fine visits with the members of the Canadian Government. While there, he had an opportunity to explain the reasons for our attitude in the Formosa matter.

As you know, I am dedicated to the idea that unless the free world can stand firmly together in important problems, our strength will be wasted and we shall in the long run be ineffective in our struggle to advance freedom in the world and to stop the spread of Communism. I believe it to be especially important that we seek to understand each other's viewpoints in Southeast Asia, because in that region we have a very delicate—sometimes dangerously weak—situation and one to which the future welfare and fortunes of the free world are definitely related. If we can achieve the kind of common understanding and thinking that we should, then I feel that there will never be any doubts as to this country's readiness to stand firmly by the side of any other free nation opposing aggression in that region. We have no possessions in that immediate area. Consequently, we cannot be accused of any support of colonialism or of imperialistic designs. We recognize situations that have been properly and legally established and we certainly want to halt Communism dead in its tracks.

To do this, one of the essentials is a strong and continuous land defense of Formosa. This can be done—certainly under present conditions—only by Chiang Kai-shek and his troops. This in turn means that their morale and their vigor, their training and equipment, must all be adequately assured. Until the time comes that they themselves feel that their morale can be sustained, even though their forces are withdrawn from all of their outlying positions, we must be exceedingly careful of the pressure we attempt to apply to Chiang to bring about such a result.

Except for this one feature, I agree entirely with the thoughts you have expressed in your former letters on this touchy subject, and I hope also that you have no difficulty of seeing the importance of this morale feature in Formosa.

As to the "portrait." Since Mr. Stephens has come back I have had no opportunity to meet with him to go over the work he did on my behalf. However, in the meantime I discovered a small black and white print of a portrait of you that was painted some years ago. In order to obtain some practice in the task I had set for myself, I have painted a small canvas, using this portrait as a guide. I do not know the name of the original artist, but it is a picture of you sitting in a straight-backed chair, in a panelled study, and holding a cigar in your right hand. Considering my lack of qualification in this field, it did not turn out badly and I have had a color photograph made of it, which I am forwarding with this letter.[2]

Actually, I have not had time to complete every detail of this particular canvas because I must say that it is difficult for me to give a fairly realistic impression of the stripes in a statesman's trousers. I could wish that, at least for the day you sat for that portrait, you could have worn your wartime "zipper suit."

With my affectionate regard and my most prayerful wishes for your continued good health and happiness.

As ever,
Ike

1. Churchill's mother, Jenny Jerome, was American. She married Churchill's father, Lord Randolph Churchill, in April 1874.

2. Enclosed with the letter was a color reproduction of Churchill's portrait by Eisenhower, with the inscription, "With apologies to my friend Winston. From Ike."

EISENHOWER TO CHURCHILL

March 29, 1955

Dear Winston,

I have no doubt that you and your Cabinet find it necessary, just as we do, to ponder daily on the world situation and to calculate as carefully as you can every move to be made as you strive to straighten out some specific portion of the tangled mess that we call international relations.

Of one thing I have always been completely confident—that you are as fully dedicated as I am to promoting between our two governments and our two peoples clear unity of purpose and common understanding of the obstacles we face so as to double our strength as we push forward in the search for an honorable peace.

It is because of this confidence in our common intent—indeed, I hope I may say our indestructible personal friendship—that I venture to bring up an apparent difference between our two governments that puzzles us sorely and constantly. Although we seem always to see eye to eye with you when we contemplate any European problem, our respective attitudes towards similar problems in the Orient are frequently so dissimilar as to be almost mutually antagonistic. I know that you could make the same observation regarding us; possibly this fact troubles you and your associates just as much as it does us.

I beg of you not to think of this letter as a complaint, or as any effort to prove that we are right and you are wrong. In writing to you in this vein I am interested in one thing and one thing only—how can we and our two governments come closer together in our thinking so as to achieve a better result in matters that are serious and fateful for both our nations? I know that frankness on my part will not be interpreted as accusation or recrimination.

The conclusion seems inescapable that these differences come about because we do not agree on the probable extent and the importance of further Communist expansion in Asia. In our contacts with New Zealand and Australia, we have the feeling that we encounter a concern no less acute than ours; but your own government seems to regard Communist aggression in Asia as of little significance to the free world future.

As I once explained to you, we are not interested in Quemoy and Matsu as such. But because of the conviction that the loss of Formosa would doom the Philippines and eventually the remainder of the region, we are determined that it shall not fall into the hands of the Communists either through all-out attack or, as would appear to be far more likely, through harrassing [sic] air attacks, threats and subversion.

The only way in which pressure of the latter type can be successfully resisted is to sustain a high morale among Chiang's forces. The danger of internal subversion and consequent collapse in Formosa is always present; Chiang feels this keenly and we believe it necessary to help him combat it.

In fact, we feel this is vitally important to the interests of the entire Western World.

Of course I would personally be very happy, both as a political leader and as an ex-soldier who may have a bit of competence in the strategic field, to see Chiang, voluntarily and in accordance with what he believed to be his own best interests, withdraw from Quemoy and the Matsus.

But I am just as unwilling to put so much pressure on him that he might give up the entire struggle in utter discouragement. It's at this point that you and ourselves seem to part company. But we cannot understand how the free world can hold Formosa except as Chiang provides the necessary ground forces.

Another apparent difference between us that added to our bewilderment occurred in connection with Foster's recent visit to the Far East. He urged the Government of Laos, while it still has the ability to do so, to clean out the areas in that country where Communist elements are establishing themselves in some strength. The Laos Government is fully justified in taking such action under the terms of the Geneva agreements. When Laotian officials expressed to Foster some concern lest such action on their part provoke attack from the Viet Minh and the Chinese Communists, he assured them that aggression from without would bring into play the Manila Pact.[1] This would mean assistance from the other signatories of the Pact to preserve the territorial integrity of Laos.

Some time after this conversation, we heard that both the British and the French Ambassadors in Laos informed that Government that under no circumstances could Laos expect any help against outside aggression, under the terms of the Manila Pact, if such aggression should result from their own efforts to rule their internal affairs.

As a result, we have a situation in which the Communists, in the affected areas of Laos, grow stronger and stronger, and we face a possibility of ultimately losing that entire territory to the Communists, just as we lost North Vietnam.

Another point bothers us. This country believes that the existence of the ChiNat Government confers upon all of us one advantage that is not often publicly noted. Throughout the Far East there are great numbers of "emigre" Chinese. These people, in most cases, possess sort of a dual citizenship—one pertaining to the country in which they reside; the other to China. Up to date, millions of these people have preserved their allegiance to Chiang and have not become Communist cells menacing the countries where they are now residents. This affects the Philippines, Indonesia and, of course, other areas such as Malaya and Hongkong.

This is another fact that points to the very great desirability of sustaining Chiang's prestige and the morale of his followers. If the Chinese National Government should disappear, these emigre Chinese will certainly deem themselves subjects of the Chinese Communist Government and they will quickly add to the difficulties of their adopted countries. Indeed, where their numbers are quite strong, I believe that their influence might became decisive and that no outside aid that any of us could bring to bear could prevent these regions from going completely Communist. Do not such possibilities concern you?

As we consider such developments and possibilities, it seems to me we cannot fail to conclude that the time to stop any advance of Communism in Asia is here, now.

We have come to the point where every additional backward step must be deemed a defeat for the Western world. In fact, it is a triple defeat. First, we lose a potential ally. Next, we give to an implacable enemy another recruit. Beyond this, every such retreat creates in the minds of neutrals the fear that we do not mean what we say when we pledge our support to people who want to remain free. We show ourselves fearful of the Communistic brigands and create the impression that we are slinking along in the shadows, hoping that the beast will finally be satiated and cease his predatory tactics before he finally devours us. So the third result is that the morale of our friends crumbles.

Of course it is easy to say that this is a gross overstatement of the case. Because the ChiComs have no great fleet and cannot now attack across the seas, it is natural to underestimate their potential strength and the fearful eventual results of the crumbling process. So I believe it critically important that we make a sober estimate of what we are up against.

Two decades ago we had the fatuous hope that Hitler, Mussolini and the Japanese war lords would decide, before we might become personally involved, that they had enough and would let the world live in peace. We saw the result.

Yet the Communist sweep over the world since World War II has been much faster and much more relentless than the 1930's sweep of the dictators. I do believe that all of us must begin to look some of these unpleasant facts squarely in the face and meet them exactly as our Grand Alliance of the 40's met our enemies and vanquished them.

You and I have been through many things where our judgments have not always been as one, but, on my part at least, my admiration and affection for you were never lessened. In this long experience, my hope is rooted that the two of us may bring up some thought or idea that could help us achieve a personal concord that could, in turn, help our two governments act more effectively against Communists everywhere.

My warm greetings to Clemmie, and, of course, my very kind regards to yourself.

As ever,
Ike

1. The Southeast Asia Collective Defense Treaty was signed in Manila in the Philippines, September 18, 1954, establishing SEATO.

CHURCHILL TO EISENHOWER

April 1, 1955

Thank you so much for your letter of March 29. Am pondering; will write.

Winston

CHURCHILL TO EISENHOWER

April 7, 1955

Thank you so much. All you said I deeply value.[1] Looking forward to writing.

Kindest regards.
Winston

1. Eisenhower issued a statement on the occasion of Churchill's retirement, which took place on April 5, 1955.

CONCLUSION

What light does the Churchill-Eisenhower correspondence from 1953 to 1955 throw on the historical issues of the time? In the Introduction some questions were raised on a number of central matters, and an assessment is offered in the Conclusion of the extent to which the correspondence adds to our understanding of these matters. Did the Anglo-American "special relationship" become closer and more intimate in the Churchill-Eisenhower era or did the special nature of the relationship gradually wane? How realistic was Churchill's aim to hold a summit meeting and seek a détente with the Soviet Union and how valid were Eisenhower's reservations? How far did Churchill succeed in restraining what he viewed as the extremes of a volatile American foreign policy? Does the correspondence reveal Churchill as an old man clinging to power for too long or does it reveal a world figure continuing to make a valuable contribution in his Indian summer? What evidence does the correspondence reveal with regard to the evaluation of Eisenhower as a statesman?

Answers to these questions have been advanced in the growing secondary literature on Churchill and on Eisenhower. There has been a considerable outpouring of books on Eisenhower, most of which have revised the assessment by contemporary intellectuals of Eisenhower as an amiable, ineffective, golf-playing mediocrity and presented him as a wise, capable, and shrewd leader.[1] Books which cover Churchill's peacetime administration have for the most part presented Churchill as a leader well past his prime in these years, but they have judged him reasonably benignly.[2] An important source for these works have been memoirs, diaries, and collections of letters.[3] The Churchill-Eisenhower correspondence is much more substantial than those sources, most of which, although they contain incisive insights, are relatively thin. On the other hand, the presidential papers of Eisenhower or the personal papers of Churchill, let alone the entire body of government documents in the British and American archives, are so overwhelming in quantity as to be beyond the capacity of an individual reader. The Churchill-Eisenhower correspondence therefore forms a valuable collection of documents which give depth and detail on the major issues of international affairs of the time within a manageable compass. Furthermore, the correspondence provides the fascinating perspective of the two statesmen in their maturity. It is significant that both Churchill and Eisenhower, after the intensity of their experiences in the Second World War, were in less demanding positions in the late 1940s, allowing them time for reflection before the period when they were simultaneously in office. The correspondence is perhaps for this reason pensive and philosophical in many places as well as concerned with everyday situations. In this respect the Churchill-Eisenhower correspondence differs somewhat from the Churchill-Roosevelt correspondence, which, while immensely rich in its coverage of virtually all aspects of the World War II relationship and dealing with events of more immediate vital significance than the issues of the 1950s, is concerned to a greater extent with day to day matters and is, consequently, generally less reflective.

Toward the end of the correspondence Eisenhower writes of "our indestructible personal friendship,"[4] and the correspondence makes abundantly clear the mutual affection between the two men and the fundamentally close relationship between their two countries, despite differences on various issues. In their years in office there were expressions of bitter Anglo-American discord in the press and in exchanges at the bureaucratic level between the British and American governments on such matters as China, economic issues, and atomic energy. Personal relationships at the higher level were more distant in the days of Anthony Eden, John Foster Dulles, and ambassadors Roger Makins and Winthrop Aldrich than in the preceding era of Dean Acheson, Ernest Bevin, and ambassadors Oliver Franks and Walter Gifford. The Churchill-Eisenhower relationship—and the correspondence itself—was consequently of great value in symbolizing and embodying Anglo-American amity. In this broad sense Churchill's relationship with Eisenhower strengthened the so-called Anglo-American special relationship. On substantial matters of policy, however, the evidence of the correspondence suggests that the two nations were growing further apart. Churchill's preference for a meeting with Eisenhower at Bermuda without the French, for example, was overridden by the Americans with their growing concern for allies other than Britain, especially France and West Germany. Churchill's efforts to secure an increase in atomic information for Britain met with some limited success, but it fell very far short of his wishes for the fruition of the atomic partnership of the World War II era. Churchill's efforts to draw the United States into joint Anglo-American negotiations with the Egyptian government met with no success at all.

The gap in economic and military power between Britain and the United States was relentlessly widening, and this determined the relationship between the two countries to a much greater extent than personal diplomacy through personal meetings or correspondence. Subjects which are not raised in the correspondence are in some ways as significant as those which are covered. McCarthyism, for example, which was a very important cause of Anglo-American stress at the popular and press level in these years, is not mentioned, no doubt for reasons of tactfulness on Churchill's part. More significantly, economic issues are scarcely mentioned, apart from a few letters on East-West trade. Yet economic issues caused bitter disagreements between Britain and the United States at the bureaucratic level over American aid policies, and it was Britain's economic decline, despite the easing by 1953 of the acute balance of payments crisis which Churchill inherited in 1951, which fundamentally determined the relationship more than any other single factor. Professor Michael Howard, writing of "the special relationship," has suggested that "Churchill's attempt to restore the relationship with Eisenhower when he returned to office was humiliatingly rebuffed."[5] The evidence of the correspondence, it might be argued, shows that Churchill succeeded to a certain degree in utilizing personal diplomacy and personal correspondence to compensate for Britain's declining power, but there were severe limits to the degree to which this was possible.

The limits of British influence were reflected also in Churchill's relative lack of success in his efforts to restrain what he considered to be the extremes in American policy. He was particularly unsuccessful on issues relating to the Far East. As Eisenhower perceptively observed, "Although we seem always to see eye to eye with you when we contemplate any European problem, our respective attitudes towards similar problems in the Orient are frequently so dissimilar as to be almost mutually antagonistic."[6] In the crisis over Quemoy and the Matsus in early 1955, Churchill was completely unable to influence Eisenhower on a policy which the British considered to be extremely dangerous. Churchill had little influence over policy in ending the Korean War, especially when Eisenhower was prepared to threaten stepped-up military action and to make veiled threats to use the atomic bomb. On Indochina, Churchill's role was decisive in destroying the American plan for united action in the form of a coalition to stiffen French resistance. But it is a dubious claim that Churchill restrained Eisenhower from military intervention in Indochina, since Eisenhower was almost certainly opposed to such military intervention, favoring united action as a deterrent and not as a means for intervention. On policies in Europe, there was less need for British restraint on the United States and the two nations worked together more easily. Eastern Europe, another subject conspicuous by its absence in the correspondence, did not prove to be an area of danger, as Republican bombast regarding "liberation" and "roll back of Communism" proved to be little more than rhetoric. On Germany, policy differences on EDC were happily resolved with Eden's initiatives, which brought West Germany into NATO. On most issues, the Anglo-American relationship was one of consultation, cooperation, and partnership, as, for example, Eisenhower sent Churchill a draft of his "Atoms for Peace" speech and his speech to the American Association of Newspaper Editors of April 16, 1953. But the partnership was becoming increasingly a relationship between senior and junior partners. On the crucial issues on which Eisenhower was determined to have his way, such as Quemoy and the Matsus, Churchill's influence was of little weight. Churchill had feared that a Republican administration might bring on a world war. That it did not was due perhaps to a slight degree to Churchill's restraining influence, but to a much greater extent it was due to Eisenhower's own relative moderation, his skill in diplomacy, and the absence of extremes in the response from the Soviet and Chinese side.

Churchill's greatest disappointment was his failure to arrange with Eisenhower a summit meeting with the Soviet Union. The correspondence provides eloquent testimony to the importance which Churchill attached to this matter in his final years in office. Many of his letters on the subject have a clear Churchillian ring. "Fancy that you and Malenkov should never have met," he wrote to Eisenhower, for example, "when all the time in both countries appalling preparations are being made for measureless mutual destruction."[7] The correspondence provides evidence of the bitter anti-Soviet feelings which Eisenhower had acquired by the early 1950s, whereas in the war and early postwar years he had shown a much more conciliatory attitude. Eisenhower revealed his innermost feelings toward the Soviet Union in the 1950s in letters to Churchill with references such as "the stupid and savage individuals in the Kremlin" and "the evil conspiracy centering in the Kremlin."[8] Yet there is interesting evidence that Eisenhower was not totally unsympathetic to Churchill's aspirations regarding a summit. In early July 1954, for example, when Churchill surprised Eisenhower as well as his British Cabinet colleagues by his approach to Moscow after the talks in Washington in June 1954, Eisenhower wrote in very sympathetic terms with regard to Churchill's possible lone journey to Moscow.[9] It might be speculated that, although Churchill did not win over Eisenhower with regard to a summit meeting in the short term, his views sank in and influenced Eisenhower in the longer term, because at the end of his presidency in 1959 Eisenhower met Khrushchev at Camp David and arranged a summit in Paris and a visit to Moscow, although this was, of course, aborted by the U-2 affair in May 1960.

With regard to Eisenhower's personality and reputation, the correspondence adds further evidence to support the revised, favorable reassessment by historians. The correspondence reveals little of a personal nature. Eisenhower was a quietly self-confident and self-contained man who kept his inner feelings closely guarded. His correspondence with his friend, Swede Hazlitt, reveals as much of a personal nature as Eisenhower was ever likely to reveal on paper. His correspondence with Churchill, although a personal correspondence as opposed to government to government communications, dealt largely with political matters, and aside from a clear indication of affection for Churchill and occasional references to such matters as painting and golf, the letters contain no insights into Eisenhower's personal nature. Eisenhower's letters do, however, make very evident his intelligence and his sound grasp of the issues. Many of the long letters to Churchill provide conclusive evidence to repudiate the view that Eisenhower was a weak, ill-informed president who abrogated responsibility to others such as John Foster Dulles.

With regard to Churchill, the correspondence provides fascinating evidence of his deepest aspirations as the sands of time ran out on him. He was frustrated by old age and failing health, and his letters were his best outlet for expression of the deepest wishes to which he would have aspired with all his vigor if his age and health had allowed. Eisenhower noted in his diary in February 1953 that the retiring American ambassador to Britain, Walter Gifford, had informed him that Churchill "is really stretching, if he has not outlived his usefulness."[10] Following his stroke in June 1953, visiting Americans sent differing reports to Eisenhower on the state of Churchill's health. In October 1953 Dulles reported that "Churchill's mental and physical condition seemed almost normal."[11] But in November 1953 Winthrop Aldrich reported that Churchill was "in very poor condition" and that Admiral Arthur Radford, who had been with Aldrich on a visit to Churchill, had been "shocked by the impression he created."[12] By June 1954 Aldrich reported that "He has good days and bad days but the former are becoming rarer."[13] Eisenhower felt uneasy in personal meetings with Churchill, especially since Churchill refused to wear a hearing aid and Eisenhower therefore had to shout at him all the time in conversation.[14] Eisenhower was much more comfortable in exchanges with Churchill in correspondence and, although Eisenhower clearly felt that Churchill ought to have resigned and given way to a younger man, there is no reason to doubt Eisenhower's frequently stated expression that he liked to receive Churchill's letters. The letters reveal Churchill's continuing mental agility and wit, such as his reply to Eisenhower's rather extraordinary suggestion that Churchill should choose freedom from colonial rule as a subject for a farewell speech. Churchill replied that on that subject "I must admit I am a laggard. I am a bit sceptical about universal suffrage for the Hottentots even if refined by proportional representation."[15] Churchill's concentration span was becoming shorter and more confined only to the subjects which greatly interested him. His letters to Eisenhower were on topics of very great interest to him and which did not overstretch his concentration span as in conversation. They are like the last drops of vintage wine from a musty old bottle.

Correspondence between Churchill and Eisenhower continued after Churchill's retirement, but it became less substantial and less regular. On the eve of the Geneva summit conference in July 1955, Eisenhower realized the irony that the summit meeting which Churchill had so wanted was taking place so soon after his retirement, and he took the time to write to Churchill. "As you know," Eisenhower wrote, "I feel sure that the Western nations could not, with self-respect, have earlier consented to a Four Power Summit Meeting. Yet I cannot escape a feeling of sadness that its delay brought about by the persistent hostile Soviet attitude toward NATO has operated to prevent your personal attendance at the meeting."[16]

At the time of the Suez crisis in 1956, Churchill wrote to Eisenhower that "There is not much left for me to do in this world, and I have neither the wish nor the strength to involve myself in the present stress and turmoil. But . . . whatever the arguments adduced here and in the United States for or against Anthony's action in Egypt, to let events in the Middle East become a gulf between us, would be an act of folly, on which our whole civilisation may founder."[17] But Churchill's health steadily declined, and the interchange of letters became intermittent and insubstantial.

In 1965 Churchill died at the age of ninety. Eisenhower came to England for the funeral and he read one of the lessons. The cortege then made its way to Churchill's final resting place in Bladen in Oxfordshire. In a broadcast tribute, Eisenhower closed with the words, "And now to you, Sir Winston, my old friend—Farewell." Four years later, in 1969, Eisenhower died. The two great men had battled and triumphed in war. In the years when they were simultaneously in power, 1953–55, they had striven, in sometimes differing ways, for peace, stability, and the protection of the national interests of their respective countries. The legacy which they left for posterity and for the historical record was extraordinarily rich. One of the jewels of that legacy was the remarkable correspondence between them.

Notes

1. Stephen Ambrose, *Eisenhower*, 2 vols. (New York: Simon and Schuster, 1983–84); Robert Divine, *Eisenhower and the Cold War* (New York: Oxford University Press, 1981); Richard Melanson and David Mayers, eds., *Re-evaluating Eisenhower* (Urbana: University of Illinois Press, 1987); Charles C. Alexander, *Holding the Line: The Eisenhower Era, 1952–61* (Bloomington: Indiana University Press, 1975); Elmo Richardson, *The Presidency of Dwight D. Eisenhower* (Lawrence: Regents Press of Kansas, 1979); R. Alton Lee, *Dwight D. Eisenhower: Hero and Politician* (Boston: G. K. Hall, 1986). All of these books present, with some reservations, the revised, favorable view of Eisenhower. An exception to this trend, repeating the older interpretation of Eisenhower as a weak mediocrity, is Piers Brandon, *Ike* (London: Secker and Warburg, 1987).

2. Martin Gilbert, *Never Despair, 1945–65*, vol. 8 of *Winston S. Churchill* (London: Heinemann, 1988); Henry Pelling, *Winston Churchill* (London: Macmillan, 1974); Anthony Seldon, *Churchill's Indian Summer, 1951–55* (London: Hodder and Stoughton, 1981); John Young, ed., *The Foreign Policy of Churchill's Peacetime Administration, 1951–55* (Leicester: Leicester University Press, 1988).

3. John Colville, *The Fringes of Power: Downing Street Diaries, 1939–1955* (London: Hodder and Stoughton, 1985); Charles Moran, *Winston Churchill: The Struggle for Survival, 1940–65* (London: Constable, 1966); Dwight D. Eisenhower, *Mandate For Change, 1953–56* (New York: Doubleday, 1963); Robert Ferrell, ed., *The Eisenhower Diaries* (New York: W. W. Norton, 1981); Sherman Adams, *First Hand Report: The Inside Story of the Eisenhower Administration* (New York: Hutchinson, 1962); Emmet John Hughes, *The Ordeal of Power: A Political Memoir of the Eisenhower Years* (New York: Macmillan, 1963); Robert Ferrell, ed., *The Diary of James C. Hagerty: Eisenhower in Mid-Course, 1954–55* (Bloomington: Indiana University Press, 1983); Robert Griffith, ed., *Ike's Letters to a Friend, 1941–58* (Lawrence: University Press of Kansas, 1984).

4. Eisenhower to Churchill, March 29, 1955.

5. Michael Howard, "Aftermath: 'The Special Relationship,' " in *The "Special Relationship": Anglo-American Relations since 1945*, ed. William Roger Louis and Hedley Bull (Oxford: Clarendon Press, 1986), p. 388.

6. Ibid.

7. Churchill to Eisenhower, August 8, 1954.

8. Eisenhower to Churchill, February 9, 1954; Eisenhower to Churchill, March 22, 1955.

9. Eisenhower to Churchill, July 12, 1954.

10. Ferrell, *The Eisenhower Diaries*, p. 230.

11. Dulles to Eisenhower, October 16, 1953, WFIS, Box 16.

12. Ambassador in UK (Aldrich) to State Department, November 6, 1953, WFIS, Box 16.

13. Ambassador in UK (Aldrich) to State Department, December 22, 1953, *FRUS, 1952–54*, 6:1066.

14. Ferrell, *The Diary of James C. Hagerty*, p. 77.

15. Churchill to Eisenhower, August 8, 1954.

16. Eisenhower to Churchill, July 15, 1955, WFIS, Box 18.

17. Churchill to Eisenhower, November 23, 1956, WFIS, Box 18.

Classified Letters

Classified Letters

Churchill to Eisenhower,	June 20, 1953
One page regarding Korea.	
Churchill to Eisenhower,	June 27, 1953
Three pages plus a three-page attachment regarding the publication of documents relating to the Duke of Windsor.	
Eisenhower to Churchill,	July 2, 1953
One page regarding the publication of documents relating to the Duke of Windsor.	
Churchill to Eisenhower,	December 30, 1954
Three pages regarding France.	

Partially Classified Letters

Churchill to Eisenhower,	February 7, 1953
Eisenhower to Churchill,	August 20, 1954

Sources of Letters

Identical copies of most of the letters are located in the Whitman File, International Series, Boxes 16–17, Eisenhower Library, Abilene, Kansas, and PREM 11 1074, Prime Minister's Papers, Public Record Office, Kew, Surrey. Listed below are the locations of letters which are not to be found in both of the sources.

Churchill to Eisenhower,	February 7, 1953	WFIS, Box 16, partially classified
Churchill to Eisenhower,	April 12, 1953	PREM 11 1074
Churchill to Eisenhower,	April 13, 1953	PREM 11 1074
Churchill to Eisenhower,	April 15, 1953	PREM 11 1074
Eisenhower to Churchill,	May 26, 1953	WFIS, Box 16
Churchill to Eisenhower,	May 29, 1953	PREM 11 1074 WFIS, Box 16, partially classified
Churchill to Eisenhower,	June 12, 1953	PREM 11 1074
Churchill to Eisenhower,	June 14, 1953	PREM 11 1074
Churchill to Eisenhower,	June 19, 1953	PREM 11 1074 WFIS, Box 16, partially classified
Eisenhower to Churchill,	June 22, 1953	WFIS, Box 16
Eisenhower to Churchill,	June 23, 1953	WFIS, Box 16
Eisenhower to Churchill,	June 25, 1953	WFIS, Box 16
Churchill to Eisenhower,	June 26, 1953	WFIS, Box 16
Eisenhower to Churchill,	June 26, 1953	WFIS, Box 16
Churchill to Eisenhower,	July 1, 1953	PREM 11 1074
Eisenhower to Churchill,	July 6, 1953	PREM 11 1074 WFIS, Box 16, partially classified
Eisenhower to Churchill,	August 8, 1953	PREM 11 1074
Eisenhower to Churchill,	October 16, 1953	WFIS, Box 17
Eisenhower to Churchill,	November 29, 1953	WFIS, Box 17

Eisenhower to Churchill,	January 25, 1954	WFIS, Box 17
Churchill to Eisenhower,	March 24, 1954	PREM 11 1074
Churchill to Eisenhower,	April 1, 1954	PREM 11 1074
Churchill to Eisenhower,	August 8, 1954	PREM 11 1074
Churchill to Eisenhower,	September 18, 1954	PREM 11 1074
		WFIS, Box 17,
		partially classified
Eisenhower to Churchill,	December 27, 1954	WFIS, Box 17
Churchill to Eisenhower,	January 11, 1955	PREM 11 1074
Churchill to Eisenhower,	January 12, 1955	Martin Gilbert,
		Never Despair,
		1945–65, pp.
		1090–91
		WFIS, Box 17
		PREM 11 1074,
		classified
Eisenhower to Churchill,	January 25, 1955	WFIS, Box 17
Churchill to Eisenhower,	February 15, 1955	PREM 11 1074
Churchill to Eisenhower,	March 18, 1955	PREM 11 1074
Churchill to Eisenhower,	April 1, 1955	WFIS, Box 17
Churchill to Eisenhower,	April 7, 1955	WFIS, Box 17